SENSELESS ACTS
OF BEAUTY

SENSELESS ACTS
OF BEAUTY

Cultures of Resistance since the Sixties

—————◆—————

GEORGE McKAY

VERSO
London • New York

First published by Verso 1996
© George McKay 1996
All rights reserved

Verso
UK: 6 Meard Street, London W1V 3HR
USA: 180 Varick Street, New York NY 10014–4606

Verso is the imprint of New Left Books

ISBN 1–85984–908–3
ISBN 1–85984–028–0 (pbk)

British Library Cataloguing in Publication Data
A catalogue record for this book is available from the British Library

Library of Congress Cataloging-in-Publication Data
A catalog record for this book is available from the Library of Congress

Typeset by M Rules
Printed in Great Britain by the Bath Press

This book, my first, is dedicated to my mother, Maran McKay,
a fine feminist and socialist

CONTENTS

ACKNOWLEDGEMENTS

I owe thanks to those people who've read and commented on parts of this book, shared the project with me, written about it for me: Emma McKay, Penny Rimbaud of Crass, Bruce Garrard of Unique Publications, Jo Waterworth, 'Alan Beam', Don Aitken of Festival Welfare Services, Jon Savage, Simon Frith, Lisa McKenna, Maran McKay (junior), Jamie McKay, Richard Barnes, Tom Cahill, Mary Anna Wright, Alex Plows and Becca Lush and Phil of the Dongas Tribe, Ian Donald, Sam and Steff on the Freedom Trail, Gibby of Justice?, John of Bristol FIN – and Ailsa McKay, who turned up halfway through.

I also want to thank: Ardis Cameron, Steve Staines of Friends and Families of Travellers Support Trust, G. of Crass, Thomas Harding and *Undercurrents*, Alan Lodge (Tash), George Robertson, Ruth Levitas, Lyvinia Elleschild, Sandra Bell, Jude Davis, John Moore, Kevin Hetherington, DJ Weasel and *Eternity* magazine, Nicholas Saunders, Dave and DS4A, a group of ravers I let down one night in Norwich, Wenda Shehata, Keith Mann, Liberty, Helen Prescott and *Creative Mind*, Alan Rice, various unknown people from Justice? for written comments on the manuscript, Chris of Dongas Hotline, Donga Jai, Greg Piggot, Tim Pearson, Camilla Berens of Freedom Network, Sylvia Ayling, Catherine Muller, Barbara Bryant, Calvin Hoy, Ian Brownlie.

At Verso, special thanks are due to Malcolm Imrie for commissioning the book in the first place and for advice and support throughout. I also want to thank Pat Harper, Stefanie Schmiedel, Laura Pearson, Gareth Pritchard, Jane Hindle, Isobel Rorison, Alexandra Grüebler.

Finally, at the University of Central Lancashire, I want to thank the Department of Cultural Studies, Peter Edge and Michael Doherty of the Department of Legal Studies for helping to curb some of my wilder ideas about the Criminal Justice Act, and library staff for continual support.

All errors, flights of fancy or daft moments of utopian desire are my own.

Picture acknowledgements

The covers shown pp. 17 and 18 are from booklets published by Unique Publications, Glastonbury; thanks to Bruce Garrard for permission to reproduce them. The publicity poster p. 28 is from a compilation of Freek Press site letters, published by Suburban Guerrillas, 1989; thanks to Trevor Hughes. The photograph p. 37 is by Ian Wallace, the map p. 46 is by B. van Loon, the photograph p. 55 is by Harry Hart; thanks to Richard Barnes for permission to reproduce all three from *The Sun in the East: Norfolk and Suffolk Fairs*. The map pp. 62–3 is by Sheena; thanks to Bruce Garrard for permission to reproduce it from *Rainbow Village on the Road*. Thanks to Crass for permission to reproduce the illustrations pp. 75 and 80. The poster p. 92 is by Gee Vaucher; thanks to the artist for permission to reproduce it. The photographs pp. 121 and 122 are by Alan Lodge; thanks to the photographer for permission to reproduce them. Thanks to *Eternity* for permission to reproduce the magazine cover p. 124. The photograph p. 144 is by John Stillwell; © the Press Association. The book cover p. 151 is Clare Zine's *The End of the Beginning: Claremont Road, E11 Not M11*, Leeds/London 1995. The photograph p. 153 is by Alex MacNaughton; thanks to the photographer for permission to reproduce it. The photograph p. 157 is by Greg Piggot; thanks to the photographer for permission to reproduce it. The cartoon p. 174 is from *Aufheben*, no. 4, Summer 1995.

CHRONOLOGY OF EVENTS

1970   Phun City, *International Times* free festival

1971   hippy camp at Cinnamon Lane, Glastonbury
first Pilton Free Festival (became Glastonbury Festival)

1972   first Windsor Free Festival
first Barsham Faire, Suffolk
Festival Welfare Services founded
miners' strike

1973   Windsor Free Festival

1974   first Stonehenge Free Festival
last Windsor Free Festival, broken up by police
miners' strike
Albion Free State manifesto

1975   Watchfield Free Festival, the only officially aided free festival ever, is held as replacement for Windsor
Stonehenge organizer Wally Hope dies

1976   Tipi Valley is established, Dyfed, Wales
last Barsham Faire
Bungay May Horse Fair

1977   two sevens clash: the year of punk
Sex Pistols' 'God Save the Queen' tops the charts in Jubilee week, the official
celebrations marking the twenty-fifth anniversary of the Queen's coronation

1978   Crass form, release first record
first Albion fairs, in Suffolk and Norfolk
first Rougham Tree Fair, Suffolk
Rock Against Racism carnivals in London

1980   bikers clash with Crass and punks at Stonehenge Free Festival
urban riots in Bristol
New Age Gypsy Fair, Inglestone Common, Avon
Festival Welfare Services identifies forty-seven festivals across Britain

1981   Greenham Common Peace Camp, Berkshire, is set up
first Glastonbury Campaign for Nuclear Disarmament Festival
urban riots in cities across Britain

1982   group of vehicles leaves Stonehenge Free Festival and turns up at Greenham
Common Peace Camp – it is dubbed the Peace Convoy

1984   miners' strike
last Stonehenge Free Festival. Peace Convoy splits to Montgomery, then to
Moon Fair in Cumbria, then to Nostell Priory near Leeds; clashes with police
there
Crass disband; their last gig is a miners' benefit in Wales

1985   Rainbow Fields Village is evicted from Molesworth Common air base
Battle of Orgreave: police versus striking miners
Battle of the Beanfield, near Stonehenge: police versus the Peace Convoy
Peace Convoy at Greenlands Farm, Somerset

1986   Peace Convoy is blockaded at Stoney Cross, Hampshire

1988   acid house/rave scene declares the Second Summer of Love

1990   Poll Tax riot in Trafalgar Square, London

1991   Earth First! groups are set up in the UK

1992   Dongas Tribe forms at Twyford Down anti-M3 protest, Winchester, Hampshire
Castlemorton free festival/megarave
Exodus Collective forms in Luton, Bedfordshire, holds first free party
Yellow Wednesday at Twyford Down

1993   government backs down on proposed road through Oxleas Wood, London
protests against M11 link, east London: George Green and the Chestnut Tree,
Wanstead

1994   large protests at M11, M65 in Lancashire, M77 in Glasgow: Wanstonia and
Pollok Free State declare independence
Dongas Tribe goes on the Freedom Trail
groups opposed to the Criminal Justice Bill (CJB) such as Justice?, Advance
Party, Freedom Network flourish
anti-CJB riot in Hyde Park, London
introduction of Criminal Justice and Public Order Act
Claremont Road protest, east London, flourishes, is evicted

1995   animal rights protests spread: blockades and demonstrations against the
export of live animals take place at Shoreham, Brightlingsea, Coventry airport
Cosmic Tree Village, an anti-M65 camp, is set up in Stanworth Valley,
Lancashire
animal rights campaigner Jill Phipps dies at a demonstration
The Mother megarave (Castlemorton II) is thwarted
'University of Road Protest' is set up at protest camps in Devon

And so on . . .

INTRODUCTION

THE CULTURE(S) OF RESISTANCE

I am an anarchist!
I'm the anti-christ!
Well sort of . . .

Chumbawumba, 'Love Me'[1]

Fancy a bite to eat? We won't have a burger, there's a McLibel demo outside the shop. We certainly won't buy veal – RIP Jill Phipps. Can't really go for a spin, since we're boycotting petrol stations and motorway extensions. People are living in trees at the end of the road. Head for a train, past the patchwork of travellers' buses and trucks parked up on waste ground by the station. Give them a wave. Have a laugh at the slogans on the defaced billboards. Catch sight of a TV shop showing the news of the Home Secretary's country house invaded by the homeless. Britain's changing. Great, isn't it?

> The agents of this change are those typically categorized as creatures of the social wildlife: travellers, ravers, squatters, crusties, hunt saboteurs, animal liberationists; or, more overtly pejoratively, rioters, trespassers, or just plain good-for-nothing layabouts.[2]

These people form the subject of this book. In the 1990s in Britain there are an increasing number and variety of cultures of resistance, living what one road protester calls 'the DIY lifestyle'. New agendas are being set, often outside the traditional framework of British constitutional politics, and employing and developing strategies of direct action. Can we say that these groups constitute a politics of the disenfranchised, wherein the youth and marginals left out of Thatcher's revolution find their voices and use them to express their resentment and opposition? To an extent this is

1

so, though I'm wary of negating a sense of agency on the part of activists and others involved, of implying that they are just another product of Thatcherism. Also, I'm more concerned with tracing the links and sometimes tensions between present cultures of resistance and those of the recent past; the direct action politics of eco-radicalism, animal rights, the campaign against the 1994 Criminal Justice and Public Order Act (usually known as the Criminal Justice Act) and so on have not just sprung from nowhere to fill some post-Thatcherite vacuum. Interestingly, the scenario in which the significant politics of the time take place outside the standard political arena was itself being talked about over twenty-five years ago, as Theodore Roszak's sixties classic *The Making of a Counter Culture* illustrates. This was first published in 1968, and in it Roszak describes the political stalemate in Britain in perhaps surprisingly familiar terms, with the parliamentary parties left behind, reacting to events after the event: 'the Labour Party, angling always for the now decisive middle-class vote, is little more than Tweedledum to the Tories' Tweedledee'.[3]

So, in the 1990s we see the largely single-issue, direct action phenomenon of the new protest or, for those less materialist, New Age politics. The dangers of single-issue political action are that it diverts from class analysis, from economic challenge, or simply from having any wider perspective. These same dangers have been seen as its strength, too: it does indeed operate outside the traditional framework of left and right. New spaces have been opening up, which isn't always a comfortable situation, even for other political activists: what might be embraced with exhilaration is distanced with suspicion. (As Stuart Hall and Martin Jacques admit in their book on the New Times, 'The Left does not much like venturing into uncharted territory. It is filled with suspicion.'[4]) On the other hand, single-issue politics at their best move beyond their central focus to include larger concerns anyway. Consider the single-issue politics of hunt saboteurs: both a simplistic animal rights direct action coalition and a brilliantly chosen territory on which to fight, one that aims at fundamental aspects of Britishness – land ownership, class privilege, the display of wealth, even (especially) the very image of rural England itself (all those pubs called the Horse and Hounds, all those biscuit tin lids). Where did the single-issue explosion come from? Whether the environment, road protest more specifically, the range of animal rights protests, the coalition opposing the Criminal Justice Act – what are their origins? Where do the radical youth cultures of hippy, punk, rave fit in? (Is rave radical?)

Any analysis of recent youth movements and cultures that seek to challenge majority culture has the touchstone of the 1960s. There are many 1960s, but the version I particularly have in mind is the one of student demonstrations, anti-Vietnam protest, the women's movement, May 1968 in Paris, Woodstock and the later Isle of Wight, *International Times* and *Oz*. That decade is important not only from the perspective of the mid-1990s, a time when the 1960s are constantly being referred to and even rewritten (though often enough minus the politics), but for the periods in between too, for the 1970s when punk happened, for the 1980s when the Peace Convoy roamed the land. In fact, one of my arguments is to take issue with what might be an accepted view of the sixties – whether on the part of today's moral majority (minority) or on the part of veterans or students of the time – as producer of 'the failed generation', as the West's social experiment, or as a flirtation on the part of the West's radical youth with utopian possibility. This book sees the sixties as a beginning not an end. Of course, positing the sixties as a beginning has its own limitations: Anthony Esler's classic and committed book from the period *Bombs, Beards And Barricades* set out to show that youth revolution or counterculture is not by itself a new thing, indeed it extends far back beyond 1945 and the end of the Second World War.

> Practically everything our insurrectionary youth have tried – from New-Left militance to hippie-style withdrawal from society, from the campus revolt to the commune movement – has been tried before. The crucial importance of the Youth Revolution of our times lies not in its alleged uniqueness, but in that very continuity with history which the Movement itself – and most of its critics – have so vehemently denied.[5]

Esler's book ends where this one starts. He concludes: 'The Youth Revolution is not fading away. It is, in fact, a growing force in history.'[6] The optimism displayed here is perhaps justified by virtue of the book's contemporaneity: like Roszak's *The Making of a Counter Culture, Bombs, Beards And Barricades* was written during or soon after the events it describes. These books are infected with the heady drug of possibility of the time (that's what makes them so good). Retrospective analyses of the period are altogether less forgiving, not only because they are more sober but also because they are influenced by the changing perspectives on the period: in Esler's 1971 book the counterculture 'is not fading away'; Elizabeth Nelson's 1989 study opens '[m]ore than a decade after the fading away of the counterculture'.[7]

There is a way in which the sixties counterculture has a sad rather than nasty habit of turning its sense of failure, its bad karma, onto whatever's come next. An article from the mid-seventies is pessimistic in its view of the result of the counterculture. Sociologists Daniel A. Foss and Ralph W. Larkin argue that 'in its place have risen "post-movement groups" which embody various aspects of the vision of the 1960s youth movement (including the fantasy that they are dissident), but in every case have withdrawn from conflict with the larger social order'.[8] In effect, they claim, the sixties ended with a retreat into New Age mysticism or cultism – they cite as examples of this 'fragmentation of the youth culture' Hare Krishna, Guru Maharaj Ji, Scientology, et cetera.

> Whereas freaks had found meaning in maintaining a position of defiance and opposition to the 'plastic world', post-movement groups find meaning in escape from the complexities and incongruities of the material world (or the world of the mind) into a more transcendent simplified view of the cosmos independent of material reality.[9]

This may well have been the case in the United States, a republic notoriously reluctant to champion its own radical traditions, but in Britain activists tended to remain active. For instance, a survey of the militant organizations of the early Campaign for Nuclear Disarmament (CND) movement of the late 1950s onwards showed that 'these activists had gone on to a variety of other single-issue and/or community action campaigns rather than into "orthodox" politics' – or into cults or mystic groups.[10]

The narrative that proclaims the failure of the sixties counterculture is frequently repeated in books about it. Dates in titles of books signal this: Elizabeth Nelson's *The British Counter-Culture, 1966–73*, Nigel Fountain's *Underground: The London Alternative Press 1966–74*, Alan Beam's *Rehearsal For The Year 2000 . . . 1966–1976*. The cut-off dates alter, but there's a general reluctance to pursue the alternative project via any actions of the next generation. Yet these book titles imply only a short – indeed shortening – gap between the bemoaned 'end' of the counterculture and the straggly dyed green shoots of the next youth antagonism, punk rock. Fountain and Nelson are particularly guilty here: the focus of both their texts is the underground press, yet neither even mentions the explosion of fanzine culture that accompanied and contributed to the energy of the punk scene, clearly a prime example of an underground press. Not all hippy activists or writers about the scene are so myopic. In 1972, the underground publication *Frendz* optimistically proclaimed, 'if flower-power has gone to seed then germination must soon begin. And what King Weeds they'll be.'[11] In 1982, writing a paean to the life of Stonehenge Free Festival organizer Phil Russell, aka Wally Hope, hippy Penny Rimbaud of the anarcho-punk band Crass wrote:

> A year after Wally's death [1975], the Pistols released 'Anarchy in the UK', maybe they didn't really mean it ma'am, but to us it was a battle cry. When Rotten proclaimed that there was 'no future', we saw it as a challenge to our creativity – we knew there was a future if we were prepared to work for it. It is our world, it is ours and it has been stolen from us. We set out to demand it back, only this time they didn't call us 'hippies', they called us 'punks'.[12]

From the perspective of rave culture in the mid-1990s, another hippy veteran, Fraser Clark, picks up and radically extends the history of youth cultures of resistance:

> Ever since they managed to blackball the Hippy to death, the correct mode of Youth (as hope and conscience of the culture) has been systematically schizo-phrened from its historical roots. And we're talking about roots that go back through the punks, hippies, rebels, beats, bohemians, socialists, romantics, alchemists, the shakers and the Quakers, witches, heretics and, right back in the roots, pagans.[13]

One of the things hippy and punk had in common – at least in terms of my construction of them – was an oppositional impulse, an idealism or rhetoric of idealism. For both, politics and culture were, or could be, or should be, the same thing. In *The Assault on Culture*, Stewart Home points out that, 'In retrospect, punk also appears as a very straightforward progression from the sixties, whereas at the time it was perceived as a break.'[14] *Senseless Acts of Beauty* seeks to show in turn that, rather than being lost in what Jon Savage calls an 'explosion of negatives',[15] traces and activists from late 1970s punk rock have re-energized political activity and cultural radicalism since. What I'm doing, then, is uncovering links of resistance through actions, lifestyles and cultural production from the legacies of the hippies and punks onwards. The language of utopian desire can be seen in the ringing slogans of the culture of resistance over the years:

1960s: Be reasonable: demand the impossible
1970s: Reality's a substitute for utopia

1980s: Fight war not wars, destroy power not people
1990s: Go and commit a senseless act of beauty.

Utopian desire doesn't go away – it may even be stronger than ever today.

Culture(s) of resistance is a term offered in both the plural and the singular. Cultures of resistance feed the culture of resistance. Put another way, subcultures feed the counterculture – the range of subcultural movements from hippy through punk through rave and others contributes to the increasingly resistant lifestyle or perspective of counterculture. It's fair to say that *counterculture* is a rather unfashionable term today. While many of the styles of the hippy sixties have come round to being acceptable again, counterculture as a term and as a concept seems to have been sidestepped. Is counterculture too located in that period alone (or is it simply too overtly political for the fashion-centred nineties)? I'm arguing that it's not: one of the aims of this book is to reclaim the power of the notion of counterculture, partly to show that the utopian project of the sixties is still with us – in fact never really went away – and partly to signal that the traces and strands of resistance the book uncovers form some sort of larger and longer-lasting achievement, a significant challenge to majority culture. While not disagreeing with the fact that, as the critic Sarah Thornton notes, 'the vast majority of British youth subcultures, past and present, do not espouse overt political projects',[16] I emphasize that I'm not looking at *all* subcultures, only at those that I'm constructing as oppositional or politically radical. The deliberately and unashamedly partial narrative of *Senseless Acts of Beauty* seeks precisely to privilege those moments of culture and protest that have been most overlooked in recent cultural history. This book is intended as an antidote to the marginalization – disappearance, even – of cultures of resistance by youth and others in contemporary Britain.

While Lauren Langman can write in some 'notes on post-industrial youth' that 'the [1960s] counterculture is not a genuine culture, since it lacks its own historic tradition and its own economic base', I'm arguing that the post-1960s culture of resistance is in a stronger position altogether.[17] The historic tradition, in the form of networks built over the years, is one of the things I'm tracing through the book. Economic power – if it really is so important – can be seen in its negation through free festivals, the flaunted supercheap independent production and performance of the anarcho-punk scene, and 1990s 'lifestylism'; more straightforwardly, it's present in the rise of green consumerism. Langman also distinguishes between counterculture and subcultures more widely:

> The counterculture seeks a fundamental transvaluation of ethics, alternate life styles, and transformations of consciousness. The 'youth culture', as we call it, is more of an ideology, theme, or style than a clearly designated group. . . . [A]dherents of the counterculture may well be a minority of youth when we consider all the squares, greasers, surfers, hot-rodders, bike-freaks, and such.

To update this last point in relation to Britain: adherents of the culture of resistance may well be in a minority when we consider all the teds, mods, rockers, skins, casuals, grunge fans, etc., etc. To what extent are subcultures and counterculture the products of generational difference? Does each generation of youth simply do its own thing differently, rejecting that of its mothers and fathers, or big sisters and brothers? There are connections, surprising ones maybe, that belie a straightforward generational reading of events over the past three decades: individual activists like Penny Rimbaud or Fraser Clark move through from one moment to another – hippy to punk, hippy to rave; the space of the free festival scene is re-energized by punk, is transformed by rave culture; the lifestyles of New Age travellers are co-opted and politicized by peace campaigners or road protesters.

One central way in which cultures of resistance define themselves against the culture of the majority is through the construction of their own zones, their own spaces. These can be distinguished in part through the subcultural elements of music, style, or favoured drugs (if any – there usually are), but space itself is vital. In an interview with Jon Savage, bassist Pete Wright of anarcho-punk band Crass describes the opening up of space in late 1970s punk in musical terms:

> Wright: I went to see Television play, and [Tom Verlaine] stopped halfway through a guitar phrase, which no one had done for like ten years. He'd played exactly what he wanted, and the rest was space, and the same happened socially. Everyone was filling in bits and making sure everything was done, and then people were stopping and creating little bits of space. That's what I think was reverberating.
> Savage: That's very interesting, because you also had dub reggae, which had lots of space – the main thing was to drop out.[18]

Writing about the rave scene, Sarah Thornton makes a more general point: 'underground crowds are attached to sounds' – popular music is key in the identification of the zone.[19] (This isn't always a positive attribute. As we'll see, differences in musical taste can lead to violent tensions within countercultural zones.) Wally Hope, original organizer of the Stonehenge Free Festival, was a firm believer in the connection of youth, music and social change in the early seventies:

> Our temple is sound, we fight our battles with music, drums like thunder, cymbals like lightning, banks of electronic equipment like nuclear missiles of sound. We have guitars instead of tommy-guns.[20]

Of course, part-time utopias like the bohemian coffee bar scene, carnivalesque areas like the early open-air jazz festivals themselves bear traces of the countercultural zones or spaces I look at. These though are prior to 1960s counterculture, the counterculture of the hippy generation I take my cue from. The idea of the culture of resistance forming itself in part around the construction of a zone or space is one I develop from texts such as Hakim Bey's *TAZ: The Temporary Autonomous Zone, Ontological Anarchy, Poetic Terrorism*, which uses the term in the widest possible sense:

> The sixties-style 'tribal gathering', the forest conclave of eco-saboteurs, the idyllic Beltane of the neo-pagans, anarchist conferences, gay faery circles. . . . Harlem rent parties of the twenties, nightclubs, banquets, old-time libertarian picnics – we should realize that these all are already 'liberated zones' of a sort, or at least potential TAZs.[21]

Bey lists some of the characteristics of the TAZ:

> 'pirate economics', living high off the surplus of social overproduction – even the popularity of colourful military uniforms – and the concept of *music* as revolutionary social change – and finally their shared air of impermanence, of being ready to move on, shape-shift, re-locate to other universities, mountain-tops, ghettos, factories, safe houses, abandoned farms – or even other planes of reality.[22]

Note that what might normally be ascribed as a sign of failure – impermanence – is in this anarchist philosophy celebrated as a symptom of ubiquity – of Ubi-ness, as it might have been seen at Windsor Free Festival. The down side of this seemingly perverse but typically anarchist approach is straightforward enough: endless transgression, little or no transformation. The spectacle of rebellion replaces the possibility of revolution, if you like. I'm suggesting on the other hand that we *celebrate the spark of transgression*,[23] see in its spreading flash the ongoing possibility, even see *with* its spreading flash. (The trouble with writing about things New Age is you get infected with its rhetoric.)

I think it's as well briefly to explain the range of social and cultural material I'm dealing with here. Through their forms of social and political organization, their clothes and language, their magazines and records, their e-mails and faxes, cultures of resistance are difficult to pin down. Their autonomy can be compounded by their transitoriness, and features like these may be central to their very identity: autonomy and anarcho-punk, transitoriness and New Age travellers – they go hand in hand. Many aspects are interrelated, and on occasion I have to introduce a feature before I explore it later in depth since it touches on the material I'm currently dealing with. For instance, I discuss the Peace Convoy in the chapter on free festivals, but look at it more closely in the later chapter on New Age travellers. I'm balancing the effort to offer a clear and largely chronological line with the desire *not* to construct an over-arching master narrative that might smooth out contradictions, tensions, gaps. The book looks at both lifestyle and direct action politics of young and not so young people since the 1960s: 1972 is a more accurate starting date, this being the year of the first Windsor Free Festival and the first East Anglian fair at Barsham. Lost narratives, partial utopias, the odd temporary nightmare, political confrontation, radical culture through music, style and forgotten books are all uncovered and analysed. This is the first time many of the actions and cultural projects mentioned here have been given the critical attention I know they fully deserve. It has been a joy to write – I've read about and met some seriously uplifting people! Believe me! If you get half the pleasure and inspiration out of reading it as I did writing it then I've done my job.

1

THE FREE FESTIVALS AND

FAIRS OF ALBION

(1) *Albion is the other England of Peace and Love* which William Blake foresaw in vision –
a country freed of dark satanic mills and similar Big-Brother machinations. . . .
(6) The dispossessed people of this country need *Land* – for diverse needs, permanent
free festival sites, collectives, and cities of Life and Love, maybe one every fifty miles or
so, manned and womaned by people freed from dead-end jobs and from slavery in
factories mass-producing non-essential consumer items.
(7) We beware of substitutes: Beware!: *Reality's a substitute for Utopia.*

Albion Free State manifesto, 1974[1]

I'm fascinated by Albion Free State.

Judge Boveen, during a Windsor Free Festival trial in 1975[2]

So were an increasing number of older and younger people in Britain in the mid-
seventies. Anarcho-punks talk of the 'loose network' of people and actions around the
country, and, as we'll see, this is a recurring feature of radical youth and subcultural
moments in Britain. In the Albion Free State manifesto of 1974, a group of London-
based hippy activists and hedonists proclaimed the end result of their activities as
'being a *network* (which already exists in embryo) of *independent collectives and communities*, federated together to form the Albion Free State'.[3] There are any number of
loose networks, which themselves form more loose networks, connecting up and
antagonizing one another in fuzzy order. It's this loose network of loose networks that
I'm tracing through the book, and that I'm suggesting can be seen as forming some
sort of decentred, autonomous counterculture. (I'm already trying to have my master

narrative and eat it here, a struggle that takes place through the entire book.) That is, all kinds of varied styles, subcultures, radical interest and protest groups, from different generations, each with their own or no agenda, the length and breadth of Britain, have been notably busy this past couple of decades, forming alliances, forcing confrontation, surprising themselves and each other, doing things on the quiet, living it . . . I want to look now at a couple of related loose networks, the *bricolage* or patchwork structures and events of free festivals and fairs, which have sprung up in rural areas, which have brought the city to the countryside.

From Windsor Free to Stonehenge

Touch, we touched the very soul
of holding each and every life.
We claimed the very source of joy ran through.
It didn't, but it seemed that way.

David Bowie, 'Memory of a Free Festival'[4]

I'm a materialist, but I've always been glad I was blessed by some pagan shaman type in the stones at Stonehenge in the summer of 1984. (In that year of all years, *anything* helped.) Chillums were passed as he went round with his pint mug of stones's mud, his finger dipping into it, then touching your forehead. Fifteen years before, even the early Bowie was touched by the spirit of free festival, gazing at the illusion, uncovering the hippy roots of proto-punks Aladdin and Ziggy.

Trace the free festivals of Britain backwards and you end up in two places, the USA during and after the summer of love in 1967, and Britain itself, with its own longstanding history of seasonal and nomadic festivals and fairs in the country and the city. Amerika and Albion. I'm interested in the different kinds of events these two antecedents spawned in the free festivals and fairs, part of the early *and* the long-lasting countercultural activity in Britain. It's clear that the American hippies were a key source of inspiration. 'The [American] Hippies . . . constituted themselves as walking critiques of bureaucratic rationality,' write Daniel Foss and Ralph Larkin retrospectively. The hippies' critique – well, Abbie Hoffman's – was a reconfiguration of the notion of *revolution* as 'a spontaneous anarchic explosion of individuals and emerging collectivities pursuing unrepressed and joyous development in an increasingly uncompromising fashion'. Foss and Larkin continue:

> By the late 1960s 'freakified' youth were exploring new aspects of self-hood which they had never previously thought existed. Indulgence in drug experiences, sex, communal activities, be-ins, sit-ins, demonstrations, riots, busts, trips with no destination in particular, not only gave subculture members a set of common experiences, but also opened up vast new capacities of self-hood for exploration.[5]

Where did all these 'new aspects of self-hood', these possibilities of subjectivity, lead to? A beautifully (naïvely: same thing) optimistic assessment of the near future that would be created by 1960s American 'post-industrial youth' is offered by Lauren Langman in 1971. Her unconditional future tense brooks no doubt, signals the sense of potential in the air of the period, shows the range of countercultural concerns. In the near future there 'will be':

(1) Decreased military spending . . .
(2) Genuine concern for the environment . . .
(3) Subsidy for those who wish to experiment with life styles . . .
(4) Greater redistribution of wealth.
(5) An end to 'victimless crimes', e.g. consenting sex acts, gambling, prostitution, drugs.[6]

Langman's list is not *altogether* inaccurate – though we should be wary of confusing rhetoric with political action, especially in relation to the United States's policies on the environment and the poor – but what has the 1960s counterculture resulted in and been replaced by? In America, by deadhead capitalism, a child of the time who touched a joint but fortunately didn't inhale, by the moral majority and by the backlash movement – against feminism, welfare, political correctness . . . Think of Gil Scott-Heron's lines in his classic 1981 protest song 'B-movie' which, though we hoped otherwise at the time, can be seen to have such prescience: 'Civil rights, women's rights, gay rights – it's all wrong.'[7] In Britain, the sixties were followed by the destruction of the unions, seemingly endless years of Thatcherism voted in again and again by the English, raft upon raft of new legislation covering up prejudice – and, well, punk rock, a resurgence of interest in anarchism, free festivals and fairs, the rave scene, the increasing amount and even respectability of direct action protest.

Free festivals are most notoriously framed in America in 1969 by the utopia of Woodstock and – a mere four months later – the dystopia of Altamont, Hell's Angels murdering while the Rolling Stones play 'Sympathy for the Devil'. One writer in the underground *International Times* viewed things in this way: 'Woodstock is the potential but Altamont is the reality.'[8] According to Elizabeth Nelson, 'Although Altamont hardly stemmed the flow of free festivals in Britain, it almost certainly affected the attitude of the British counterculture to what might be termed the festival idea.'[9] I'm not sure about this: Woodstock and Altamont are so early in the timetable of British free festivals, they've almost been and gone before the British scene is in any way established. (It may be that the influence of Woodstock is felt later, when the movie is released and distributed in Britain. Nigel Fountain similarly suggests that the *film* of the 1967 Monterey festival exported the romance, the desire of such events to Britain.) In 1969 the British scene is utterly embryonic; in fact, free festivals in Britain are one activity that can clearly be said to have outlived the hippy counterculture from which they sprang.

There is an earlier American film influence on the development of British music festivals, namely the films of Newport and other jazz festivals. In spite of the vagaries of climate, Britons too wanted to experience *Jazz on a Summer's Day*. '[S]ince the early 1960s the British had gathered in wet fields to hear jazz, [and] 1968 had seen an outbreak of small festivals, with even a fair-sized event (12,000) on the Isle of Wight, ... [but] 1969 was the year that rock festivals took off in Britain.'[10] Blind Faith at Hyde Park in June, the Rolling Stones there in July, Bob Dylan on the Isle of Wight in August. It's ironic and apt that the free festival movement in Britain rather stumbled into existence – the White Panthers helping the fences come down at the final Isle of Wight in 1970.[11] Another event that quickly turned into a kind of free festival, what may have been Britain's first consciously organized along non-profit-making lines, was Phun City.[12] This event was organized by the then underground writer Mick Farren, inspired by what he saw – following Woodstock in August 1969 – as the utopian possibility of connecting counterculture with rock music. The event was publicized through the underground press, including one of the most widely circulating hippy-politico magazines, *International Times*. July 1970 was the date, described retrospectively by Nigel Fountain as the underground's 'Indian summer'. Shambolic organization and finances, court injunctions and the local drugs squad led what was originally planned as a profit-free enterprise to end up effectively as a free festival, with between three and ten thousand people – depending on who you read – camped in the woods by Worthing, Sussex. There was free music, free food, even free drugs: at least one dealer 'sold dope until he had covered his costs. Then he gave it away.'[13]

Actually, the early free *festivals* – as opposed to simply one-off free concerts – were commercial events which either went wrong, or were challenged or overwhelmed by their audiences:[14] a month after Phun City the final Isle of Wight festival attracted upwards of a quarter of a million people, many of whom were unhappy about the rip-off prices for admission and food, and about the general musical organization. Within a couple of days the fences were torn down and a free festival was declared (just like Woodstock complete with food shortages), outside the now physically guarded VIP enclosure.[15] The following summer, underground rockers the Edgar Broughton Band planned to take the idea of festival on the road. A free tour of British seaside towns was organized. The resort of Blackpool, a self-proclaimed centre of pleasure and indulgence, reacted strongly to the possibility of such subversives coming, and 'slapped a ban on all such free shows for the next 25 years'.[16]

> Free festivals are practical demonstrations of what society could be like all the time: miniature utopias of joy and communal awareness rising for a few days from grey morass of mundane, inhibited, paranoid and repressive everyday existence. . . . The most lively [young people] escape geographically and physically to the 'Never Never Land' of a free festival where they become citizens, indeed rulers, in a new reality.[17]

The political margin of the early free festival scene in Britain was crystallized by one particular yearly event, special because of its almost founding status, its means of organization, its setting and the way in which it attracted ever-increasing numbers of festival-goers. This was the Windsor Free Festival, which took place in 1972, 1973 and, finally, 1974, when the event, by now deemed too illegal, was broken up by police action. Windsor Free has partly entered countercultural legend because of the way it was conceived and organized. As with Stonehenge a couple of years later, the sheer audacity of its beginnings is quite extraordinary. In *Rehearsal For the Year 2000*, Alan Beam explains that 'Bill "Ubi" Dwyer, tall, upright & honest, and in temperament as fierce as an army colonel, is "by the grace of God, originator and co-ordinator of the Windsor Free Festivals"'.[18] With Ubi's great story, who knows or cares what's fact and myth, but here's a version I've cobbled together from different sources.[19] In the early seventies Ubi was living in a commune in a squatted fire station in Fleet Street in London. Tripping on acid in Windsor Great Park he had a Blakean vision of a communitarian utopia, which he thought he could bring to life by holding 'a giant festival in the grandest park in the kingdom, seven miles long!' Why hold it at Windsor? Because it's an effort to reclaim land enclosed for hunting by royalty centuries before – an updating of seventeenth-century Digger strategy, challenging the later seizure by George III of Windsor common land. Ubi strikes at the heart of the British Establishment and property-owning classes. Accounts of the numbers of invitations distributed and of people attending fluctuate wildly. 'For August 1972 Ubi invited four million people to Windsor Great Park but only a few thousand turned up. They spent a few days in a copse and hardly anyone noticed them.' One slogan of the Windsor Frees was PAY NO RENT. The second festival was also a rally for the legalization of cannabis, and 10,000 to 20,000 people turned up for nine days of (what's so funny about) peace, love and understanding in the shadow of one of the British royal family's several estates. The Queen was invited, but wrote declining to attend. The fact that she *did* reply was taken by Ubi 'as a form of encouragement. . . . [W]hile not exactly enthusiastic, this letter was not actually hostile.' The Windsor Frees were publicized by a leaflet campaign organized by Ubi – in a neat irony, at one stage he was working for Her Majesty's Stationery Office during the day while distributing stationery against her majesty and her privilege and property during the evenings. For what became crunch year, 1974,

> 300,000 leaflets were distributed in Britain and overseas, British Rail arranged to lay on extra trains, and 300 bands offered their services free. Ubi decided that to accommodate all the bands there should be 6 stages spread throughout the site, with 6 stage managers, each with a team working with him. He also arranged with the United Nations that they should use the festival to hold an Ecological Fair.

The UN couldn't get it together, but many thousands of others did, including some unwelcome but perhaps not unexpected gatecrashers, a large contingent of police (eight hundred, according to Alan Beam). But more on that later.

The South-west of England, with its comfortable climate and ancient landscapes, and its accessibility from London and the Midlands, soon became the favoured region

The underground press tells of the struggle for Stonehenge Free.

for free festivals. In 1971 the first Glastonbury Fayre had been held, with its pyramid stage, at Worthy Farm.[20] The same year as the final Windsor Free, the first Stonehenge festival also took place. Stonehenge was to become the longest-lasting annual event in the counterculture's calendar, in two ways. First, by growing to spread over the entire month of June each year, and second by virtue of surviving for over a decade. This was a squatted event celebrating the summer solstice, hatched by Phil Russell aka Wally Hope with help from friends including some who would later be involved with anarcho-punks Crass. Penny Rimbaud recalls Hope's 'ludicrous plan . . . to claim back Stonehenge . . . and make it a site for free festivals, free music, free space, free mind', inspired by Ubi and the Windsor Free Festivals.[21] Kevin Hetherington describes 'the host of meanings given to Stonehenge' as a social space:

The struggle continues.

an important archaeological site, a temple, an ancient astronomical instrument, a tourist attraction, a symbol of ancient Britain as culturally and technologically skilled, a New Age site of worship, part of England's cultural heritage, a node in a system of powerful ley lines, and the site of an annual rock festival.[22]

Latching onto the solstice rituals of Druids at Stonehenge which themselves go back only to the turn of the century, the hippies invent an instant and powerful tradition. Squatter and original Hyde Park Digger Sid Rawle pinpointed the historicity in a letter to *The Times* in 1978, which explained: 'We come to Stonehenge because in an unstable world it is proper that the people should look for stability to the past in order to learn for the future.'[23] Rimbaud describes the exhilarating contradiction of

Stonehenge: 'Wood-fires, tents and tipis, free food stalls, stages and bands, music and magic. Flags flew and kites soared. Naked children played in the woodlands, miniature Robin Hoods *celebrating their material poverty.*'[24] The utopian celebration of poverty at Stonehenge became an annual event for hippies, then for punks, then for travellers too until 1985 when, with tactics honed during the miners' strike, backed by the respectability of English Heritage, police trashed the convoy on its way to the stones.[25]

Stonehenge Free Festival, June 1984

With its peculiarly unimpressing stones. Maybe on Midsummer's Eve when the druids dance it'll seem more exciting. Hitching was great and we get here real early – only four hours from Nottingham, and straight to the gate. Just coming up a hill and round the corner in a retired Lord's faithful Vauxhall we first see the two sights. On the left of the road the ramshackle rocks looking like lost fainting guards, and on the right the shimmer silver through the heat haze of the hundreds of tents and tipis. It's frightening and exhilarating. All you do is walk through the gate and you're part of some other. This takes a surprising amount of nerve.

Your first sight is the decrepit twig and polythene benders lining the entry path selling all kinds of drugs. Brazen flaunting of authority – when will something give? Everyone is selling everything here – small business free (man) enterprise lives and thrives. Get down to Stonedhenge Maggie see your utopia. I saw a big bus full of equally decrepit hippies though who had a big sign (small, actually) saying 'Fuck all for sale'. Tents are everywhere, mingled like allotments with hired vans, stolen cars, ancient buses, predominantly British bikes, nudes (alive), nudes (dead), and human/dog shit. For a supposedly ecologically aware subculture there is much live wood burnt and litter everywhere.

There's a main stage, shaped like a pyramid, with a dope-leaf motif five feet high at the front, two or three smaller stages in ramshackle tents with PAs tipped out of coaches. There are more interesting sideshows. There are some fine-looking hippy women here with long hair, long legs flashing through thin baggy dresses. Someone is atop a theatre company transit van adjusting a flag made from a patterned dress, ones like sold in Head In The Clouds. I've yet to see any band that's not completely mediocre. The hippies don't mind though. Their idea seems to be to sit in a field with many a similar type for all the summer months and destroy brain and body cells.

I got up and had a wash in a trough and went back and sat and lay in the almost oppressive heat for what seemed like the rest of the day. No one has watches. Only the St John's people are busy, well them and the dealers. For breakfast a cup of tea and a jam buttie, as the sun belts down melting me like margarine. The guy in the tent next to ours blares out superloud headache-inducing guitar hero heavy metal.

Gets claustrophobic, though. You see strange unfamiliarized faces in the throng – clean village girls up to see the annual strangeness, American tourists camera-ready and in vain for rocks, youth unused to atmosphere. Men and women walk round naked, like at the Isle of Wight all those years ago, yeah? I am a quick wreck, approaching white-corpse-with-red-eyes. I don't find the atmosphere of this festival so free, more oppressing or intimidating a bit. Dunno, maybe I'm just feeling the collective force of challenge that a two-generation (hippies and punks) alternative can offer, and that might not be an altogether enjoyable experience.

Last night was it I fell asleep before the summer solstice dawn rose. Eventually we go to see the stones, and the druids (looking remarkably like a bunch of smashed ramshackle hippies) were performing one of their ceremonies. It wasn't very pagan, though I did get blessed by one chief man with a daub of holy mud on my forehead. Bongos and assorted drums beat out an earth rhythm, which all right did have the hypnotic effect of feeling sort of like mother nature's heartbeat or whatever. We were inside the broken rings, sitting on the stones, right in the middle of any force that might call upon us or forth from us.

I begin to feel really more free and comfortable and I suppose peaceful here, after a couple of days and the dawning of familiarity. It is so alternative in many ways – are the drugs both symbol and cause of freedom? Like when the ceremony is on at the stones, it's one of the few times that they actually take away all of the fences and let anyone and everyone wander round and touch the rocks where and as they were once touched by the people who made them. We who gather here in Nineteen Eighty-Four for Christ's sake! are a challenge and alternative to what normally goes on, and that generates fear (viz. police helicopter constantly buzzing overhead, weary and war-worn from picket duty, and some of the pubs in the village signing refusal to serve festival-goers).

When you look round at the hippies and punks here you see how merging they have become over the years, which is maybe a surprise to many of the young people who first came alive with punk (like me), seen as a movement against everything hippy stood for. The thing is that a lot of the 'punk' musicians were older and from that hippy generation. Amalgamation maybe inevitable because both came to offer youth alternatives, and there are a finite number of variations on the basic theme of alternative lifestyles. Bands like Crass and Poison Girls had a lot to do with uniting the two, because of the combination of their anarchist/pacifist/vegetarian politics and their (early, at least) aggressive punk sound. They are good because they actually live their alternative, their independence (like through their record company set-up). When you look at the throngs of young people here (very few stray sixties survivors) the punks & hippies even almost dress the same, esp. the women, with their long frilly skirts, varied tops, bare and dirty feet, dark skin and easy smiles, tons of belts and bangles to herald their arrival. Sometimes only the hair colour tells the difference. The hippy blokes wear straight trousers (hardly any flares at all), punk blokes have long hair. It is just so powerful and present (what I mean is the fact that it's actually happening, it's actually here and now, alive) – intense presence of unification of ideas and lifestyles here is a positive, enervating, almost tangible feeling. I love it here. I am comfortable and at ease and I suppose peaceful in this place. It's good to spend three hours working up to a walk round the site, the stalls, dealers, people drugged up and down, people normal, dusty roads with home-dug speed bumps to slow down dodging British motorbikes, signs for dope everywhere, stages with crews incessantly fixing up equipment but never a band playing.

It's important to emphasize, through the story as I've told it so far, that free festivals in Britain were *not* a central part of the 1960s counterculture – they'd hardly got going when the sixties ended. The political engagement of rock music as a whole at the time is questionable. George Melly notes in *Revolt into Style* that 'the spring and summer of 1968, the time of the great "demos", of the "battle of Grosvenor Square" . . . was surely the moment when you might have expected pop to provide the anthems, the marches, the songs for the barricades. In fact it did nothing of the sort.'[26] Free festivals have some origin in the sixties, yes, but it's really the mid-seventies that they become common and popular – Windsor Free culminating, Stonehenge beginning, both in 1974. Free festivals thrive throughout the seventies, and (debatably) inspire different though related events, such as the East Anglian fairs I look at below. What's the point I'm leading to? That the acme of the free festival scene was during the short period leading up to the beginning of punk, and during some of the most active years of punk – the late seventies, even early eighties. Free festivals thus quickly became a site of negotiation between generations of sub- and countercultures, as well as a site of contestation between festival-goers and the majority culture. Below we'll see that the neat and tidy sound of 'sites of negotiation and contestation' is misleading – Windsor Free in 1974, and events at Stonehenge in 1980 and nearby in 1985 illustrate the tensions and violence involved.

I'm suggesting that the free festival is a significant event at which, peaking in the period of subcultural transition from the mid-seventies to the mid-eighties, the hippy and the punk came together. It's a site of negotiation and transformation between radical subcultures. Their radical nature needs stressing: both hippies and punks leaned towards anarchist cultural politics, and the quarter-organized chaos of a free festival offers an easy homological fit. This isn't necessarily the case with all subcultures: I have a striking image in my head from a late 1970s Reading Festival – the respectable, commercial side of the rock festival scene. Rabble-rousing punk type Jimmy Pursey of Sham 69 is holding hands onstage with a bemused-looking Steve Hillage, once of Gong, proclaiming solidarity between 'the punks and skins and longhairs!' At this very moment, with a sense of irony I didn't know they possessed, Sham 69's main followers rise as one from among the sitting afternoon masses. There is an instant swarm of Crombies, Harringtons, Air Wair, cropped hair, as hundreds of skinheads rush to the stage, kicking others out of the way, chanting 'Jimmy is our lee-ea-der!' or some other such crap, throwing cans and punches. Hippies and skinheads do *not* form counter-cultural utopia here . . .

So what kinds of cultural products do justify my argument about subcultural nego-tiation and transformation? There are my own contemporary comments from my diary of Stonehenge, above. The B side of an early single by the Fall, themselves per-haps surprisingly involved in free festivals bearing in mind Mark E. Smith's reluctance to be easily located or categorized, catches a sense of the continuity. At the end of 'Repetition', recorded in 1977, Smith sings (sort of), 'Groovy blank genera-tion, swinging blank generation'.[27] The groovy, swinging late sixties meets the blank generation of the late seventies in a repeat performance. Smith's delivery suggests that this is an occasion to sneer at a lack of imagination: 'same old blank generation' means repetition is a wholly negative process for him. There's another musical text that reflects more clearly and more positively the early hippy/punk mix of free fes-tivals and free tours. *What You See . . . Is What You Are* is an album released in 1978 on an independent punk label, Deptford Fun City Records.[28] As the handwritten sleeve notes inform us, it's a live recording 'made on Mickey Mouse cassette recorders on the Summer '78 free tour'. One side features the hippy/space cadet band Here & Now, the other the original punk band Alternative TV, led by fanzine innovator Mark Perry of *Sniffin' Glue*.[29] Both bands played on the tour around Britain, stopping off with roadies and dogs and friends on 'the big red bus' at festivals and free con-certs, joining each other on stage for chaotic, feedbacking encores. The cover photo captures just such an occasion. The back photo shows everyone involved posing in

WHAT YOU SEE...

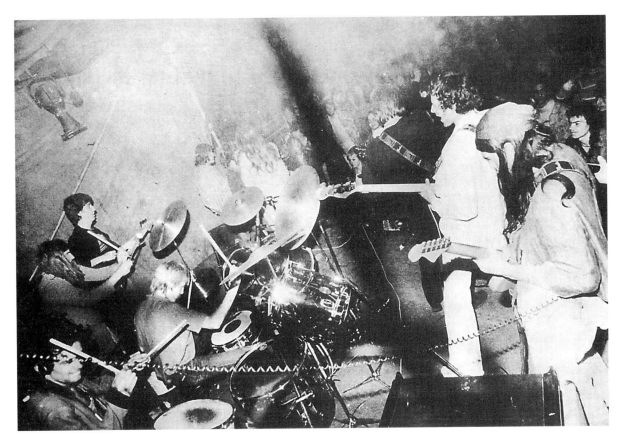

IS WHAT YOU ARE

Love and peace meets hate and war: the hippy/punk crossover on the 1978 free festival circuit.

front of the bus, in a flat festival field with the odd tent, transit van and motorbike in the background. All are smiling, sort of. The sleeve notes at the end maintain the utopian aspect of the entire project: 'Thanks to everyone who *gave* cos thats the way its going. Go with it.' The only disappointment is that the destination board on the bus doesn't read NOWHERE. The musical trajectory of Alternative TV itself shows a shift. In 1977, they offer short and direct studio singles like 'How Much Longer', a song whose lyrics are about subcultural styles and rivalries, presented in a standard verse–chorus structure:

> How much longer will people wear
> Nazi armbands and dye hair
> Safety pins, and spray their clothes
> Talk about anarchy, fascism and boredom?
>
> Well you don't know nothing, and you don't really care.
>
> How much longer will joss sticks rule
> They have their hair long and stringy and wear jesus boots
> Afghan coats, yeah making peace signs, maaan
> Talk about Moorcock, Floyd at the Reading Festival?
>
> Well you don't know nothing, and you don't really care.
> The punks don't know nothing, the hippies don't know nothing . . .
> Well we all don't know nothing and we all don't fucking caa-aare![30]

Competing subcultural styles and discourses (not just what they wear, but also the different things they talk about) are treated as both serious and daft: they're all-important for people who 'know nothing'. The self-ironizing delivery parodies the Sex Pistols at the end. On *What You See . . . Is What You Are* from a year later, Alternative TV offer a rare flower from the dustbin, a punk epic, one that works. 'Fellow Sufferer' is a eleven-minute piece centred around a slow repeated bass figure and a clicking guitar sound suggesting that, as the lyrics say, 'time is passing'. Over these is Perry's London voice, talking/singing about the events of 1977 to 'Gillian', the woman he addresses in the song. There's no chorus, rather a long slow narrative offered live to a free audience. He repeats words, takes his time, in a performance that's not punk, but comes from it and is in part about it, and that's not hippy, but wouldn't have been possible without the space and style of 1960s rock.

When we were soldiers on the same route
Encouraging each other to fight, to fight!
Oh lord god we were knights
The knights of the future
The knights of the future
But our armour
Our armour – it melted in the hot sun
The summer of seventy-seven, it was so hot
The armour, it just melted
And we were left, just standing.[31]

To my own surprise, I think the British hippy movement has been misrepresented, and the main villain in this misrepresentation is the subculture that came after hippy, that initially shoved it out of the way: punk. We've heard a great deal over the years about, say, the organization of punk bands like the Sex Pistols by Malcolm McLaren or the Clash by Bernie Rhodes, the behind-the-scenes organizers being almost as well known as the bands themselves. What's lost is the fact that, only a very few years before the anarchist-influenced activities of the likes of McLaren, individual hippy activists were themselves doing quite breathtakingly cheeky and subversive things: look at Ubi and the Windsor Frees, or Wally Hope and Stonehenge, or Alan Beam and Albion Free State. Even more interestingly, the motivations of Ubi, Hope, Beam are less transparently commercial than those of McLaren and Rhodes trying to capture fame and fortune in the music industry. From this perspective it's possible that punk in its early days is a diversion from the subversive utopian impulses of the preceding counterculture – that it *is* the 'explosion of negatives' Jon Savage describes it as. In this reading, punk opens with a retreat from (hippy) engagement – 'I hate hippies,' said Johnny Rotten – into a hedonistic, narcissistic space of the individual . . . maybe in the way that rave is seen to replicate at *its* beginnings a decade or so later, now rejecting the sloganizing politics of punk and post-punk. Is this the way that oppositional counterculture functions today? Opening with an attention-grabbing burst of self-indulgence, of ego energy to distance the generations, before its more aware political types express their voices and ideas?

Stamp on them

The free festivals were anarchist celebrations of freedom, as opposed to socialist demonstrations against oppression and, as such, presented the authorities with a new problem – how do you stop people having fun? Their answer was predictable – *stamp on them.*[32]

The subversive politics of pleasure hoped for by Ubi Dwyer at the Windsor Frees provoked what Crass saw as the 'predictable' reaction from the authorities, one which would be repeated near Stonehenge a decade later, and at other small and large festival gatherings up and down the country year in, year out. In court a few months after the festival, with terrific aplomb suing the Chief Constable of the Thames Valley Police for damages incurred during the police action (and winning!), Alan Beam described the night before the police clearing of the Windsor Free:

I told how it was like a medieval fair, or a gathering of North American indians, and that each group of tents had its own flag, that the peoples were gathered almost in tribes, with the people from Nottingham in one group, and those from Stoke-on-Trent in another, and that I went round every camp fire on the site. 'It was like . . .'

The Judge broke in with a very well-timed prompt: 'like Agincourt perhaps?'

This was exactly what I'd been going to say – 'Yes Sir, it made me think of Agincourt, except we had no king and we weren't expecting a battle the next day.'[33]

A battle there was, though, one that would provoke sympathy for the festival-goers and criticism of the police. In the early morning of 29 August 1974 a large contingent of police broke up the third, the last, the biggest Windsor Free Festival. As Penny Rimbaud of Crass put it, 'The days of flower-power were over, the pigs were out grazing in the meadows.'[34] Eight hundred police, in fact. The site was cleared, in spite of there having been negotiations between police, Crown Estate Commissioners and festival organizers as to its precise location in Windsor Great Park (it had been moved on police orders from the south end to further north, away from the royal residence), in spite of the 1974 festival having already been going quite peacefully for five days, and in spite of an apparent assurance from police that the festival could continue until its advertised last night on Sunday, 1 September. Festival-goers were woken up and ordered to leave the site. Not all did, determined to resist this surprise police action. Indeed, one of the key issues in the aftermath of events revolved around precisely why the police thought it necessary to employ an element of surprise. Surely calm negotiation would have far more peacefully and successfully cleared the site, if that was the only aim of the exercise? The suspicion was that the festival, now in its third year, was becoming too large, and that its size increased the provocation perceived by the Establishment on behalf of the royal family. The spectacular flourishing of the culture of resistance needed to undergo the first of its periodic curtailments. As anarchists Crass saw it, 'Tens of thousands of people had come to ensure that Her Royal Majesty remained unamused and she, in turn, was waiting in the guise of a massive police presence.'[35] Fighting took place sporadically through the day, especially near Stage A, and it became clear that, while apparently tightly structured and controlled in units and zones, the police operation quickly went out of control. Wally Hope, fresh from the first Stonehenge Free Festival, described something of what he saw: 'the police dragging away a young boy, punching and kicking him, I saw a pregnant woman being kicked in the belly and a little boy being punched in the face. All around the police were just laying into people.'[36] The activation of an old suspended sentence as well as new charges saw Ubi Dwyer jailed; his sentence included the first ever conviction for the offence of incitement to commit a public nuisance. That was the end of Windsor Free, but the three annual Windsor Frees were the beginning of a serious countercultural way of life.

Even government could on occasion be aware of this. The Stevenson Committee's 1973 report to the Department of Environment states:

> These young people have been expressing a need to get away from their immediate environment and the inhibitions and limitations of everyday life – particularly in our towns – to a situation in which they can experiment socially, come face to face with new ideals and concepts of life and decide for themselves what they wish to accept or reject.[37]

It appears that not all chief constables read government reports in order to work out their strategies, or that they understand 'coming face to face with new ideals and concepts of life' as punching in the nose and pulling out the hair – the two assaults Alan Beam and friends sued the Thames Valley Chief Constable over and won, a story

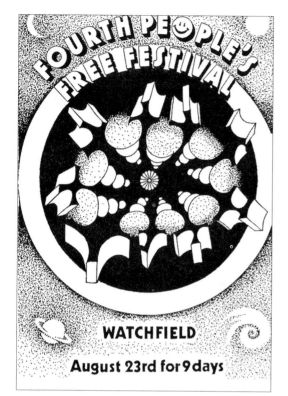

The Windsor Free moves to Watchfield in 1975: the only free festival ever organized with help from the government.

gleefully recounted in Beam's *Rehearsal for the Year 2000*. The 1976 follow-up report from the Department of Environment's Working Group on Pop Festivals surprisingly perhaps offers an even more glowing review:

We agree with the Stevenson Committee that pop festivals – whether commercial or free – are a reasonable and acceptable form of recreation. . . . [F]ree festivals in particular are developing an interest in a number of activities – for example, theatre, folklore, mime, rural arts and crafts, alternative technology and experimental architecture. . . . We think that festivals can offer useful experience to young people in living away . . . from the facilities of modern society.[38]

Such amazingly positive views from government reports[39] confirm the toleration stated in an anonymous leaflet about free festivals and counterculture from 1978, that 'Britain has been virtually the only country in the world to tolerate free festivals.'[40] Ominously though, the leaflet continues: 'There is no certainty that this toleration will continue.' On occasion, toleration needs to come from within as well as from without. Stonehenge Festival ran each June from its inception by Wally Hope in 1974 to its enforced demise in 1985. As the festival grew in size so did tensions between groups of festival-goers. Sometimes there was no need for the authorities of the majority culture to do the stamping – the venerable tradition of subculture wars would supply its own violence. As with mods and rockers, or with punks and teds, subcultural energy can divert itself from what I'm arguing can be seen as the constructively utopian to the simply self-destructive. The American precedent here of course is Altamont.[41] Tensions exploded at Stonehenge in 1980 between punks and bikers, when anarcho-punk band Crass attempted to play the festival. As we've seen, members of Crass had been involved in originally organizing the festival with Wally Hope, and they had had a long-term dream to 'play the festival as a kind of memorial to him'. The presence of Crass at Stonehenge 'attracted several hundred punks to whom the festival scene was a novelty; they, in turn, attracted interest from various factions to whom punk was equally new'.[42] The process of subcultural negotiation I mentioned earlier was about to take place. From being a relaxed summer evening, around the main stage things suddenly changed.

> [A] group of bikers stormed the stage. . . . Bikers, armed with bottles, chains and clubs, stalked around the site viciously attacking any punk that they set eyes on. . . . There were screams of terror as people were dragged off into the darkness to be given lessons on peace and love. . . . Meanwhile, the predominantly hippy gathering, lost in the soft blur of their stoned reality, remained oblivious of our fate.

Crass were attacked and many of their punk fans were beaten up by Hell's Angels and other bikers with little sense of history or gratitude who saw punks poaching on *their* territory. The gap between countercultural theory and practice is here widened by subcultural rivalries, focusing on musical and generational differences. The free festival as 'miniature utopia of joy and communal awareness' was never more distant. As *New Musical Express* reported things:

> . . . a group of middle-aged bikers went on the rampage, attacking every punk they could lay hands on. . . . Penny Rimbaud, who was one of the people who started the Stonehenge Festival in the early 1970s, was particularly bitter at the bikers' attitude. 'They said they didn't want punks taking over *their* festival, they only wanted to hear "real" music. This is supposedly an *open* festival, of peace and freedom.'[43]

A quick-release flexi-single by Crass in the same year called 'Rival Tribal Rebel Revel' looked at this violence which was too close to home in the subculture wars. 'It's in the mirror that the real war starts,' pacifist Crass sang.

Squatting in the West End of London in 1985, I pick up a copy of *Time Out* containing a black and white advert which includes the following words: 'STONEHENGE: the National Trust and English Heritage regret to announce that the free festival will

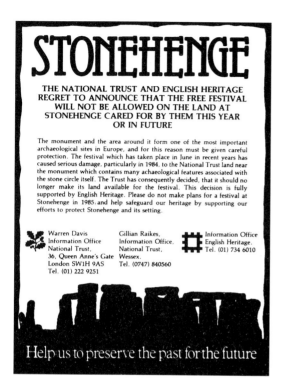

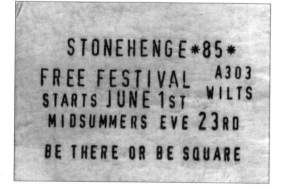

Competing advance versions of Stonehenge Free Festival in 1985, leading up to the Beanfield.

not be allowed on the land at Stonehenge cared for by them this year or in future. . . . Help us to preserve the past for the future.' Presumably, preserving the past refers to the grotty exhibition centre, a joyless tunnel under the road, admission charges, police or private security guards patrolling the strengthened fences round the stones. Is this the heritage of an England that's survived Orwell's year? I pick up a small bright orange street sticker, peel it from a lamp-post in Camden Town, a roughly duplicated thing that says: 'STONEHENGE * 85 * FREE FESTIVAL STARTS JUNE 1ST MIDSUMMERS EVE 23RD A303 WILTS BE THERE OR BE SQUARE.' I stick both texts in one of the books I have on Stonehenge, a recent history that mentions the free festival once. These competing narratives of the future of the festival will be more starkly played out later that year during what becomes known as the Battle of the Beanfield.[44] The book *A Time to Travel?* challenges this heroic description of the events of June 1985 that followed the police's Operation Daybreak:

Though popularly recalled as the 'Battle of the Beanfield', it was, more accurately, a cowardly attack by armed men on family groups including many women and children.[45]

This time they didn't even get to hold the festival, but the entire convoy of travellers, which, as I show in Chapter 3, had been subject to a cat-and-mouse routine with various police forces up and down the country for much of the previous three years, was trapped and, frankly, taught a lesson. Hardened by urban riots, the miners' strike, protest at peace camps, the intransigence of Thatcherism, and the blatant disregard for authority the Peace Convoy displayed, the police made little pretence at self-control as they tried to uphold court injunctions banning travellers from approaching the stones.

While at the Windsor Frees the direct provocation to the Establishment is manifest – setting up camp in the Queen's backyard – it's more difficult to position the ancient stones of Stonehenge as being a symbol of Englishness that needs the utmost protection. Why should these stones be the site for such struggle? Plainly not because they're central to the Establishment – they'd only been 'owned' by the state since 1918, and just prior to their donation the Bomb Squadron 'had twice demanded the destruction of the stones because they were a potential air hazard'.[46] Or was it damage to the nearby Bronze Age earthworks that was the cause of concern? Apparently at the 1984 festival these had been dug up for an oven, or for rubbish tips and longdrops (trench latrines), though it's surprising there are any earthworks left given the wanton 'archaeology' carried out by wealthy amateurs over the previous couple of centuries. Besides, if this was the problem, why not simply supply a few hundred skips and portaloos? It wasn't the stones or the earthworks that the alliance of English Heritage, the National Trust, the police and Wiltshire County Council set out to protect through court injunctions and their brutal enforcement – it was the irritating summer cycle of the convoy and of the hugely popular free festival that they set out to get. The convoy and the festival: two birds with one stone, at the stones.[47] It was time to stamp on the counterculture again, which hadn't gone away but which had chilled out a little, been re-energized by punk, and got itself back on the road.

> One image will probably stay with me for the rest of my life. I saw a policeman hit a woman on the head with his truncheon. Then I looked down and saw she was pregnant, and I thought: 'My God, I'm watching police who are running amok.'[48]

A familiar enough scene, by now. The problem for police was that these words were spoken not by a reporter or by a member of the convoy or of the general public, but by the Earl of Cardigan, owner of Savernake Forest, secretary of the local Conservative Association, all-round pillar of the Establishment. Cardigan had given the police permission to use Savernake Forest for a forthcoming operation to deal with the convoy.

On its way to Stonehenge for the festival, the convoy was herded into the forest by police overnight as a containment measure. *Observer* journalist Nick Davies was travelling with the convoy, and he continues the story of the next day, Saturday, 1 June 1985:

> The Convoy slept late, and it was early afternoon before a long chain of 140 rumbling, wheezing buses, vans, ambulances and cars started to curl out of the forest, south [to] Stonehenge. . . . It was a pleasant ride. Lunch-time drinkers waved from the village pubs; the Convoy stopped to buy crisps and apples. In front and behind, dozens of riot police in reinforced vans rode with us.

At a well-chosen spot for an ambush, a junction of three roads between the villages of Shipton Bellinger and Cholderton, the police set up a number of simple gravel road-blocks which quickly and effectively prevented the convoy from moving forward or back. As things ground to a standstill, people were trapped in their vehicles, their homes, down a country lane. Shouting and jeering was followed by limited violence as the police tried to force travellers to comply with the High Court injunctions by the strategy of smashing windscreens and windows with their truncheons.

Without a way forward or back, and in order to escape the destruction of their vehicles, the leading buses and vans swung right, through a hedge and a wooden fence into a nine-acre field. Here there was 'an ugly stalemate' for a few hours, with vehicles driving round the field, at the police and veering away, and other vehicles which the police had commandeered being used as battering rams. The *Observer*'s Nick Davies was himself arrested during the initial police trawl through the vehicles. In the paper on Sunday, 9 June 1985, he wrote an eyewitness account of the 'rural riot', a police operation that ended as 'a chaotic whirl of violence'. Buzzing overhead, a police helicopter 'barked down encouragement from a loudspeaker: "You're doing a great job. That's the way they like it."' Negotiations failed: according to travellers because police wouldn't allow a withdrawal back to the forest, and according to police because travellers insisted the festival at Stonehenge would go ahead. This stalemate lasted until early evening when the police helicopter announced: 'Those who wish to leave without trouble should drop their weapons and walk out.' Some women and children, men and dogs did leave; many stayed and were involved in a pitched battle with the hundreds of riot police. According to the *Sunday Times*, in a report otherwise clearly reliant on police sources, 'When the final coach came to a rest after about 20 minutes, some 40 or more police smashed its windows and dragged out its occupants, who appeared to be offering no resistance.' In the end, everything that could be smashed was, from stabbed radiators to stabbed yoghurt pots; some pet dogs were destroyed on police orders. Over 500 arrests were made, largely for public order offences (years later charges would be thrown out of court *en masse*); the Earl of Cardigan, who had originally given the police permission to use his land for the operation, was so shocked by what he witnessed that he now turned it over to the convoy as a sanctuary.

Many who took part later saw the Battle of the Beanfield as a turning point:

> Looking back, you can see why they did it. At that stage the whole lawless anarchy of the Stonehenge thing was really alarming a lot of people. It was getting bigger all the time. . . . I think the police were bored and hyped up after the miners' strike and they'd learnt a lot of things from that, a lot of tactics. . . . The Conservatives are the party of law and order and we were an annoying thorn in their side, a whole troop of crazy people going out and rejecting everything they believe in and encouraging others to join them. It was the yuppie era. That's what was being rammed down people's throats – that's what you were meant to be and we were the total opposite of that. It worked though. . . . After the Beanfield . . . it wasn't that great mass movement again.

So thought one traveller, Jay, who was at the Beanfield.[49] Is it coincidence that the two most shocking acts of state violence against irritant cultures of resistance should take place in close proximity to large-scale police mobilization around industrial action? The miners' strikes of 1972 and 1974, which effectively brought down a Conservative government, and that of 1984–85, which *almost* brought down the Conservative government,[50] are surely important factors in the treatment of the free festivals during these times. If one 'enemy within' (Margaret Thatcher's description of striking miners in 1984) wins a struggle against the state – the miners against Edward Heath in 1972 and 1974 – the state elects another enemy, an easier one to flex its muscles at – Windsor Free in 1974. If the state thinks it has disposed of one enemy within – the miners in 1984–85 – it demands another small victory to feel good about itself – the Peace Convoy at the Beanfield in 1985. Seumas Milne describes 'the much-reported nation-wide deployment, the 11,000 arrests, the road blocks and large-scale use of force by the police' during the 1984–85 miners' strike;[51] nationwide surveillance, mass arrests, the use of force, and restrictions on freedom of movement are all strategies adopted by the police for dealing with the convoy, too.[52] On the other hand, this may be too con-spiratorial, or at least in danger of ignoring dissimilarities between the two, such as the fact that police liaison on a national basis is much stronger in the 1980s than it was in the 1970s, and that the urban riots of 1980–81 themselves play an important role in changing police tactics.

According to Elizabeth Nelson, 'festivals reflected a new kind of consumerism':

> Indeed, it could be argued that many of those 'in' the counter-culture were there chiefly as consumers, spectators more than participants. . . . And ironically for the British counter-culture, which was trying to reject what it saw as straight society's acceptance of the 'American way of life' – including American con-sumerism – it became imbued itself to a large extent with what might be termed the 'American way of the alternative future'.[53]

While this may be the case with rock festivals in general, I don't think it's true of the British free festival, that illegal, subversive, and sometimes very dangerous place. Nelson's thesis also misses the significance of the ancient British tradition of festivals, seasonal, nomadic and otherwise, which contributed to the development of the fairs in East Anglia.

'A fair field full of folk': East Anglian fairs: engagement or nostalgia?

> It was simply a space that was being created in a field . . . that was without fear. As soon as you came in the gate, you became a part of a community that was giving, and it didn't matter what you could give, because the whole essence of the effort was that it was almost structureless.
>
> Keith Payne, an early organizer, on the Barsham Faires[54]

'*Almost* structureless' – yes, when compared to the majority culture, clearly less so in relation to the far more autonomous zones of the free festivals. In 1971 a group of friends in Norfolk and Suffolk, some recently arrived, decided to explore 'the pos-sibilities of somehow connecting the hidden wealth of energy, laughter and skill in this area'. Theirs was specifically a rural project – more, an avowedly rural project: the site of an event was quite literally to be a field. Round a pub table they formed a grandly titled organization, the East Anglian Arts Trust, which developed and organized fairs until around 1977–78, when Albion Fairs was set up, involving many of the same people. The shift of name is interesting: on the one hand, the locale widens to embrace the entire country, on the other there is a retreat into the ancient, even mythical. The East Anglian fairs took place throughout the period that saw subculture move from hippy to punk, throughout the 1970s and early 1980s. These fairs were a cross between revivals of historic folk events and displays of (to some extent, subversive) energy by younger country people. Of course, all kinds of folkloric events have been revived or still survive in the twentieth century, from May Day celebrations in Padstow, Cornwall, to Appleby Horse Fair in Cumbria,[55] but the East Anglian fairs do not (only) function as a nostalgic yearning for a (possibly invented) more close rural community of the past. It's worth noting that these fairs were and are legal, too, unlike the mostly squatted free festivals. There's none of the confrontation that sometimes comes with free festivals.[56] Richard Barnes, author of *Sun in the East*, recently drew the following distinctions for me between fairs and free festivals:

> At a free fest you might have the fun of sledge-hammering a police car into shreds with your mates from a city squat, while at a Fair you have to keep mildly responsible, because if things get out of hand you won't get access to the site again. Personally I like to see all types of people at a Fair – and that doesn't happen at fests.[57]

Sandra Bell, another early organizer, has emphasized to me the importance of the relationship with local people and their involvement in the fairs. The fairs spread, or sprang up at similar times, across the country, to Wales and the South-west – both rather better known than East Anglia as centres of interest in all things New Age – and to the North, and combined with local events and organizers in those places to produce a vigorous strand of hippy countercultural activity.

It's worthwhile mapping the development of the East Anglian fairs to gauge their significance and the extent of their contemporary countercultural thrust. From 1972 to 1976 Barsham Faire became a unique annual event in rural Suffolk, which took months to organize and lasted for the public a long weekend. From 1976, things began to expand across Norfolk and Suffolk, first with the Bungay Horse Fairs and Rougham Tree Fairs, and with the Albion Fairs, which were designed as a kind of movable feast of activity across the summer countryside, attracting thousands from local villages and towns alike. If you were unemployed during those summers you'd follow the Albion trail from fair to fair, in your own truck or bus if you had one, and meet up with friends at a different site each week. Sometimes the dole office would even go on strike – its timing for once impeccable – and your giro would be sent out automatically. If you were unfortunate enough to have a job during those summers, you wanted to jack it in. Anyone who's been to a fair has their own collection of images. Clusters of horse-drawn carriages and tipis are later overtaken by clusters of FG trucks and vee-dub campers (to the consternation of some early fair-goers, who saw them as organic, engine-free zones). Tents from army surplus to benders occupy space between the vehicles. Latecomers fit in on the edge of the lane or, worse, near the longdrops. Site crews are tanned and important, have been on site the longest, know when the next lot of pine splits is being delivered for firewood.[58] The atmosphere changes as the day passes and punters come and go. Mid-afternoon it's a cross between a lull in a rock festival and a village fête, kids watching Punch and Judy (the Professor starts non-violently until shrieks of protest force change), the vicar doing the rounds, people haggling at stalls selling jewellery, second-hand clothes, flicking through campaign leaflets from Green Deserts, Libertarian Education. In the evening from a marquee or the big top comes music maybe by the Hank Wangford Band – what sort of music? Country, because that's where we are, and because the musicians' surnames, like Wangford, are taken from Suffolk villages. In future years it'll be the Liberators, playing heavy white reggae from Blakeney in north Norfolk. Late night it's chillums and hot knives in a truck, joints and brandy coffees passed round fires, people tripping on acid avoiding the too-packed beer tent selling lovely flat warm ale. Self-designed and traditional ceremonies celebrating fertility, the elements, rooted to nature and ecology, are watched and participated in in the darkness and before sunrise. That's an East Anglian fair.

Tree Fair, Rougham, Suffolk, September 1985
Soaked in the sublime degeneracy of a fair. Many people left today, it's much more relaxed tonight. Last night was too crowded, too frantic, festival fraughtness like Stonehenge, the city of them all. Too many dancing legs as we sat exhausted on the floor of the big top while the Liberators played.

Fairs interrogate modernity: a horsedrawn wagon and the Albion truck at Sun Fair, Lyng, 1980.

As with most organizations there were a number of motivating factors for the people involved in East Anglian Arts/Albion. Keith Payne, over from the USA, explained that 'The idea of Barsham came from California. . . . The real inspiration was coming back and responding to merry old England.' The 1960s American countercultural events, festivals such as at Monterey, Woodstock, Altamont, were mediated and diluted in 1970s Britain – or is it extended? I suggested above that the shift in name to Albion Fairs signals a retreat from the contemporary to the ancient or mythical. The shift can be read differently, less critically, to suggest that the use of 'Albion' illustrates a desire for a truly alternative society, even an alternative history, a dub version of Britain. The *Guardian* reported from Barsham Faire in 1974, showing that the fairs were developing a national profile: 'The spirit of Notting Hill 1967 is as strong at Barsham as that of the mistier past.' Albion is in the air: Alan Beam's *Rehearsal for The Year 2000* tells of a sixties-style episode in 1974 in London, when a derelict cinema is squatted and a community free festival is held. The cinema is rechristened Albion Free State Meat Roxy, and bears on an outside wall

> the large slogan 'How much longer must our lives be dominated by prussian horse cripplers and nebbishes from cobweb corner? Let us found a new nation under god, Albion Free State'. And on the front of the Meat Roxy there was still John's picture of 'Albion's capital', the Tor at Glastonbury.[59]

Another fair-goer also roots the fairs in the sixties:

> in East Anglia would blossom a temporary travelling coincidence of jugglers, musicians, vegetarians, non-animal circuses, heavy horses, painted caravans, tipis, alternative capitalists, naturists and real beer freaks. Like some impossible dream dreamed in the Summer of Love.

Nostalgia begins to multiply: the historical references of the Barsham Faires are several: an initial medievalism, a pre-Industrial Revolution agricultural ideal, the 'dream' of the (first) Summer of Love. Versions of Olde England are comfortably mixed with the 1960s, producing energy and humour, even some politics, maybe. Albion as constructed is an earthy, mystical, mythical Blakean alternate world of British history, all mists and Merlin, using a language whose words are spelled with extra *e*s on the end to signal the link with a constructed past: Follye Fayre, Faerie Fair.[60] The first Barsham Faires were modelled on 'a medieval fair, which meant you couldn't have anything that was modern, no cars, no electricity. . . . And all the stall-people . . . had to build their own stalls too.' Whatever politics functions here in the early 1970s is a politics of rejection of technology, a contribution to a hippy organic ideal through a parody of history. It also, though, predates the punk ethos of DIY. Early fairs were themed and the admission charge was reduced if you were in costume, which could be anything from Dark Ages beggar to buxom wench to Viking.[61] One of the reasons the Middle Ages was chosen was that it was cheap and easy to dress in costume suggestive of that period: cheerful rags and playful poverty, cheap jokey styles of fashion, splashes of colour from other worlds wallowing in incongruity – and this is *before* punk! Carry On History meets *Lord Of The Rings* in a postmodern romp through images and distortions of England.

Links with the past in the choice of sites themselves are also seen as important to their success – the Stonehenge effect, if you like. Keith Payne argues that 'more than anything else this revival of old atmosphere was responsible for the success of the Fairs'. He offers as examples the fact that Barsham church paddock had once been a stone circle, the Bungay Horse Fair 'had two Bell Barrows on it and was in alignment with "The Mount", a huge conical mound in a wood, half a mile distant where twenty leys meet'. I'm not so sure that it's a 'revival of old atmosphere' as the invention of a new one, even if this new one is in part developed from a tradition. The combination of a partial traditional narrative – of rite or site – with a contemporary turn is evident also in the ceremonies that became a regular feature of fairs. Many ceremonies were celebrations of the elements or of nature. The best known were those designed and carried out by Bruce Lacey and Jill Bruce, a couple of performance artists from London whose tipis would be set apart from the main camping area, surrounded by arranged branches, skulls, a tethered goat, a vaguely druidic atmosphere. They would celebrate fertility, fire, the weather, using corn dollies, an Earth Goddess, white flowers as sperm, burning straw ignited by the sun's heat – a serious/funny mixture of Cecil Sharpe and Robert Graves. Bruce Lacey explains that 'in the midst of everyone getting drunk and listening to bands, Jill and I always felt we were getting to the magic core, expressing the very soul of what the fair was all about'. At something as freely structured as a fair there's always the potential for things to get out of hand, especially at fire-themed fairs. At Thornham Magna the beer tent burned down one year; I think I recall Bruce Lacey shooting a burning arrow up into a windy night sky during one of his rituals – several hundred in the audience must have been hoping as I was that it wouldn't land on *my* tent.

Fair organizers, then, foregrounded the *situatedness* of their events: the sense of locality, of landscape, of rural tradition and history was central to the East Anglian fairs. The social and cultural hegemony of urban space, the idea of the city as hero and site of modernity (and postmodernity, in spite of its claims to focus on the margins), is challenged a bit by things like the fairs. The British countryside, ignored since the Romantics, since Hardy and the Edwardians, was claiming back some territory, was interrogating the limits of enclosure.

It was also the beginning of the movements of young people leaving the cities, hoping to find a more harmonious life, a natural order. And it did not take much to focus where people went to – the country was the country if you lived in the cities. And it took only one good event to draw the urban mind to the possibilities of rural existence.

This situatedness is also evident in the specifically agricultural slant of the horse fair. Prior to its revival, the last Bungay fair had been held in 1934: a May fair at which horses were traded, ponies and traps ran up and down the high street, farmworkers and their families had a day off work – the town was at carnival to celebrate the turning out of farm animals to summer pasture. The Bungay May Fair was held again in 1976, at Mettingham Castle, organized by the East Anglian Arts Trust. It was modelled in part on the still-surviving Appleby Horse Fair, held each June in Cumbria. On the Saturday there was a horse auction, and horse and dog races, and on the Sunday there was a service for horses. Rural writer Adrian Bell expresses his surprise and pleasure at the success of the revival, which took a tradition, a memory, and made it contemporary, out of time: 'Harness-makers were discovered, saddlers, farriers too, all operating in this England of the electronic eye'. Here, at a reinvented horse fair, the thrust of anti-technological politics, of an implicit eco-radicalism, is most keenly felt. Keith Payne reflects on the sheer energy, even danger involved in these events:

> the Bungay May Horse Fairs . . . had a truly anarchic quality which you put up against yourself more than any amount of acid and street theatre. . . . They were raw, encouraging the wilder elements of the community to come together. There was an explosive feeling about (unlike the 'convoy' who seemed like ghosts by comparison) – the horses and gypsies kept the sparks flying. The police suddenly realized that the so-called hippies had sided with the troublemakers and begun to make life difficult.

A more explicit eco-campaign within the fairs was that run by Green Deserts. Based at the village of Rougham in Suffolk, and responsible for the Rougham Tree Fairs from 1978 to at least 1985, Green Deserts employed fairs as a consciousness-raising and income-generating series of events. As signalled in the names of their fairs, forestry was the focus of the campaign, both through the effort to help local people combat desertification (and thus poverty and starvation) in North Africa and through the encouragement of native broadleaf species in Britain. Green Deserts's publicity proclaimed that 'trees link our activities at home & abroad'; it was a single-issue campaign and action group which directed itself towards a much wider agenda. As it put it:

> Green Deserts pursues a development path leading towards local self-reliance in food, fuel and shelter. Trees, crops and technology should be chosen to meet specific needs and avoid creating a dependency on fossil fuels, foreign expertise or unobtainable spare parts.

Earlier organizations that combined music, youth and awareness of problems of global privilege like Green Deserts became rather overshadowed during the showbiz hullaballoo of Band Aid and Live Aid in the mid-eighties. Yet it's clear that the events that raised funds for Green Deserts – fairs – themselves contributed to the understanding of the problems Green Deserts worked to solve. There's a direct connection between the issues of the campaign and the events that publicize the issues. East Anglian fairs employed 'local self-reliance in food, fuel and shelter' (among other things) in order to raise awareness that encouraging this to happen elsewhere in the world can help challenge wider problems. A Green Deserts fair was intended to be both an opportunity to highlight the issues and, in part, a working illustration of potential solutions. The Green Deserts leaflet, the tree fair itself – both are texts intended to politicize you about global inequality and local ecology. Keith Payne again:

> So seeds were planted in East Anglia, and some of these seeds blew very far away, to Devon, Cornwall and Wales. . . . Barsham was finished and new fairs came along, and are still going on, and some of these are very good. But the fairs now are fairs of the 80s, being put together by people from the late 70s, whereas Barsham was a fair of the 70s somehow crystallizing energy from the people of the 60s.

Silver Moon Fair, Nenthead, Cumbria, August 1984
The silver moon's beauty warms. Up in the hills where the air is so fresh it catches in our unclean throats like city smoking. We need the fresh biting air of the mountains and heathers and we have it, all around us, here and now, everywhere! We eat air like men.

Nature is Class A. I lost time on my second day among the allotment patchwork of tents, trucks, and buses. I saw a person wearing a watch. These words took a long time to write at this wonderful fair.

How far did the fairs alter in order to accommodate the next generation's cultural energy of resistance? I want to look at this, particularly in relation to the emergence of the Peace Convoy, which was viewed with suspicion by many of the East Anglian fair people. Audience and atmosphere began to change – fair-goer Chris Challis saw it in terms of the relation between style and ideology: 'it seemed like there were fewer manes and more spikey mops in magenta. More politics, less ritual.' An article-cum-editorial in the community paper the *Waveney Clarion* of October 1982 deals with the future of the fairs, positioning the Peace Convoy as almost a symbol of the crisis of the Albion Fairs organization, now a decade old:

> Are [fairs] a meeting place for the 'Alternative Society'? More seriously, are they short-lived demonstration models of a life-style which can embrace everyone and whose tolerance we'd like to see extended into everyday life? . . . In the midst of these philosophizings the Peace Convoy has appeared to many to be a minor distraction, but to others to sum up the problem in a nutshell. Just what is to be tolerated?

It's a little like the critique of Mikhail Bakhtin's notion of the *carnival*. Bakhtin suggests that, say, the old harvest festival when landowner and farmworker swap roles for the evening can be read as a subversive moment in which fixed social roles and mores are overturned. Mike Weaver, involved with Albion Fairs, pinpoints the perennial problem of carnival, that carnival merely functions as a safety valve to upturn order that order may be maintained. 'What's wrong', he asks, 'in having a good time? Nothing – but does it create overall positive effects or does it on a major level reinforce the status quo?' For Weaver, 'the fairs must remain in essence subversive'. To be effective, fairs must refer outside themselves, not exist solely as insular, narcissistic concerns.

Planning the coming summer's events in January 1983, another 'wider reality' impinges on fair utopia: 'although it won't be a fair, there will be a picnic at Lakenheath, quite close to the Americans and their weapons, one of the many things going on in 1983 for peace and disarmament, a wider reality'. You might say about time too – after atavistic indulgence comes an engagement with the real world again, a massive symbol of which occupies East Anglian land, a bit like the fairs in fact, with the transformed fields, customized vehicles and strange buildings of rural US Air Force bases. Can we read this activity in any way as a result of the questions being asked by the Peace Convoy of the cosy set-up of Albion Fairs? Probably not: it's more the result of actions inspired by dedicated groups of anti-nukes women at the gates of Greenham Common – another site of open-air, rural resistance.

The Peace Convoy coincided with the Albion Fairs' demise. So does this make the convoy responsible? Plenty of people I spoke to affirmed that view: if the Peace Convoy turned up to a Green fair, its members would intimidate punters out of money, rip other fair-goers and organizers off, squat the land a month after everyone else had left and, when they did go, leave burnt-out cars and piles of rubbish behind for someone else to clear up. Quite soon, the Peace Convoy put people off holding fairs altogether. I don't dispute this. What I do say though is that the convoy isn't a cause of the end of the fairs, rather the convoy is both in part a product of events and attitudes like the fairs, *and* a symptom of the increasingly intransigent rhetoric and policies of Thatcherism, to which the fairs were also opposed. Everything vaguely or coherently alternative was more difficult to achieve under Thatcher, became more extreme in its responses: why should the fairs be immune to wider social change? Back to the *Waveney Clarion*:

> Are the Fairs to be small-scale and local, or large-scale and national . . . are they to be Fairs or Festivals? . . . On the road, used to Free Festivals, without local ties, etc., the Convoy undoubtedly bruised the Spirit of Albion badly at the outset.

To blame the Peace Convoy is to misrepresent a symptom for the cause, which is even worse when you bear in mind that some of the ideals and ideas of the convoy – as autonomously formed – were direct extensions of the activities of the fairs: land, alternative society, travelling, impermanence, even the initial connection with gypsies through the Bungay Horse Fairs leads to a travellers' lifestyle. The NIMBY, not-in-my-back-yard, aspect of blaming the convoy for destroying the fairs is worrying too:[62] the danger is that what started as an alternative use of the land referring back to common ground and rural traditions begins to replicate the jealous possession and exclusion of middle England. Billy Freedom of the Peace Convoy voiced its bewilderment at the way they were being treated by the elders of the counterculture in 1982: 'When we arrive at these fairs they are making us into a separate ghetto. We find all the things we had hoped for years ago but we are still outcasts because we carry a political ethic into society.' Was the East Anglian 'alternative society' beginning to finds things becoming a bit too alternative? Maybe when the city comes to the countryside it doesn't only stumble on solutions, it also dumps some of its problems.

It's my argument that the free festivals and the Fairs of Albion were central and ongoing features of the British culture of resistance, features that originated during hippy times and that were altered and re-energized by successive subcultural developments. These temporary autonomous zones interrogate the limits of majority culture, producing on occasion moments of violent reaction from within and without. Anarcho-punk band Crass, those archetypal hippy–punk crossovers, put it better when they took issue with punk's unimaginative and inaccurate sneer at hippies as 'boring old farts':

Critics of the 'hippy generation' would do well to remember that the majority of . . . alternative bookshops, printing presses, food shops, cafés, gig venues etc., are still run, for the benefit of us all, by those same hippies; old maybe but, because of the enormous efforts many of them have made 'to give hope a chance', not boring.[63]

2

O LIFE UNLIKE TO OURS! GO FOR IT! NEW AGE TRAVELLERS

They call themselves new age travellers . . . we call them new age vermin.

Paul Marland MP

By the end of the 1970s a regular summer circuit had been established. From May Hill at the beginning of May via Horseshoe Pass, Stonehenge, Ashton Court, Inglestone Common, Cantlin Stone, Deeply Vale, Meigan Fair, and various sites in East Anglia, to the Psilocybin Fair in mid-Wales in September, it was possible to find a free festival or a cheap community festival almost every weekend.

Young people from traditional travelling families began to come into the festival scene and people from the cities began to convert vehicles and live on the road. . . . [T]he habit of travelling in convoy caught on. . . . So the New Traveller culture was born, emerging into public view at Inglestone Common in 1980 with the 'New Age Gypsy Fair'.

Festival welfare worker Don Aitken[1]

Veteran traveller and Green activist Brig Oubridge dates the origins of the convoy as a national idea more specifically to 1976: 'That summer was the first in which there was a full programme of Free Festivals from June to September, and the convoy was simply a means of moving from one site to the next. . . . [It] was an enjoyably sociable means of travel, carrying the festival atmosphere along with it.'[2] The festival scene and the development of New Age travellers are directly related. Many travellers identify a local or national free festival as the pivotal moment, when the possibility of a kind of change, of something different, was glimpsed, when energy, a good time and some

The movable feast of the Albion Fairs, 1978.

sort of community became woven together, within reach. The festival was usually Stonehenge,[3] though following Albion's effort of the summer of 1978 – an entire series of fairs moving eastwards across East Anglia from Cambridge to the sea at Lowestoft, almost every weekend through the summer – 'a travelling fair . . . across the realms of Albion'[4] also encouraged movement in convoy. There's a practical side to a convoy, too, as Brig Oubridge points out: quite apart from sociability and security, with all the old vehicles 'there were always plenty of people to help out in case of breakdowns'.

Clearly, one way of explaining New Age travellers is to identify them as a product of times of domestic crisis and increasing legislation in Britain: for example, during the mid-seventies the legal procedures for evicting squatters were eased, forcing more people onto the roads, and squatting itself was made even more difficult under the 1977 Criminal Law Act.[5] Long-standing squatting communities, as in areas of Hackney in London, or Argyle Street in Norwich until early 1985, often extended to include truck- and bus-lined streets where travellers park up for the winter – literally parallel communities of houses and vehicles. The boom in urban squatting from the late sixties was itself a response to an ongoing housing crisis and, like squatters, travellers produce their own solutions to homelessness when few others are offered by the government.[6] Thus, activists in the Dutch squatting scene of the 1980s noted that 'the *bricolage* constructed . . . [is] in accordance with the transformation and transience appropriate to an often nomadic lifestyle that rejects permanence and stability as ideals'.[7] When Tory minister Norman Tebbit suggested in the eighties that the unemployed should 'get on their bikes' to look for work as his own father had done during an earlier period of mass unemployment, little did he realize the swelling of nomadic lifestyles that was actually taking place in Britain.[8] Ironically, in terms of the economy, Jay points out that he and other travellers are

> probably the least affected people in the whole country by recession. I mean we live in a permanent recession anyway so it doesn't make a lot of difference. . . . Everything we buy apart from food and petrol just about is second-hand or traded, the whole black market economy.[9]

The New Age travellers of the nineties commonly describe themselves as 'economic refugees' . . . 'refugees seeking shelter. That's how I see myself, as a refugee.' Sociologist Kevin Hetherington mentions that 'there are even some [New Age travellers] who have taken up living in caves in Spain'. But despite such perceptions of neo-barbarian difference, the actions of the New Age travellers are not historically unfamiliar, even in recent history – for instance, during the Second World War Londoners and Bristolians fleeing aerial bombardment damage lived in nearby caves.[10]

Despite being sprayed with silage by a farmer; despite putting up with 'fuck-off looks' as well as far more physical manifestations of hostility; despite being harassed for 'producers' by police, that is, to produce vehicle documents at a local station within seven days; despite suffering periodic attacks of what one calls 'straight sickness' – why aren't I in a house, with a flushing loo, running water, a telly, pubs and cinemas nearby? – despite all that it's not all negative. As well as rejection and exclusion, travellers emphasize the attraction of the New Age traveller lifestyle, as in the Romantic pleasure of rural living. While 'rural Britain is for the rich', says traveller Shannon, 'if I want to live with space around me and trees and hills and woods, the only possible way apart from sleeping out is to buy a vehicle and live in that'. Jay concurs: 'your outside space is just as important as your inside space in my view. . . . That feeling of space and privacy to me is worth a lot.' Space and privacy, precious commodities, simple desires. Jeremy of the Levellers, himself a traveller, says that 'the appeal is quite romantic. It's the English dream really, isn't it? – the fantasy most English people have: trees, fields, all those images from *Tess of the d'Urbervilles*' – including Stonehenge again.[11] There's an image here of New Age travellers as contemporary scholar-gypsies, retreating from 'this strange disease of modern life' as Matthew Arnold put it in the poem 'The Scholar-Gypsy', or as updates from the fiction of George Borrow.[12] It is ironic that while the Thatcher government championed Victorian values it was giving free rein to the violent harassment of groups of such atavists. The government's imperfect grasp on history helped Thatcher out here, though: the Peace Convoy was described by her home secretary in June 1986 – one year after the Battle of the Beanfield – as 'a band of *medieval* brigands'.

The fact that early East Anglian fairs had seen the revival of horse fairs at Bungay links the fairs as well with a traditional travelling community, gypsies. So, are New Age travellers related to traditional gypsies, and if so, how?[13] Under the Caravan Sites Act 1968 gypsies are defined as 'persons of nomadic habit of life, whatever their race or origin, other than a group of travelling showmen, travelling together as such'. As the National Council for Civil Liberties (NCCL) has observed, 'It is vital to note that this is a definition *by lifestyle*', not by race or other origin. In 1986 the government reported that a total of 10,592 gypsy caravans were recorded in the country, and there were around 4,000 places for those caravans on legal sites. Less than 40 per cent of traditional gypsies were supplied with legitimate spaces, though the Caravan Sites Act puts a legal duty on councils to provide 'adequate accommodation' for 'persons of nomadic habit of life'.[14] Add, by official estimates, 8,000 New Age travellers and their 2,000 vehicles in the 1980s and 1990s and the already inadequate provision comes under even greater strain. When approached by the NCCL to explain how it could distinguish between New Age travellers and gypsies for the purpose of providing sites, the Department of the Environment replied, 'it is not considered that there is any duty under the 1968 Act for local authorities to provide a site specifically for the Peace Convoy'. The main reason given was that 'the Act is concerned with the provision of *caravan sites* not tenting and camping sites' – the sheer variety of convoy vehicles and living spaces became the government's let-out clause.[15] Kevin Hetherington observes that:

> Just as has been the case with Jews and gypsies down the centuries, the 'New Age travellers' are hated not because they are always on the move but because they might stay and 'contaminate' through their ambivalence and bring all manner of horrors upon the 'locals'.[16]

Do we need to interrogate further the casual comparison between ancient and modern wanderers? Does, for instance, the fact that there may be a degree of self-marginalization on the part of the New Age travellers contribute to their difference from traditional gypsies?

27 May 1995

The old veedub starts despite the early summer damp, and we drive to a salt marsh a few miles from Lancaster for a walk. In a triangle of rough grass by the Stork at Conder Green are unexpected splashes of colour and life – bright red wooden wagons, horses, a gleaming caravan. Gypsies. They must be making their way up to Appleby, to the horse fair in early June. I didn't know this was common land. A perfect opportunity: here I am trying to work through the connections between New Age travellers and gypsies and here are some gypsies who I can try asking. Two middle-aged men are sitting round a smoky fire by a wagon enjoying this sudden sun. I approach them, keen to start up a conversation, uncertain of their reaction. A kettle's on a firestand made from horseshoes welded together. Harnesses are out, halfway through being cleaned. Bedding is being aired.

We chat for an hour. One's a rag-and-bone man from Bolton, the other – a Highlander with a sense of irony – says he's currently 'a gentleman farmer'. He lives in Preston. Basically they have no interest in or sympathy for New Age travellers. They are hard-working men who despise these people for their sponging, their laziness, their filthy lifestyles, their provocative flouting of the laws of the land, their drug taking, their music, the way they rip up hedges for firewood, their dangerous vehicles, their begging, their filth again, the length of their dreadlocks . . . I couldn't have got a more negative reaction from talking to the members of a Conservative association or the National Farmers' Union in Wiltshire!

They do see though that they may be demonizing New Age travellers in the same way that Gorgio [non-gypsy] society has demonized them in the past. That contradiction doesn't bother them. Possibly New Age travellers have made gypsies more acceptable – anyone would rather have a few lovely horse-drawn caravans pull up near them for a few days than a band of filthy, noisy travellers. They agree with each other that the hippies from the sixties who live with horses and wagons are quite different from today's New Age travellers; a hippy couple even travelled and worked with one of them on the road in a larger group years ago.

The variety of names for the New Age 'trailer trash' betrays the extent of majority culture's distaste for and distrust of them: crusties, drongos, mutants, hedge monkeys, brew crew, soap dodgers, giro gypsies, brigands. In a sense, as with the gypsies complaining about their flaunted dirt and dreadlocks, New Age travellers attract such abuse and invective. In sociological terms, this means that they '*deliberately* assume "risk identities", . . . celebrate chaotic and expressive lifestyles', as Kevin Hetherington puts it.[17] The gypsies I talked to are correct about the plural nature of New Age travellers. Simon of Bedlam rave sound system neatly distinguishes ravers from the older generation of hippy travellers: 'We're different from them. They sit there admiring their crystal and we'll sit there admiring our vinyl, know what I mean?' Crystal power of hippies versus material vinyl of ravers' records. Traveller Shannon elaborates on generational distinctions and motivations:

> Whereas in the early eighties it was mostly alternative-y type people who picked an alternative lifestyle, now it's people who are basically fucked off with the city. . . . It's not the rosy rainbow hippy scene it was in the seventies and eighties, people trying to live in love and peace. . . . [T]hat isn't going to exist in the nineties.[18]

Addressing the local majority culture in rural Glastonbury, travellers Grig and Tosh also highlight urban space as the source of contemporary tension, not just between travellers and the majority culture, but between groups of travellers themselves:

> A lot of the travellers are coming out of the cities with nowhere to go. . . . They get full of the 'brew' and go around making a nuisance. . . . We can't chuck out our 'drongos', any more than you can yours.[19]

It seems as though at one extreme are the idealists from the sixties, still living in horse-drawn wagons, or in tipis, living the organic life in touch with the land and with local communities, and at the other are the 'brew crew', the 'drongos', young urban homeless who merely fulfil the prophecy of the Sex Pistols' 'No future for you!', and their injunction 'Get pissed. Destroy!'

The increasingly unsympathetic treatment of New Age travellers by local authorities and police itself contributes to hardening attitudes. For example, since 1993 two police intelligence units in Wiltshire and Cumbria have been dedicated to the national coordination of intelligence on travellers, known as Operation Snapshot. Its aim is to collate on computer information on around 8,000 travellers, including details of trucks and living spaces, friends, nicknames, and so on. These are people who haven't even *done* anything yet! And what would they do, anyway, that could justify such a scale of surveillance? Meet up in some fields for a week or two, get out of it a bit? I'll remind you that in 1975 the (Labour) government provided a site for the People's Free Festival; by 1995 the (Conservative) government has potentially criminalized the lifestyle of the people who organize and go to free festivals.

But what is this New Age that these people are travelling through, or taking us to? The complexities of the term themselves need unpacking. In case you didn't know it, we are currently in the New Age. A global ritual called the Harmonic Convergence took place on 17 August 1987 to signal – among other things – the end of the nine cycles of hell which followed the thirteen cycles of heaven in ancient Mayan cosmology.[20] Apparently postponed from the late sixties, the dawning of the Age of Aquarius was finally here, endorsed by the wackier fringe of Californian celebrities, people like Shirley MacLaine. Andrew Ross captures the American New Age well: an 'eclectic and colourful mix of healers, psychics, holistic foodsters, folk metaphysicians, psychotechnologists, UFO contactees, crystal therapists, dolphin advocates, channelers, and a roster of New Age stars such as Timothy Leary'.[21] The 'new generation/With a new explanation' sung of by Scott McKenzie in 'San Francisco (Be Sure To Wear Some Flowers in Your Hair)' in the summer of 1967 was, twenty years on, really beginning to get things together on a global scale. And today you can buy New Age music from its own shelf in record stores (ambient synthesized sounds cross with world music samples and folk melodies), high-street bookshops have massive New Age sections (on runes, crop circles, the birth of the inner child), head shops sell fewer Rizlas and chillums now than crystal necklaces and moody posters of Ayers Rock. New Age travellers are the gloriously downmarket end of the commodification spectrum.

But political critic Stuart Hall asks:

> How new are these 'new times'? Are they the dawn of a New Age or only the whisper of an old one? What is 'new' about them? How do we assess their contradictory tendencies – are they progressive or regressive? . . . If we take the 'new times' idea apart, we find that it is an attempt to capture, within the confines of a single metaphor, a number of different facets of *social change* . . .[22]

Pat Kane identifies 'a much wider and deeper culture of the irrational: a culture which we often dignify with the term "New Age", but which should properly be called occult'.[23] I'm not sure how far *New Age* can be called a term of dignity (any more), but possibly we should indeed be making greater use of the term *occult*, in its original sense of *hidden (from sight), concealed*. In this sense, occult groups and events are those this book revolves around: hidden or marginal figures and narratives. Though their etymologies are in fact entirely different, occult sounds like it ought to be connected to *culture*, too, even to *counterculture*.[24] Occulture as a term for New Age's culture of resistance? Kane continues:

> After the convulsions of the sixties and seventies, the new right gained power by turning the counterculture's individualism against itself: freedom redefined as the freedom to consume aggressively. New Age and occult cultures represent an alternative politics of the individual.

Like Pat Kane, Nigel Fountain locates the impulse originally in the sixties:

> In the 1960s the young dropped out, in the 1980s they are dropped out. Two decades after drugs were supposedly a tool to heighten reality, and offer visions of the future, in the 1980s they are an escape from the present, and a replacement for the future. Across the decades the lost army of travellers still makes its pilgrimages to Glastonbury.[25]

Why so negative? Why must they be described as 'lost'? Apart from the romantic construction of drug use here by Fountain – writings about the sixties by people from the sixties are full of such nostalgic acid flashbacks – there is the larger issue about the degree of active choice involved. For Fountain one difference between 1960s and 1980s youth is that in the sixties there was the clear possibility of conscious decision on the part of dropouts. Dropping out could be seen as a critical indication of power. In the eighties and beyond, for Fountain, dropping out is passive, a symptom of powerlessness. Exploring this kind of dynamics of power, American writer Ron Sakolsky suggests that 'Some will contend that oppressed groups do not "drop out"; they are pushed out.' He goes on to discuss 'the heady freedom of disappearance' that can be the result of such exclusion.[26] Surely there's a politics there?

Jeremy of the Levellers disagrees: 'We weren't a movement, just a bunch of pissed up people, some so nasty not even I would talk to them.' Others, though, clearly *are* politically engaged, such as Don, after witnessing the eviction of Rainbow Fields Village at RAF Molesworth in February 1985:

It was a decision. It was right and wrong. It was good and evil. It was that strong. Anyone who was slightly spiritual, or slightly feeling, they could see that there was a line to be drawn there. They were standing there in their black suits with their riot shields, with their batons, with their commanders, with their orders, not even knowing why they were there and what they were doing. And you'd see a few long-haired people with bright coloured jackets ambling around playing music, sitting round fires, smoking a bit of dope, having a laugh, being good people, helping each other out. And then twenty, thirty foot away you've got a line of five hundred riot shields and three hundred more around the corner on standby.[27]

Yet even Don's had enough of the struggle: 'Living on the road making a statement all the time is boring,' he now says. Bruce Garrard, a committed New Age activist and writer, who runs Unique Publications in Glastonbury, outlines his plan of action for 'building the new society'.[28] It's patently a deeply political approach – one which, I'm arguing, clears some or most of the mist of mystical rhetoric from the term *New Age*. He'd disagree perhaps, reluctant to be entirely materialist, or to have his Avalonian utopia more rooted in anarchistic tradition. His first two actions are 'withdrawal (from conventional politics and social structures), reassessment (from a standpoint on the extreme fringes of society)'. These are the conscious actions of self-marginalization that other countercultural figures in this book (Ubi Dwyer and Wally Hope, Crass) display, of dropping out rather than being pushed. But the standpoint he refers to on the extreme fringes of society is also that of other marginal groups who've been pushed rather than dropped out, maybe – some of the squatters, travellers.

From Tipi Valley to the peace camps

Contact with the Earth is not a metaphor in a tipi. When I sit down I can feel the skin of our Mother under my bum.

Patrick Whitefield, *Tipi Living*[29]

In Dyfed in South Wales there is a valley of traveller-type people, living in a community that's one of the longest-surviving alternative traveller lifestyle sites in Britain. This is

Tipi Valley, Teepee Valley, sometimes Talley Valley, north of the A40, the old Roman road. Like Stonehenge, Tipi Valley has strong associations for New Age travellers, many of whom have made their pilgrimage or simply ended up there at some time while on the road. Before terms like *New Age travellers* or *the Convoy* were in use, groups travelling from festival to festival were known simply as Tipi People, whether they lived in tipis or not. Tipi Valley became more established in 1976 when some derelict farmland was bought by a group of festival-goers aiming to extend the festival season by establishing a long-term eco-friendly community. The Tipi People originally thought (hoped?) they would not need planning permission since their dwellings were not permanent structures. The nowadays 'world-famous'[30] Tipi Valley is a precarious community, partly by virtue of its autonomy, but also because of the regular efforts on the part of the authorities to end it. For instance in the mid-eighties the local district council tried to used the planning laws to evict the inhabitants of the entire village, claiming an unauthorized shift from agricultural to residential land use.

Patrick Whitefield describes the seasonal routine of the village:

> The tipi village in Wales is situated in a little valley. In summer time the tipis are scattered over the surrounding hillsides, many of them on circular terraces cut to give a level pitch on the steep ground. In winter they come together in an intimate circle deep in the valley, and if the weather is very cold everyone may move into the big lodge to eat and sleep together, sharing each other's warmth and one great big fire, which takes less wood than a lot of smaller ones.[31]

Turning up at a psilocybin festival in Wales in 1980, traveller Shannon describes the instant hit of power and difference he felt on first seeing this utopian merging of landscape and lifestyle:

> At the bottom of the valley there were all these tipis and benders with smoke rising out of the top of them. It looked like some picture of the Rocky Mountains in Colorado hundreds of years ago. The pine trees, the tipis, the sunset, it was gorgeous. It was something totally new to me – people living in benders, spending the whole year in them, just tarpaulin and rugs and cloth, trying to live in a way totally different from society. And the energy it had to it then was extraordinary.[32]

Welsh tipis at Tree Fair, Rougham, 1982.

The Native American origin of tipis has itself been raised within the context of the political issue of homelessness in the United States. Arriving at one of the 'tent cities' that sprang up in the urban USA in the eighties, Dick Hebdige found a single tipi amongst the shacks, dominating with its size and surprise. The Manhattan tipi, he wrote,

is the landmark focus of this alternative development – its single distinguishing feature. It towers over the other makeshift shelters – a cone of dirty undyed fabric held upright round a tall, treelike wooden pole. . . . Made by the homeless for the homeless after a 'primitive' design that dates back long before New Amsterdam was acquired from the natives for the legendary handful of beads, Tent City's tipi is both an invocation and an indictment – an invocation of the history of expropriation and genocide which accompanied the founding of the nation and an indictment of a system that continues to uproot, 'vanish' and dehumanize the ghosts that (against all odds) go on dancing at its margins.[33]

The Manhattan tipi makes use of the USA's past to comment on its present; the Welsh ghost dancers (to pick up Hebdige's reference) also survive at the margins against the odds. Tipi Valley illustrates again that the travelling lifestyle picks up nomadic traditions and historical forms. For tipi purist Whitefield, 'moving is very much part of what tipi living is all about, treading gently upon the land, allowing the pitching spot to recover and green over again before returning'. As with New Age travellers and elements of gypsy tradition, there's a strong mimetic impulse, one that seeks both to imitate *and* to shift tipis' context, no matter how unfavourable the new circumstances might seem. George Borrow's *Wild Wales* is surely an unforgiving place to set up a canvas community imported from the plains of American history – isn't that effort to triumph over climatic and social obstacles a utopian one? Even the official report of the public enquiry in 1985 into the status of Tipi Valley is sympathetic: 'the degree of visual intrusion or environmental damage or traffic hazard which results from a limited tipi presence in the valley bottom [is] minimal. . . . In relation to the local ecology their presence seems to be beneficial rather than harmful.'[34]

It may be that the adoption of the tipi lifestyle as model is a more self-consciously politicized choice than that of gypsies: after all, the Native Americans' great struggle has been against the dominant white culture of progress, industrialization and capitalist grasping in the USA, and for equitable distribution of land and respect for traditional skills and folk rituals. A repoliticized living space contributes to the romantic construction of alienated people, of marginals. Possibly the sheer otherness of this chosen living space – in racial, geographical and historical terms – helps to signal the degree of rejection the inhabitants of Tipi Valley wish to display to mainstream society; or maybe it's just easier to feel you're on the social warpath if you actually live in a tipi.

The utopian possibility of the version of Tipi Valley I've just given, from the outside, is undercut rather by an insider's recent description of it: internally, it's a working site of tension, which is seen even in the layout.

There's something pretty magnificent about the sight of a load of tipis stuck together. In Talley, people were split at the time. There's the centre village, with about twenty people in it, which has been there for a long time and is pretty much self-sufficient. But there was a lot of friction between the centre village and the people on the outside where there were vehicles and first-time tipi dwellers and a lot of people with romantic ideas of what it was going to be like. . . . If you go there and walk into the middle, it's lovely, but if you walk towards the outside there's bags of rubbish, just left lying around, and more shit around.[35]

Tipi Valley thus duplicates some of the social problems and structures it has sought to remove itself from: deliberately placing itself at the margins, away from the centre of majority culture – almost from *any* culture – it has developed into a central space inhabited by *authentic* veterans and idealists, surrounded by its own marginal types, problem cases. There are other problems, too. Helen Prescott, editor of the environmental magazine *Creative Mind*, described to me her surprise at the general lack of vegetable cultivation and organic activity she saw on a week's visit to Tipi Valley, all the more remarkable in her view when the amount of land available is considered.

More insistently nomadic New Age travellers were those in the Peace Convoy – the most-publicized and largest group of travellers during the 1980s. In the media it was usually 'the so-called Peace Convoy': the amount of sheer venom packed in to that small hyphenated word 'so-called' when used in connection with the convoy is extraordinary. As we've seen already in relation to the Battle of the Beanfield and from some of the people at the East Anglian fairs, antagonism towards the Peace Convoy came from both sides. In a way, that's what's so interesting about it. The Peace Convoy interrogated what had become the comfortable binary framework of social establishment (parliament, landowners, the military and police) and established alternatives (the Campaign for Nuclear Disarmament, the fairs). New spaces were opening, were parked up on for a couple of months as participants waited for the inevitable eviction to come through. A circuit of temporary autonomous zones. A movable feast of folk devilry, one ripe for demonization by the many, for romanticizing by the few. The National Council for Civil Liberties explains in its *Stonehenge* report that over the years 'It became a festival feature that travellers living in vans, buses and trucks would leave the site in a convoy that moved on to the next free festival. Travelling by convoy gave a sense of safety and security. In 1982 the convoy moved on to Greenham Common Peace Camp and "Peace Convoy" was stencilled on the side of some of the vehicles – a title that has persisted.'[36] The North East Anarchist Federation's bulletin number 9 of Autumn 1982 includes the following report written by 'a Doncaster comrade', which illustrates the connections between travellers, the free festival scene and the peace camps:[37]

PEACE CONVOY'S ENTRY TO GREENHAM

On the 30th June, the peace convoy of approximately 150 buses, vans and cars, which one TV programme called a 'tatty circus', left the site where the TV cameras were to record the final moments of the Stonehenge People's Free Festival '82.

A couple of hours or so later saw the convoy pulling up to the works entrance of the Greenham Common USAF base, after evading several attempts by the police to split us up into smaller groups.

The side road to the works entrance was blocked by a police motor bike and two transit vans, as well as about 20 police and three cars, some of which were parked just off the road. But it couldn't have been a serious attempt to keep us out, not with 500 of us against a mere 20 of them. After about 20 minutes of discussion and confrontation at the roadside, with the convoy blocking the road in both directions, the first bus started to edge its way forward, and about 25 people got round the first transit and bumped it out of the way, whilst the second transit reversed away leaving the way clear for the buses to get to the site entrance. After . . . trenches which were dug by the police across the entrance of the field were filled in, the occupation of the site, yards from the base's fence, was completed, and in jubilant mood the 'Cosmic Counter-Cruise Carnival' began.

The peace camp at the USAF base at Greenham Common had been set up in September 1981; during its early days, as Brig Oubridge explains, 'only the small camp at the main gate . . . was considered to be a women-only space'.[38] In February 1982 the entire camp became women-only. The convoy's arrival that summer resulted in the Cosmic Counter-Cruise Carnival, a free-festival-like event near the Green Gate which both politicized the convoy and energized the peace camp.[39] In '20 Years of Festivals', Don Aitken points out that 'It was from the new Travellers that the Greenham women learned about benders, which proved to be crucial to their survival in the face of official harassment.' There were to be a number of such exchanges and meetings between travellers and peace campers throughout the early 1980s. In a recent letter, Rainbow Fields Villager Jo Waterworth writes of the peace camp movement that 'there was just so much interchange and mingling of ideas and ideologies, from radical christians to young punks via old hippies and the plain mentally ill. Spirituality meets politics meets new age travellers.'

The convoy that took its name from the peace camp movement meandered and broke down around England and Wales during these years. It showed itself to be less a considered political event or zone than a regular irritant to majority culture and, as I've suggested, even to majority culture of resistance. For instance, an Albion Fair meeting of October 1982 in East Anglia noted that 'problems are going to arise regarding the Peace Convoy'. Some involved in the East Anglian fairs were aware that, if it *was* a problem, the Peace Convoy was one partly of their own making. Others were less understanding, thought the convoy's interrogation of the limits of authority too deliberately provocative. As one former traveller and squatter put it to me, if you deal drugs and have DRUG SQUAD massively painted on the side of your vehicle, you shouldn't be too surprised when you get busted. Some attitudes towards the convoy became more sympathetic from 1984 onwards. During that summer, the convoy went from Stonehenge to Montgomery, to the Silver Moon Fair in Cumbria to Nostell Priory near Leeds. At Nostell Priory the cycle of violent eviction and harassment by police began that was to continue at Rainbow Fields Village at Molesworth, at the Battle of the Beanfield near Stonehenge, both in 1985, and at Stoney Cross in June 1986.

Photographer Peter Gardner writes of first coming across the Peace Convoy and the waves of police it attracted at the disused airfield at Stoney Cross in the New Forest in early June 1986: 'what was happening reminded me of groups I had photographed in remote areas of the Third World, conjuring thoughts of "minorities", "repression" and "injustice". But here in Britain?'[40] The language of authority was indicative of the rising level of official intolerance. John Duke, Chief Constable of Hampshire police, could talk apparently without concern about 'neutralizing this invasion'. Prime Minister Margaret Thatcher positively relished the opportunity for a nice little crackdown, being 'only too delighted to do what we can to make life difficult for such things as hippy convoys'.[41] But the convoy was undoubtedly also an inspiration, a spectacularly shambolic example of British subcultural nonconformity that exploded onto our television screens every summer to remind us of the possibility of a life unlike to ours. To quote the words of traveller Jay again:

> The Conservatives are the party of law and order and we were an annoying thorn in their side, a whole troop of crazy people going out and rejecting everything they believe in and encouraging others to join them. It was the yuppie era. That's what was being rammed down people's throats – that's what you were meant to be and we were the total opposite of that.[42]

Rainbow Fields Village at Molesworth RAF base became another traveller-related community signalling solidarity with a pre-existing peace camp, one that lasted longer than the Counter-Cruise Carnival thrown by the convoy at Greenham. RAF Molesworth in Cambridgeshire had been a little-used airbase since the Second World War until the decision to transform it into an American cruise missile base. The peace camp had been established two and a half years before a Green Gathering held at Molesworth in late August 1984. Green Gatherings themselves grew out of summer meetings organized by the original Ecology Party in 1980; until Molesworth they were all legitimate – often as part of the Glastonbury Festival, which still maintains the influence of the Green Gatherings through the Green Field. Unable to find an independent site that would give them permission for the 1984 Green Gathering, the organizers decided to step outside the legal framework, effectively radicalizing themselves by this decision. Rainbow Fields Village was formed in the wake of the Molesworth Green Gathering, on the opposite side of the proposed cruise missile base from the peace camp. In fact, the village was founded on an earlier site of the peace camp. Here again some New Age travellers were locating their activities and lifestyle firmly within a framework of resistance.

Bruce Garrard gave this report at the end of October 1984, when the village was still in the process of being developed:

> The village is a string of tipis, tents, vans, buses and benders, mostly pitched along the hedge which forms a natural windbreak down one side of the village field. . . . Between all these things, the gaps; filled with possibilities. . . . The village is slowly growing and changing (and if you want to join us, what we need most is more settlers). There's about 80 of us here now – travellers, peace campers, greens, tipi-dwellers. . . . Some are here to oppose cruise missiles, some to build a new free community, and some just to live here for the winter or for longer.[43]

Brig Oubridge, veteran of Tipi Valley and long-time thorn in the side of authorities up and down the land, was living at Rainbow Fields Village when the (even by their standards) massive mobilization of police and troops – yes, troops – came in the night in early February 1985 to evict them. Another hippy veteran, Sid Rawle, was there too, living in a bender. The villagers' first response to imminent eviction was to argue among themselves about what their reaction should be. Bruce Garrard sees the arguments as highlighting 'the same old division: the convoy wanted to survive, to get away from the aggro. The greens wanted to stay, to make a non-violent stand.'[44] One of the villagers called it 'the military occupation of Molesworth Common', and certainly the sheer scale of military action was the focus of media reports. Brigadier-General Edward Furdson, defence correspondent of the *Daily Telegraph*, described it as 'the largest single Royal Engineer operation since the Rhine crossing in 1944'. Another right-wing news-paper, the *Daily Express*, had a front-page article headlined 'The Battle of Molesworth', which contained an inventory of personnel: 1,500 Royal Engineers, 100 military police, 600 civilian police, infantry on reserve just in case, huge numbers of vehicles including bulldozers to clear trees, hedges, benders, buses out of the way.[45] This was an extraor-dinary overreaction, even by the increasingly authoritarian Thatcher government's standards: the net for the enemies within was being cast wider and wider. Flak-jacketed Defence Secretary Michael Heseltine sternly placed himself in the front line for the vital twin battles for British democracy and camera time. Perhaps the excess of barbed wire laid down by the sappers was a military response to the embarrassment caused by the actions of Greenham women in October 1983, when four miles of Greenham's per-imeter fence had been taken down. The sense of unreality, and of sheer danger, is captured in a moment described by Bruce Garrard, immediately after the eviction:

> We stopped off in Huntingdon to pick up some food, and walking through the shopping centre was extraordinary, bizarre: I felt like I was on acid. We'd just been in the middle of a civil war, with squads of soldiers all over the place, mud, barbed wire entanglements, searchlights, fire and smoke, and police setting up roadblocks behind us: here, people were going about their daily business, ten miles away, as if nothing had happened.[46]

The Rainbow Villagers were locked out of Middle England and evicted back into it at the same time, a vision more unsettling for Garrard than any bad drug-induced hallucination.

The booklet *Travellers In Glastonbury* gives a micro-perspective on problems with and attitudes towards New Age travellers, as well as on the history of such issues.[47] The Somerset town of Glastonbury is presented – both by New Agers and by local councils and tourist boards – as a site of ancient pilgrimage, myth and legend, most significantly perhaps in the still-flourishing annual festival. But there were travellers, dropouts, people investigating 'eastern religions, mysticism, communes, "back-to-the-land"' in the

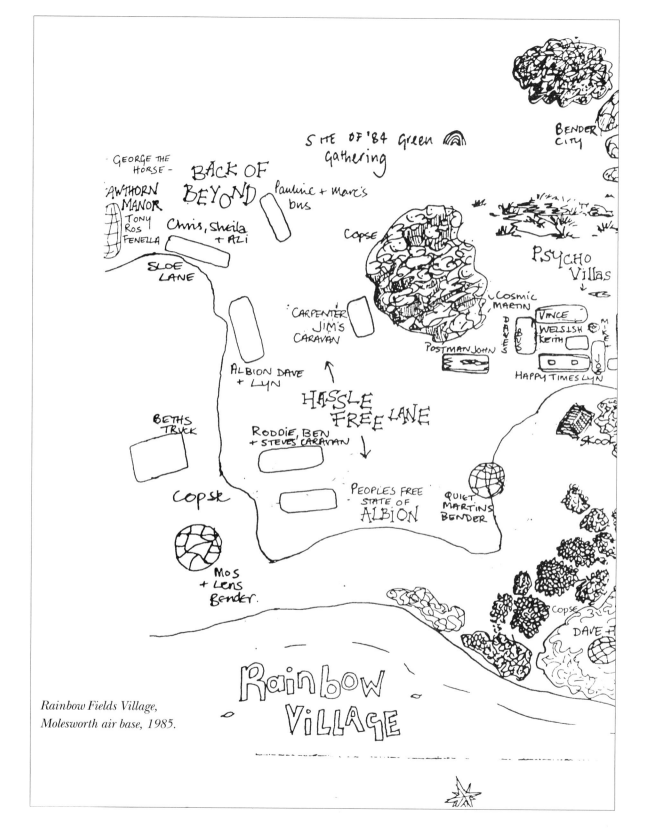

Rainbow Fields Village,
Molesworth air base, 1985.

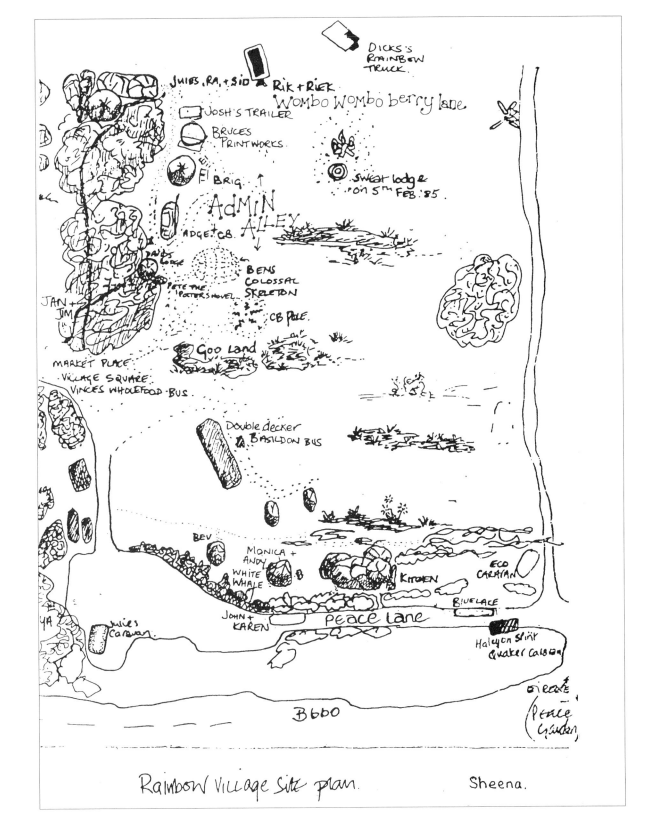

Rainbow Village site plan.   Sheena.

area before the first free festival at Pilton in 1971. There was a degree of resentment and distrust towards these incomers, even if some of them were actually Glastonians – in fact, as early as the 1920s there had been resistance to a circle of bohemians in the area, one centred around the radical composer Rutland Boughton. In the early 1970s, attraction and resentment developed alongside one another: 'Along with a vegetarian restaurant we also had the signs "No Hippies Allowed" on other cafés and pubs in the town.' New Age writer Ann Morgan argues that people like the hippies and festival-goers have been responsible for reviving the town's fortunes. 'Glastonbury was a sleepy town in decline,' she writes, 'and now everything is waking up. The alternative scene and the travellers are important parts of that.' Yet in the late 1980s prejudice came in the form of 'the notorious "Hippy Wrecker" tow truck', bought by an out-raged Glastonian to ensure that every last traveller's vehicle would be evicted.[48] In fact, it was originally planned that the cost of the Hippy Wrecker should be raised through the offer of 1,000 £1 shares to Glastonians, an idea raised by a local councillor at a council meeting. The man behind the Hippy Wrecker explained his thinking: 'We want to get the Travellers out of Glastonbury; right out. That's what my people want. I believe in giving the people what they want.'

There were other Glastonians, more charitable ones, who offered more thoughtful responses to the influx of travellers. In 1985, after Molesworth in February and the Battle of the Beanfield in June, part of the convoy, including remnants of the Rainbow Villagers, sought refuge at Greenlands Farm on the outskirts of town. Up to a hundred of the travellers making up the five hundred or so in the convoy that had been trashed at the Beanfield were the remains of Rainbow Village, now a nomadic community, a village on the road. At Greenlands Farm, Glastonians and the wider respectable con-stituency of Britain were shown the way forward by an ordinary citizen-turned-hero. Alison Collyer, a committed Christian in her sixties, opened up her farmland to the beaten and bedraggled convoy. As traveller Charley Barley put it:

> Up in the orchard all is muddy fun. We're a bit overcrowded, but there is other space we can use. Alison Collyer is showing the community what Christian charity is all about. And we are grateful to her for the sanctuary, peace and quiet she has offered us in this most difficult and frightening summer for travellers.[49]

Rainbow Village at Greenlands Farm proclaimed itself the Free State of Avalonia, as shown in the title of the booklet about events there: *The Children of the Rainbow*

Gathered in the Free State Of Avalonia at the Christian Community Of Greenlands Farm. This latest temporary autonomous zone had a nice line in the millenarian and the mundane, the cosmic and the political, and went some way to countering the memories of the 'battered bodies, battered vehicles' of earlier that year.

> We are free in our minds, and the crack is to gather with like-minded people and thus celebrate the Free State of Avalonia. . . . Anarchy is freedom is taking responsibilities for ourselves and our actions. Anarchy is not dropping rubbish around the Tor. Anarchy is disposing of roaches mindfully.[50]

Or, as the parodic 'COMMUNIQUE FROM THE PROVISIONAL HIGH COMMAND, AVALONIAN PEOPLE'S POPULAR LIBERATION EXPERIENCE' dated Guy Fawkes Night 1985 put it, 'THERE IS LIFE BEFORE DEATH.'[51]

Living spaces

> It's warm by the river, the weir keeps us clean
> The woodsmoke and cigarettes are all that we need
> Marking the dirt with twigs and simple words spoke . . .
>
> The Levellers, 'Far From Home'[52]

> I blame [the Levellers] . . . for that romantic idea of travellers that's built up; young kids have this image of buses painted like Romany caravans, people sitting round communal campfires. Anyone who's been on the road knows that's a load of bollocks.
>
> Vic, traveller[53]

In a sense the problem with writing about the Peace Convoy or the Rainbow Village on the road is that you end up offering a series of spectacular confrontations, which may only replicate the narrative approach of many erroneous media reports about the events: Nostell Priory in 1984, Rainbow Fields Village at Molesworth in 1985, the Beanfield in 1985, Stoney Cross in 1986 – these are the rural riots, largely the result of insensitive police and military operations around Britain. This is the version of traveller as outcast, as pirate even, offered by the Levellers, a leading crustie band (though some see *crustie* as a pejorative term), and originally travellers themselves. A logo on their album *Levelling the Land* shows crossed spanners beneath a rough 'folk devil' face in imitation of the skull and crossbones. The spanners signal the affinity with buses and trucks, are another example of the self-reliant DIY ethos of resistance culture.[54] The band's name, of course, itself recalls the radical republicans of the English Civil War, and clearly (and self-heroically) locates the band within a historical context of social uprising – which if you're a Rainbow Villager feeling you're in 'the middle of a civil war' at Molesworth may be accurate rather than dramatic. But what's life like on a mundane level for New Age travellers, when they're not locked in battle with various authorities?

Life is dirty. Everyone says so. In fact, dirt is a signifier of difference, of outsiderness for travellers and other marginal groups. For the Amsterdam squatters of the 1980s, according to ADILKNO (the anarcho-style Foundation for the Advancement of Illegal Knowledge), 'The clothing of the movement looked sexless (thus "masculine"), dirty and ripped. There were hard patches and nasty stains on it. . . . Squat dress resembled the work clothes of miners, chimney sweeps and tank cleaners. It looked at least as rough and filthy, only it couldn't be traded in after work for a designer sweat suit.'[55] Dirt as a focus both of (political) identity and of revulsion is seen also in earlier press reports about Greenham Common women. In *Femininity in Dissent*, Alison Young focuses on the grotesque emphasis of media representations, 'a theme of startling intensity and violence': 'It is a preoccupation to which the papers constantly return: dirt, disease, disgust positioned against cleanliness, health, approval. . . . The grotesque [body] becomes synonymous with the marginal and the deviant, the cast-out.'[56] Ann Morgan is more maternal in her description of traveller style, seeking to defuse the perception of difference in her address to other parents:

> They act tough and cheeky and a dog helps. They're your kids or mine, from different circumstances. Their hair is matted and they are grey with dirt. They have green teeth and enough mud under their fingernails to plant potatoes in. They scrape around in huge boots with no laces, smoking fag ends and slurping beer from cans. They may have a security blanket dangling around their bums and a pocketful of sweeties.[57]

August 1993
In Glasgow there have always been old blokes, drunks, trying to cadge a few coppers for a cup of tea. A couple of years ago on Byres Road though one red-faced bloke catches my eye and hones

in expertly. With a triumphant smile he says: Any chance of a fiver son, so's I can get a bevvie? He knows the cheek's worth at least 50p. Today Glasgow cheek was outdone in Bristol. By the nails outside the market, near a squatted anarcho-shop, a scruffy man too young to have been either a hippy or a punk but looking like a downmarket cross between the two ambles across. Greasy long dreadlocks, ripped combat trousers, a Dennis the Menace striped jumper, army surplus boots half-undone, an excess of pierced facial parts. In an urban-inflected West Country accent he says: Got any spare drugs, mate? So he's a crustie – I've been out of touch.

While some may be easily identifiable by their clothes and behaviour, New Age travellers as a larger community are more diverse and inventive in their attitudes, motivations and living spaces. Describing a convoy going to an East Anglian fair as early as 1978, Derek de Gale recalls a pause in the 'progress of the long and ungainly snake. Then, green under the street lighting, its windows curtained, was a double-decker bus. It seemed so English and yet the language was not of Suffolk or England.'[58] This is a good point: as familiar icons like double-decker buses are transformed, so Britain is being rewritten around its margins. We'll see later how travellers and campaigners such as the Dongas Tribe in the 1990s take such rewriting further, reinventing themselves as the nomadic 'indigenous Englanders' of the land. Those travellers who have vehicles want to tell you about the ways in which they've transformed them into homes. (Such a blurring of distinction between vehicle and home has apparently been overlooked by police: destroying homes at the Beanfield, impounding them *en masse* at Stoney Cross, the authorities contribute to rather than resolve social problems of homelessness. A darker reading – taking into account Thatcher's remark about being 'only too delighted to make life difficult for hippy convoys' – suggests that homelessness is the state's punishment for the travellers' transgressions.) Lubi converted her twenty-six-foot ex-army radar bus herself, using recycled materials, other people's waste:

We had to rip all the aluminium computer racking out. . . . Now it's got tongue-and-groove wooden floors and cupboards, and I found all my furniture in skips. I've got a low antique pine chest with a sheepskin rug in front of the wood-burner. I've got these two bits of 1920s furniture I cut up, one I put the sink into, the other I put the cooker in and I use the rest of it for a cupboard. There's material that billows all the way along the roof and it matches the curtain material and the material on the cushions on the seats.[59]

Vic describes her vehicle's metamorphosis, the 'ripping out' of an old interior and the process she herself went through in reworking the bare box:

> My first truck was a minibus with a BMC A series engine. I paid £700, quite a lot really. Looking back I wouldn't have paid that much for it – they're good trucks for doing long distances but you have to use them all the time to make it worthwhile. I ripped all the seats out, put a bed in, put a cooker in, put wood around the side, tongue-and-groove panels – a bit of a cliché, a real stereotypical traveller-truck thing to do, but it's really good insulation.

The interior transformations of these two travellers' vehicles indicate the importance of being in control of your own 'space and privacy', as Jay put it. It's more than that, though: the emphasis is on the act of transformation from what the vehicle was, from its previous function being erased ('ripped out' is the phrase both used) to it being replaced by the necessities and some luxuries of domestic life. The significance travellers put on these narratives of transformation says something about them: the work involved in the process transforms the person, is even part of the way in which you *become* a New Age traveller.[60]

Exteriors of vehicles are decorated in a variety of beautiful, provocative or deliberately unassuming ways.[61] Slogans are offered: PEACE CONVOY on the side of a double decker, FIGHT TRUTH DECAY on the side of a coach. Destination windows of former public transport coaches read STONEHENGE GO FOR IT! and MYSTERY TOUR. Other coaches have signs saying CLOSED or PRIVATE on their windscreens. Rainbows, mandalas, suns, anarchy symbols – a coach entirely covered in a painting of a romantic landscape, all trees and mountains, with a huge tarpaulin running the length of its dodgy roof. Others are more practical: CAUTION! BABY & DOGS IN TRANSIT! – a plea to majority culture rather than a provocation? Following the Beanfield many New Age travellers have learned to curb their artistic expression: 'The whacky paint jobs still exist, but lots of people retain the anonymity of their vehicle's [original] company colours.'[62] If from the outside they resemble vehicles not homes, there can be less hassle when on the road.

Not all travellers sail the 'black tar rivers' of the Levellers' road mythology in particulate-puffing diesel trucks and buses. The nomadic nature of the lifestyle can be seen in other, more flimsy, living spaces. There's even a hierarchy of transitoriness: from a tipi to a bender, for instance, is a shift to ever-greater ephemerality. Decker John lists the bewildering range of places he's called home: 'I've lived in buses, I've lived under hedges and in phone boxes, in church porches, in forests, in houses and more houses, in people's flats. I've lived on a few fixed caravan sites too.' He has a terrific sense of the simple and the improvisatory when it comes to building a home. His trailer caught fire and was destroyed.

> [So w]e put two tarpaulins in a square, two of them together to make a cross, and put a very little hole in the middle of them, the size your finger goes through, and put a rope through it. We threw the rope over the branch of a tree and pulled it up, then pegged the bottom out and that was it for about four months.[63]

A sense of the sheer variety of sites is evident in this description of the places the Travellers' Skool Bus parked up on in 1990:

6 areas of common land
6 green lanes
4 disused airfields
3 areas awaiting development
1 verge area
1 commercial festival
1 council-owned recreation area
1 farmer's field with permission
1 farmer's field without permission
1 national conference
1 field under disputed ownership.[64]

Two young women travellers offer opposite opinions on having your own vehicle. For travelling artist Lubi, who specializes in sound sculptures and has produced work for Ebbw Vale Garden Festival, the attraction 'was the self-containedness. It was all there on four wheels, and you took your whole home with you, wherever you went. . . . The idea of being completely independent, and 100% mobile' was its appeal. For Vic, on the other hand, 'when you own your own vehicle . . . it becomes more difficult. There's all the legal side of it, the maintenance, finding somewhere to park.' When Lubi first became a traveller, she noticed that travellers' sites too were gendered spaces, where ownership and power were distributed along male/female lines, possibly even more so than in majority culture. Lubi came across 'no women who owned their own vehicles. . . . [W]omen are reliant on men for a roof over their heads, and such a power play goes on.' She responded with action, echoing the women-only space at Greenham Common she's almost too young to have experienced:

> In '91 I organized a women's camp in Wales. Part of the reason for setting it up was because there weren't any networks for women. It was a new thing to have a space where women and their children could just get away and get on with living. . . . We set up communal spaces like a purple dome and we had a tipi, and a couple of women from Tipi Valley came along with their tipi too, and we did workshops on issues that women wanted to talk about.

Harry is a middle-aged woman with three daughters who has been on the road for twenty-odd years. Her eldest two have been on the road all their lives with their mum, and still are travellers: they've moved out of Harry's truck into their own vehicles. As a mother she has particular views on the difficulty with travelling life. 'The one big problem on the road is that a lot of the time there aren't any children,' she says. 'Frances is eight. Finding her someone to play with is nearly impossible. . . . There's a lot of babies and a few teenagers but there aren't actually many families with children.'[65] As well as the practical problem for Harry, there's a more general issue here about the extent to which youth culture matures and adapts as its exponents grow older and develop different expectations and priorities.

Peter Gardner notes that travellers in the South-west of England 'see thousands of acres set aside for military purposes and question the validity of the argument that there is no room for them. Surely there must be a small patch of land available somewhere for our peaceful coming together? – they ask.'[66] This question echoes the cheeky demand in the Albion Free State manifesto of 1974 for 'permanent free festival sites, collectives, and cities of Life and Love, maybe one every fifty miles or so' up and down the land.[67] Walking onto a lay-by, a piece of industrial waste ground, a disused quarry, some council-owned or common land, you may miss the resemblance to 'cities of Life and Love', but locating sites both temporary and permanent (or at least longer-term) is the constant struggle of New Age travellers. The Friends, Families and Travellers Support Group (FFT) is an organization that seeks to protect the rights of all travellers, whether gypsy or New Age. It too voices the need for identifiable sites, as well as for the maintenance of traditional stopping places. With the Criminal Justice and Public Order Act 1994 the prospect is not encouraging, as it actually repeals the obligation of local councils in the Caravan Sites Act 1968 to supply sites for travellers. Steve Staines, national organizer of FFT, describes the situation in mid-1995:

> The difficulties Travellers have accessing the law, combined with the available battery of legislation which is routinely used by police, councils and landowners against them and with an almost countrywide policy of denial of sites traditionally used by Nomadic Peoples, means that the position of this diverse community is steadily worsening.[68]

It's possible that travellers contribute to their own demonization: the brew crew, the younger crustie element that hangs around the edges of Tipi Valley, or begs for drugs in Bristol, represents the current popular image of travellers. Some travellers themselves might seem to revel in their alienation. (Why wouldn't you, if you're alienated?) Yet why should brew crews be seen as a problem, and one created by travellers? Alan Dearling suggests rather that they and their sites reflect the wider social situation: 'Sure, some Travellers are dirty; some get busted for dealing; some are suffering from mental health problems and drink- and drug-related problems. Unfortunately, the same is true for many other members of society.'[69] Even if hard drugs aren't present, life on site is increasingly punctuated by eviction orders, which are the standard way of moving the 'problem' on elsewhere – preferably, in the case of police and many county councils, over the border to another county's responsibility. Traveller Rabbit can see the positive side of this though: 'Suddenly everyone you haven't seen for ages is outside changing wheels and standing around with their engines in bits and everything gets going.'[70] This can be viewed as a sign of inertia: the travelling impulse as a response to external actions rather than initiated by travellers themselves. Or, more positively, it's a sign of New Age travellers' ingenuity: even the deliberate and systematic disruption of their lifestyle can be turned from a source of anger or despair into a routine of pleasure and energy.

Writing about the living spaces of New Age travellers, I've been struck by the extent to which they *are* living spaces, vibrant and imaginative. I'm most struck by this astute remark from Shannon, a traveller in the early 1990s, when the 'politics of envy' was a phrase much-favoured by the unimaginative political classes. Shannon reverses the typical poles of desire and disgust between travellers and the inhabitants of the majority culture: '. . . a lot of the hatred of travellers is out of envy'.[71]

3

CRASS 621984 ANOK4U2

One good thing about music
is when it hits you
you feel no pain.

Bob Marley, 'Trenchtown Rock'

So punk ain't going to change the world
Where's all the bands that were going to?
Maybe it's just a fashion, I don't know
But now it's . . .
Come and get your punk in Woolworth's
Bondage trousers – twelve pounds
Mohair jumpers sold next to cardigans
It always comes around.
They make it safe.

Patrik Fitzgerald, 'Make It Safe'[1]

In 1978, the Sex Pistols had fragmented, Sid Vicious was under arrest for murder and on the way to death by rock cliché in the States, the Damned, the Jam, and the Clash were trying, with varying success, to bridge the gap between punk antagonism and pop sensibility – it looked like things were being made safe again, opposition was being channelled and recuperated, rebellion commodified.[2] The beauty had been brief, the spectacle awesomely accurate. Punk singer–songwriter Patrik Fitzgerald had released early singles on a London-based independent record label, Small Wonder, including the rough classic 'Safety Pin Stuck in My Heart', subtitled 'A Love Song for Punk Music'. By the time Fitzgerald made it to recording an album, *Grubby Stories* in 1979, punk's narrative was well on the way to being cleaned up. The single piece on

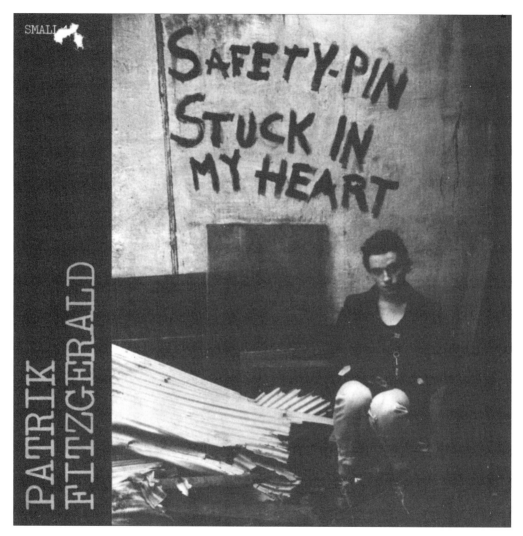

'*A Love Song for Punk Music*'.

that album that features no music, only Fitzgerald's East End voice reciting the words, is 'Make It Safe'. Its starkness of delivery underlines its seriousness – what had happened to punk's utopian possibility?

In 1978 a record called *The Feeding of the Five Thousand* was released on Small

Anarcho-pacifist Crass fight war not wars.

Wonder.[3] There's nothing remarkable about the independent release of another post-punk band's record, except that this one was by an anarchist band/collective/commune who called themselves Crass, and who were to survive and flourish as a radical underground organization in the dark days of Thatcher's early 1980s. (Their active trajectory was from around 1978 to 1984.) More than that, they were to produce a large and varied body of cultural texts, with record sales in the tens of thousands, and by my reading they are a significant and neglected example of what Stewart Home calls 'politico-cultural agitation and protest' groups.[4] In one of the few references to Crass in books academic and otherwise (one that is lengthy and admiring), Jon Savage writes:

> Their 'Feeding of the 5000' was the first of a sequence of media (records, slogans, books, posters, magazines, films, actions and concerts) so complex . . . and so effective that they sowed the ground for the return of serious anarchism and the popularity of CND in the early 1980s. It's also possible to trace the current popularity of the travelling lifestyle to Crass's huge success in the early eighties.[5]

Crass were a radical anarcho-pacifist, anarcha-feminist, vegetarian collective, and the anarchism it espoused was not the anarchy of the Pistols ('Anarchy in the UK' begins with a frightening guttural laugh by Johnny Rotten and ends with the almost comic-book 'Get pissed. Destroy'), but a lifestyle and world-view they developed through a combination of hippy idealism and resistance, punk energy and cheek, and some of the cultural strategies of the Situationists.[6] Punk itself has been charted endlessly, particularly around the Sex Pistols *circa* 1976–77. In the slightly later and somewhat ignored post-punk culture, the earlier political thrust was more keenly developed and deeply explored. Crass worked in the vibrant post-punk context of radical politics and radical musical culture which featured other bands such as Poison Girls exploring the politics of sexuality and liberation, the band Pop Group claiming to be ending despair and beginning tactics via a sort of intense jazz–funk/punk crossover, the Raincoats searching out an apparently quieter, gendered approach to rock music. These were musicians and activists who were questioning Patrik Fitzgerald's dark view of punk's development. What was different about Crass was that here was a post-punk band whose sole reason for existence was that they were going to change the world.

Consisting of around nine male and female musicians, artists, film-makers and activists living in a commune in Essex, Crass were a quite narrowly English organization (though on occasion with one American, the performance artist Annie Anxiety), problematically erasing issues of class and race (while they were themselves all white), and taking their songwriting materials from a specifically English experience. An urban, London-based perspective was offered early on. For instance, there are textual references to the Roxy club (an early punk venue), Securicor, the London Underground, and so on. Stewart Home's argument that 'the "hippies" who'd started the Stone Henge festival formed their own *punk* band – Crass – . . . [and] inject[ed] an element of *ruralism* into the movement' needs refining.[7] What Crass did was to develop provincial networks from an original London focus:

> . . . we tour[ed] far and wide throughout the UK, bravely treading where no band had trod before. . . . Hundreds of people would travel to join us in unlikely spots to celebrate our mutual sense of freedom. We shared our music, films, literature, conversation, food and tea. Wherever we went we were met by smiling faces, ready and willing to create an alternative to the drab greyness all around.[8]

Certainly there is a hippy background to Crass: drummer and key member (*not* leader) Penny Rimbaud had kept open house since the early 1970s. A former public school boy, Rimbaud was at first one of the hippies 'who were getting on with it quietly',[9] not at all involved in the public countercultural actions of hippies, for instance at the Windsor Free Festival. Public political activity was to come later, with Crass, which was the outcome of various squatters, artists, youth being energized by punk and using Rimbaud's Essex commune as a space in which to explore these new musics, events, attitudes. Bassist Pete Wright:

> I can remember right at the beginning, about a week before I got together with Steve [Ignorant, singer], sitting in a wheelbarrow out in the garden, and thinking,

something's going on that's a bit dangerous, and I'm on the dangerous side of it.

For Rimbaud, when punk turned up, 'getting on with it quietly' was no longer an option. Distinguishing between his own attitudes as a hippy and as a punk, he says: 'I'm not going to . . . grow organic tomatoes, I'm going to start throwing them at the bastards.' For other punks though, the politicizing experience had a rather different source, one more focused on multiracial urban Britain, an area Crass didn't explore. As Paul Gilroy notes in *'There Ain't No Black in the Union Jack'*:

> The street carnival, with its bass-heavy sound systems pumping out the new militant 'rockers' beat of reggae as the half bricks and bottles flew overhead, demonstrated to the punks the fundamental continuity of cultural expression with political action.[10]

Crass sidestepped much of punk's relations with black British culture, but were indeed entirely involved in strengthening the continuity of cultural expression with political action that Gilroy writes of. Dave Laing, in *One Chord Wonders*, writes of their 'significant . . . self-proclaimed anarchist politics. . . . With their own record label, fanzine and even a commune to live in (which brought inevitable accusations of "hippie" deviationism . . .), Crass attacked punk bands who had "sold out".'[11] The communal living was a utopian experiment, and contributed to the total package – right down to lifestyle, right down to living in a version of what anarchist thinker Murray Bookchin calls an 'affinity group'. There's an effort here to close the gap of rhetoric and practice, a rarely achieved thing in anarchist thought and movements. (Anarchism might be better defined less through theory and practice than through the gap between the two.) Those consciously mob-oriented anarchists Class War offered a typically double-edged compliment to Crass:

> The only band to carry the musical–political line forward was Crass. They have done more to spread anarchist ideas than Kropotkin, but like him their politics are up shit creek.[12]

Crass's anarchist politics 'are up shit creek' because of their refusal to situate their actions in the traditional labour framework of class opposition – presumably they are compared to Kropotkin, a one-time prince, to signal Class War's distrust of indulgence through privilege.

It's significant that Crass were not just a musical band releasing punk records, for it's their multiplicity of cultural and textual activity that's of interest. I want to look at their strategy of *bricolage*. By *bricolage* I am referring to 'the classic modes of "anarchic" discourse', 'the structured improvisations of *bricolage* for a theory of spectacular subculture' that Dick Hebdige has developed and explored in his classic piece of punk analysis *Subculture: The Meaning of Style*.

> The subcultural *bricoleur*, like the 'author' of a surrealist collage, typically 'juxta-poses two apparently incompatible realities'. . . . Punk exemplifies most clearly the subcultural uses of these anarchic modes.[13]

It does so because the modes of juxtaposition and subversion are so entwined in punk: the safety pin and the Queen, the bin liner on the body. *Bricolage* is a key sub-cultural notion, one I come back to again in my discussion of other marginal narratives, as it's useful for looking at styles of clothes, culture, politics. It can also be translated as *do it yourself, DIY*, a punk idea that has extended into the early 1990s. As clothes of punks, of New Age travellers, of people at free festivals, are patchworks of styles and views, so the *bricolage* of Crass is a patchwork of ideas, strategies, voices, beliefs, and so on. Crass extended the act of *bricolage* to cover multimedia and inter-textual forms. What are the elements of this *bricolage*? I want to consider a number of the devices they employed in their cultural and political practice. In turn, these are political campaigns, live performance, visual styles, and finally the actual music itself.

Crass had a number of favourite targets for critical attack, ones that they (too) often merged together in a kind of grand conspiratorial accusation as 'the system'. The breadth of their onslaught is signalled in some of their album and single titles: *Stations of the Crass, Penis Envy*, 'How Does It Feel (To Be the Mother of a Thousand Dead)?', and, in what seems like a moment of rare humour, *Christ: The Album*.[14] The Church, unemployment, patriarchy, family values, the state, war, nuclear weapons, Third World exploitation, the environment, the meat trade, these were the targets – as well as punk bands and writers who didn't live up to Crass's rigorous standards. (In a neat, almost self-effacingly earnest way they later sang, 'We're tired of living up to other people's expectations when our own are so much higher.'[15]) There was a streak of English puritanism, too: no drinks or drugs which might dissipate anger or lead to diversionary police interest. 'Whenever I wanted to do any drugs I used to have to go out [of the commune] and do it, then come back and try to act normal,' confessed singer Steve Ignorant.

The social interventions of Crass range from the sub- and countercultural to the more global. I'd say, though, that it's outside mainstream culture and society, at the margins of representation and expression, at the margins of political activity, that Crass's interventions were most significant. Members were involved in the organization of the early Stonehenge festivals – though they were hardly gratefully received when they attempted to play the festival in 1980. Crass were involved throughout with the peace movement, bringing particularly anti-nukes actions and information to different and larger groups of people than were previously involved. Their 1980 single 'Nagasaki Nightmare' illustrates this involvement, less for the music of the piece (though the insistent repetition of the word 'nightmare' by singer Eve Libertine does have a powerful defamiliarizing effect) than for the graphics and text on the seven-inch single's black-and-white foldout cover. These are complex and wide-ranging, from contemporary Japanese descriptions of the effects of the bomb to illustrations by band member G. of world leaders with and as bomb victims, from a brief history of the anti-nukes movement in Britain to the addresses of current campaign groups, from images of cowboys and US Air Force glamour to tiny cartoons such as the one showing the Queen cradling a baby bomb in her arms, from an insistent connection between gender and destruction (missile as phallus, the slogan 'MAN MADE POWER MAN MADE PAIN') to Crass's overt positioning of the listener/reader as always already politicized:

> While we rebel with marches and music and words they'll fight us back through the propaganda of 'popular' media – television and daily papers. . . . Subversives are what the whole thing is about. Subversives are all the people who want to change things. Having this record makes you a subversive. Being on a strike committee makes you a subversive. Women living outside men's rules are subversive.

The centrepiece of the cover is a map of Britain adapted from a poster by Bristol Anti-Nuclear Group. It shows the frightening scale of the nuclear project, both for domestic power and for national weaponry, and its present and potential impact on the environment and on society. Crass lay bare the insidious nature of the network. They

19454U
enola hallo
AN.OK?521984
pay no more than 45p

Crass symbol: capital/the system consumes itself or Crass self-destruct?

construct from fragments a conspiracy, instil a sense of distrust, even paranoia, into the person holding the record, so the record itself becomes a potent site for oppositional struggle.

From their earliest recordings Crass explored aspects of patriarchy through a strategy of extreme representation, so extreme that one track was originally censored by the workers in the record pressing plant, who refused to press it. This was 'Reality Asylum', an astonishing spoken piece from 1979 delivered by Eve Libertine over sound effects that constructs Western patriarchy through the master narrative of Christianity – hardly a new idea in itself, but certainly provocatively different through its rhetoric – and situates that Christianity in the wider contexts of militarism and misogyny:

HE / HE / HEAR US JESUS / YOU SIGH ALONE IN YOUR COCKFEAR / YOU LIE ALONE IN YOUR CUNTFEAR / YOU CRY ALONE IN YOUR WOMANFEAR / YOU DIE ALONE IN YOUR MANFEAR / . . . ALONE IN YOUR FEAR / YOUR FEAR / YOUR FEAR / WARFARE / WARFARE /

In 1981 an entire album was devoted to the women's voices in the band. The cover of *Penis Envy* shows on the front a sex doll in its box, on the back a meat preparation factory, and quotes from the Bible, 'This is now bone of my bones, and flesh of my flesh: she shall be called woman' – gender and sexuality, meat and death, religion, they're all there. According to Penny Rimbaud, '*Penis Envy* was an incredibly empowering record. I know that a large number of the hardcore Greenham women had come to it [the peace camp movement] through punk, through . . . us and the people we inspired.'

At least two bogus recordings by Crass surfaced into the public domain over the years, recordings intended as political hoaxes. First, under the name of Creative Recording And Sound Services, they produced a parody of the romantic love song called 'Our Wedding', which was accepted by teen-romance magazine *Loving* as a flexidisc to be given free to its readers (the publishers found out about the hoax only after several hundred readers had been sent their copies). Second, the 'Thatchergate Tapes' saw Crass embroiled in the politics of the Cold War, and of Falklands War recriminations. Put together secretly by Crass, these were edits of a recording purportedly of a telephone conversation between Ronald Reagan and Margaret Thatcher. On the tape Thatcher admits responsibility for the sinking of the Argentinian ship *Belgrano* during the war, and Reagan threatens to use nuclear weapons on Europe in order to defend the United States. Information not in the public domain was used, supplied to Crass by a sailor who was in the Falklands – it included the accusation that HMS *Sheffield* (which was hit by an Exocet missile) was effectively sacrificed by navy commanders in order to protect a nearby aircraft carrier on which was Prince Andrew. There's an oblique reference to this on Crass's 1982 single 'Sheep Farming in the Falklands':

> *The royals donated Prince Andrew as a show of their support*
> *Was it just luck the only ship that wasn't struck*
> *Was the one on which he fought?*

When the story eventually broke, the initial angle, as reported by the *Sunday Times*, amongst others, was that the KGB was responsible for the forgery. In fact, the tape had taken Pete Wright three months to produce. When the *Observer* broke with Crass's involvement, 'The world's media pounced on the story, thrilled that a "bunch of punks" had made such idiots of the State Department.'[16]

Possibly the collective's least abstract campaign was during and following the Falklands war, when Crass found themselves largely alone on the punk scene in vociferously criticizing the actions of the British government. Talking at the Essex commune, Steve Ignorant gives some idea of the pressure on Crass then, as they released the singles 'Sheep Farming in the Falklands' and, when the death toll was known, 'How Does It Feel (To Be the Mother of a Thousand Dead)?':

> That was the only time I've ever been frightened of actually living here, the only time I ever considered moving, because it's so exposed. . . . Just after we'd done 'Sheep Farming', the flexi, and I was really worried there was going to be petrol bombs coming through the windows.

The single was originally released in 1982 as a flexi-disc with no label, which gives a further idea of how nervous Crass felt.[17] According to Dave Laing, on re-release it became the best-selling punk single of 1983.[18] Questions were asked at Westminster on several occasions about Crass's records and activities, particularly during their onslaught on the Falklands War. 'How Does It Feel' was described by Tory MP Timothy Eggar, attempting to have it prosecuted under the Obscene Publications Act, as a 'vicious scurrilous attack on the Prime Minister and the government. . . . Authority', he thundered, 'has to draw a limit somewhere.'[19] Crass's strategy was precisely to interrogate authority's limits. It has to be said, though, that others in the music industry were less convinced by Crass's rhetoric and practice over the years. Rock critic Tony Parsons decried Crass for their 'gumbie-activism', while Mark E. Smith, the northern voice of the band the Fall, made characteristically plain his disapproval of 'a condescending French Resistance-type group', and commented on the post-punk music and style scene in the 1980 lyric 'Cash 'n' Carry':

> You think you've got it bad with thin ties
> Miserable songs synthesized
> Or circles with A in the middle . . .[20]

In an industry like the music business, premised on hierarchy (the charts), success, glamour, touring circuits, lucrative contracts – all of which were desired by the first punk bands, when punk had ostensibly been about getting back to roots, the street, away from the old rock dinosaurs – Crass refused to act in this way. Of all the successful punk and post-punk outfits, Crass alone managed that most difficult of manoeuvres: to avoid recuperation, to maintain political and artistic autonomy in the music industry of all places. That is such an achievement. If punk was a discourse of authenticity, obsessed with street credibility, with not 'selling out', Crass must be placed at the centre of that discourse.[21] As Colin Larkin notes, Crass 'to this day remain one of the few groups to loyally adhere to their original ideals'.[22] Where the Sex Pistols took their 'DESTROY' tee-shirts too seriously, where the Clash moved from 'I'm So Bored With the USA' to providing the soundtrack for Levis ads, for Christ's sake, Crass found, developed, explored and finally exited their own political and cultural space. They set up their own record company, produced and released all their own music, designed their own covers and texts, mostly using non-standard materials. They organized an alternative gig circuit largely around benefits for local peace groups and other radical organizations, their first live performance as Crass being at the Huntley Street squatters' festival in London in 1977. In their early successful days one idea of theirs was permanently to play the support slot at gigs – as on the first occasion I saw them, at the University of East Anglia (UEA), supporting Poison Girls.

Just as punk was dead along came real believers like I was, not like me at all, seriously earnest folks, intimidatingly serious in look and rhetoric, singing songs like 'Punk Is Dead'. At the UEA barn I stumbled across them, they weren't even on the bill. Some time in '79, near the end of the year. We knew about Crass from The Feeding of the Five Thousand *– I'd even written to them – but it wasn't until the night that we knew they'd be playing too. Not too sure even then. Was it a benefit gig for Freewheel, the radical bookshop on St Benedict's? I still have the poster somewhere, which caught my eye from being so small and difficult to read, rough red screenprint with thick ink on rough black paper. It featured intriguing slogans and totems: ANOK4U2, a flying bird with talons against a circular backdrop. It was contemporary, and flaunted that: the admission price was 79 pence. I liked that the price, the money aspect of this anarchist event, was so rooted to the date. It made it somehow less capitalistically important, just an arbitrary contemporary necessity which could as easily be gone tomorrow.*

That first time in Norwich, Crass were startling, not just to me, but to all the punks who knew about the gig and had turned up, all the more so because they were so casual about it, wandering around the half-empty hall before and after playing waiting for us to talk to them, drinking tea. Music was material to Crass, and they showed that; the performance was an object, clearly delineated, which they involved themselves in and then exited. Music happened for a while and then it didn't happen. Even a post-punk art group like Wire that we'd all seen at People's (they didn't throw paint at us) didn't manage to subvert the performance process in the way that Crass did. Looking at it from the other way, Crass didn't so much cut short in a material way the performance as extend it entirely and indefinitely, to include the pre- and post-show, the setting up of the stolen (did I make that up?) and homemade PA, the draping of flags and banners and subsequent transformation of the barn, the being looked at in their problematically paramilitary black garb and red armbands, the sexy sexless women. Either way I was totally intimidated, and deeply attracted. Here were people doing exactly what I thought punk should do, take itself seriously, be considered as a force, a creative possibility to destroy. (Bakunin vivified. Though in their early days Crass said they thought Bakunin was a kind of vodka.) For Norfolk people it was a bit like a set of alien beings dropped into our cosy country context, from some other place that ran on different rules, that breathed authenticity. There was no joy with Crass. It was the fostering of puzzlement. Norwich punks were bewildered. We weren't expecting this.

I knew in an instant that Crass were something special and, more importantly, something serious, a new shard of punk.

The shock of that first single too, I am no feeble Christ, offered in an intensely righteous way, a clearly spoken rhetoric that blurs words, coupled with the frenetic delivery of the repeated In all your decadence people die! on the other side. That's the side I listen to, doubtful only of the cheap drama of railtrack sound effects that suggest the Holocaust. The cover, too, signals difference, rough brown cardboard with staples and typed lyrics, red and black graphics, industrial grey paper insert, mysterious symbols, slogans and coded numbers.

Village halls, old theatres, tents, free festivals – all were transformed by a kind of performance art that variously bolstered, contradicted and transcended the actual music playing. I was intrigued: after that same gig I write about retrospectively above, I wrote what, judging by the response below, must have been a long letter to Crass containing my reactions to and questions about the gig. The reply I received is I think as comprehensive a statement of Crass's ideas and cultural strategies as I've seen. It's also a snapshot of their positive feelings about their activities at this still quite early stage, particularly their activities in the provinces.

26 November 1979

Dear George

Thanks for the letter. Complicated, comprehensive, sensitive, committed (and only slightly self-effacing). It's rare that we get letters where we aren't just expected to trot out a few pleasantries and 'send a badge, please'.

Perhaps I'll just go through it and write as I come to things –

Our appearance? Well, it's been about the same for about a year now. And so are most of the actual clothes. Our clothes might be the 'right' ones in Norwich, which I find slightly and illogically refreshing, but in London we look like a bunch of well-tended ragbags. So I suppose it's over to you to sort out. We're not velvet zippies, we're not the system.

Our performance? A large part of what the band can do is point out, or even give a small indication of the way things are going. Our stage appearance which is assumed, considered (but not contrived), is a charade of what people might have to deal with in 5–10–15 years' time. There isn't aggression in our performance, it's desperation. Usually we play in places where a large part of the audience are self-confessed misfits – punks, skins, National Front, British Movement, Socialist Workers Party, hippies, freaks, anarchists – and no matter how bigoted they might be in their own particular sensitive areas, they are still open, if we can put it right, to ideas. They openly admit that they *are* looking. Their commitment to the system, to the way things are done, continuing, isn't complete. . . .

I think that if the people from the town hadn't come we would have either not played or have gone over the top. I think Steve came close. That's why we don't usually play in colleges since the early days when we were pissed anyway. (We were a last minute support for the Poison Girls.) We played Chelsea. The only way I could express my disgust at the place was by pissing on a Henry Moore sculpture outside the front door – which is pretty futile.

Encourage/provoke/intimidate violence? We don't *instil* violence. At best we confront the individuals in the audience with their own violence, prejudice – in a relatively safe environment. As safe as we can make it. Ideas again. If the individual wants to deal with it he or she can in their own time.

You seem to be making an attempt to understand – yourself. I suspect that's the only thing really worth the effort to try and understand. Trying to understand Crass? I think it's possible to see anything in the band – fascist, wimps, fools, stars. . . .

And afterwards people did ask us for badges, autographs etc. and, short of autographs, we try and give people what they ask for – but if someone asks for a badge they get our badge Anarchy and Peace with the A breaking the gun; and that's loaded. Sooner or later they might try and come to terms with the symbol they've been wearing for two weeks or so. [Badge attached here to letter paper.]

Eve sang, 'in all *your* decadence . . .' and 'in all *our* decadence . . . .'.

To understand what we are doing, to have thought about what we are doing is us taking responsibility for what we do. I don't think that's superficial. We don't 'get off' on playing, we don't particularly like putting ourselves up there in what, in London at least, seem to be heavier and heavier situations. And if we don't know what we're doing, or haven't considered things then the audience is exposed.

The way we do handouts, record covers, etc smacks of care and diy.

One of the nicest things about gigs increasingly is the number of people turning up who are doing things of their own. A sort of loose network slowly builds up and information gets around. And we don't only hand out badges at gigs. We get to meet and chat with quite a few people. It's a pity we didn't get to talk to you – bit of a weighty letter this. Perhaps if you come and see us at a gig some other time – It's so much easier talking than writing.

I'm enclosing a copy of TOXIC GRAFFITTY just for the hell of it. See you.

Anarchy and peace

Pete Wright

The text of a leaflet I have from a gig in the Midlands illustrates the informative, self-conscious politicizing intent of the entire performance event, as well as the hippy-style rhetoric in the punk context:

AN 021 @ party For Anarchy + peace

. . . IN CRE@TION TO FACILITATE OUR POTENTIAL

The last time Poison Girls, Crass etc played B'ham £300 surplus was made this went towards 2 free festivals in Summerfield Park (thanks to bands helpers etc) / S.L.A.G. alarms publication of a slychiatry drugs dictionary and a anti E.C.T. 'guide' / Donation to Peace Centre + Prompt (Anti PsHciatry League). Helped buy printing equipment / submission supplements / Animal Farm vidio + lots more. This time the surplus won't be so great as all the overheads are more except the bands (£860 in all to be precise)

But the entrance is still only £1

DIGBETH CIVIC HALL

WED 22 APRIL 7.00.

CR@SS

POISON GIRLS

ANNIE ANXIETY

FLUX OF PINK INDIANS.

The leaflet explains a typical Crass event: money raised from the previous performance went both towards marginal political campaigns (mental health and animal rights) and to encouraging more music via free festivals. Opposition and subversion through activity; opposition and subversion through music itself. Crass thus sought and created an alternative audience, an alternative market, over a period of around seven years, while many other punk bands around them dissolved, moved away, went to detox units, and (sadly) eventually reformed. Their ex-centricity was self-created and flaunted, their self-marginalization a critical statement both on punk and on the capitalist music industry.

A significant part of Crass's *bricolage* was their use of the visual arts. A graffiti campaign had long been one of Crass's strategies – *Stations of the Cross* is partly so named because of their extensive graffiti on London Underground stations. Their graffiti had to be 'always neatly performed'; much of its impact came from this fact. Key non-musical members of the outfit were G. (also known as G. Sus), the visual artist throughout, and mick, the film maker. G., who had worked in the United States as an illustrator, explains: 'Stencil graffiti was very much inspired by New York cos it used to be on the pavements, which was great. Every time you'd cross the road, there was something to read.'[23] At gigs audiences were bombarded with signs and slogans – the black punk rags worn by all members ('makes washing easier', I seem to remember one explaining), the flags and banners as backdrops to the stage, displaying Crass slogans and symbols, the banks of TV screens showing film. A written text called 'Autopsy' from a record cover describes the film (again, note the constant self-reference, an earnest urgency to document, and to explain their own practice).

AUTOPSY / a break-down of the film shown at the start of most of our gigs.
businessmen / mannequins / motorway construction / technology / dead soldier in ireland / soldiers / guns / shadows / army reconnaissances n. ireland aerial photos / meat (meat lorry / two births (cutting umbilical / parthenon / british museum / oscilloscope / suicide / road accident / fighter and bomber jets / military police / westminster / stock exchange / security guard / graveyard / burnout / pornography / television / foetus / suburbs / x ray / wolf / battlefield (tanks and men) / lynching / brides and bridesmaids / mushroom cloud / beach scene / spaceman // sound breakdown / sentimental orchestral pop songs / president truman from 'why i dropped the second bomb on nagasaki' code expressions referring to little boy / baader meinhof conversation / terrorist ultimatum / birth screams / nurses voice for

treatment with injection / hubert humphries on strategic
arms limitation treaty 'frankly i doubt it' / piano piece
played by woman whose life was saved in extermination
camp by playing for nazi officers / psycho killer; talking
heads / bands: crass / why not / nipple erectors / mick[24]

The film's *bricolage* strategy is one of juxtaposition and subversion by association: this technique creates the now familiar-sounding Crass message – connected social institutions are the body, war and technology, birth, and marriage. It's an autopsy, though, not a vivisection: an examination of a (social) corpse. The second part of the film (signalled in the textual description by double obliques) leads into 'sound breakdown', a shift from the social and visual to the social and aural. There is political discourse by institutional (Truman) and subversive (Baader-Meinhof) individuals, who are implicitly linked by their 'terrorist ultimatum', their bombing activities. There is a focus specifically on music and its social role, including, interestingly enough, the connection of Crass with the American art/post-punk band Talking Heads. Talking Heads were largely apolitical (that's why they've been so popular with academics) – can we read this as Crass commenting on the inadequacy of contemporary popular music's oppositional nature?

Representations of Crass gigs in turn are used on the black-and-white record covers, which open up into posters. These too are littered with slogans and representations of graffiti – very Situationist, very 1968: 'FIGHT WAR, NOT WARS', 'BE WARNED! THE NATURE OF YOUR REPRESSION IS THE AESTHETIC OF OUR ANGER'. . . . In fact, the interdependence of the different textual aspects is foregrounded in the cultural practice of Crass – many of the sung lyrics are impossible to decipher without the lyric sheet, and the vinyl records themselves are inscribed with text, on the playout section near the centre, where the grooves are widely spaced. You actually *read* the record itself. For example, peer at the two records of *Christ: The Album* with the light in the right direction and you can read on one, 'For war there is no reason – only cruel babaric [*sic*, I think] utility,' and on the other, 'In war there is no reason – only cruel barbaric futility.' No opportunity to propagandize through text is overlooked. The cover texts offer a carefully constructed image of DIY, of samizdat, from the crammed typewritten lyrics to the stencilled slogans. The visual strategies favoured by G. include montage- and photomontage-style paintings, superimposition, multiple frames and *mise en abîme*, as well as the by-now-standard Situationist *détournement*.[25] She (G. Sus *was* a woman) uses everyday images from the media, the political world, and the body itself, and these images are resited and defamiliarized in exaggerated, grotesque, and often apocalyptic scenes. The future Crass present is a nightmare – as Pete Wright explains in the letter reproduced above, they offer 'a charade of what people might *have* to deal with in 5–10–15 years' time' – but the future they want is not. A (guardedly materialist) utopian politics is represented through dystopian cultural formations.

Even as they uncovered contradiction or duplicity in others, Crass were themselves rife with it in their own cultural activities. They produced and employed tension from contradiction – using their masculinist, super-aggressive music to sing songs of peace, protest, and feminism; their aggressively confrontational visual art to protest against, for instance, the Falklands War. Even the black clothes suggested a paramilitary air more in line with fascist than with anarchist semiotics. They explained their clothes and performance strategy in one of their numerous fanzine interviews.

> Our whole appearance is designed to be a barrage of contradictions. We try and challenge people on every ground we can. The appearance is fascist. We wear black. The symbol which hangs behind us looks like a mish-mash of different flags. . . . The audience don't get a neat little package they can swallow down and walk away from.[26]

Confronting an audience can backfire, as we've seen with their performance at Stonehenge in 1980. Their concern was both to keep the anger they felt towards what they identified and called 'the hypocrisy [that] is as appalling as it is obvious', and to channel and *represent* that anger through the music. Their aim was to construct an 'aesthetic of . . . anger',[27] rather than, say, to adopt the strategy of a previous generation of British anarchist activists, the Angry Brigade, all terrorist cells, bombs, and communiqués. (A Crass poster proclaims: 'Germany got Baader Meinhof, England got punk.') While seeking to represent anger through their cultural products, Crass avoided the standard poles of youth subcultural politics of the time: right-wing (British Movement, National Front, Sham 69, Oi) and left-wing (Socialist Workers Party, Rock Against Racism, the Clash). As they put it, 'we refused to do the most important thing, which was siding up'. The idea was that by refusing to take sides, Crass's music and performance left audiences provoked but unpositioned. This is either Crass utterly valorizing their autonomy, or a clear instance of their politics being, as Class War put it, 'up shit creek'. Penny Rimbaud explains:

There was more than ambiguity, there was a downright contradiction, between the warmth, openness and everything, and of all the punk bands we were the most mechanical, inhumane, terrorizing, much more so than the Pistols, we were a great black void full of all sorts of horrible images. A total bombardment, in total contradiction to afterwards when we would be wandering around eating marmite sandwiches and drinking cups of tea. It was that confusion that put people in the middle and said, make your own fucking minds up.

There was a self-conscious sense of built-in obsolescence, or alternatively a realization that from the beginning they would have only a certain amount of time. The end-date for the Crass project was 1984, because of Orwell's book. Their last live gig was a miners' benefit in Aberdare in July 1984. The earliest records and stencilled graffiti showed a mysterious sequence of numbers: 621984. In 1979 this became 521984, and so on in subsequent years, and these numbers were eventually incorporated into the record catalogue numbers, a countdown, a millenarian signal to the date when society would (or should, or might be) changed. But also almost a sell-by date. The singles compilation that came later – releasing a compilation is a standard enough thing to do in the rock industry, though this one was at least not marketed by K-Tel – is called *Best Before . . . 1984*. The title signals Crass's self-ironizing awareness of their music as product in the marketplace. The most common symbol Crass used is of a stylized snake that eats its own tail in a circular motion, a continuous event. Intended as a critique of capital/the system's consuming self-destruction, it works equally well as an auto-critical statement, even prediction. The strategies of capital were co-opted by Crass in a skilled way – for all their self-marginalization they would still use effective sales techniques and pitches to get their views over, their records bought, listened to, read. They foregrounded the cheapness of their self-produced and self-released records, the first single saying 'Do not pay more than 45p' on the front cover (singles at that time cost 80–90 pence). As they developed, and released the records of over twenty other anarchist and punk bands, their designer label, their radical chic corporate identity, was a statement of organization and longevity. For anarchist bands, the label the record was released on was almost as important as the music that was released. This insistent shift to extra-musical concerns was vital for Crass's flaunted autonomy: Crass Records and Crass the performing band were interlocked aspects of the same musical/political activity.

Crass lyrics and music

Texts were rewritten ironically by Crass. In terms of subjectivity, their use of pseudo-nyms (a common feature of punk) enabled them to rewrite, to transform themselves. As Eve Libertine writes, on the cover of 'Reality Asylum', 'I'll find new names for myself and a new place to stand.' Crass gave themselves names like N.A. Palmer, Phil Free, Joy de Vivre, names that resonated politically and with irony. Jon Savage (itself a pseudonym) notes this time-honoured process of reinvention, describing 'pop' as 'the one place in English society where you can reinvent yourself, where the donning of a new jacket can appear a political act'.[28] Crass also rewrote the intertexts of punk, a par-odic move that is both critical and, by the very echo, appreciative. In 1978 the Clash released a great single, one of the finest moments in the punk/reggae crossover, '(White Man) in Hammersmith Palais'.[29] Released on the multinational CBS label, it includes the following couplet (which was approvingly quoted on the cover of the Tom Robinson Band's first album, itself released on another multinational label, EMI):

Hah you think it's funny
Turning rebellion into money.

This overt and unacknowledged contradiction – that the rebellion both the Clash and the Tom Robinson Band refer to and proclaim is itself being turned into corporative investment by virtue of its very proclamation by them – was of course too much for punk purists Crass to bear. They replied with their dismissive rewriting of those lines in their own couplet:

cbs promote the clash/
but it ain't for revolution, it's just for cash.[30]

In 1980 a single was released jointly with anarchist co-conspirators Poison Girls, 'Persons Unknown'/'Bloody Revolutions', which was both a benefit record to raise funds for an Anarchy Centre in London and a retrospective protest against the trial of four anarchists on conspiracy and bomb charges. The cover folds out to form a poster that is an ironic rewriting of one of punk's best-known images, famous publicity shots of the Sex Pistols from around the time of 'God Save the Queen'. (Crass's parody has itself become one of punk's best-known images.) The four punks are redone: Johnny

Crass redraw the Sex Pistols in a cover poster for the single 'Bloody Revolutions', 1980.

Rotten has Thatcher's head on his shoulders, and is drinking a glass of wine rather than a can of beer; Sid Vicious is the queen, with one chain around his/her neck and another holding a corgi nearby; the pope is wearing Steve Jones's clothes, and has 'MUM' tattooed in a heart on his upper arm. . . . The rebellion's become the Establishment? Ironically, Crass were attacked from both sides over this poster: HMV stores banned their record, presumably on the basis of its treacherous and blasphemous potential, while G., who was responsible for the artwork, says 'the most violent reaction . . . came from punks who thought it was a heresy against the Pistols'.

I want to look now in more detail at a couple of musical texts by Crass. It's here that I justify the epigraph I use from Bob Marley, those beautiful impactful lines: maybe pacifist Crass make a music that *does* hit and *is* painful. . . . This piece, 'Women', is from their first record, and it illustrates their extreme rhetoric and musical approach, as well as their insistent connections of feminism, pacifism, capitalism. (With the lengthy quotations from Crass texts, I approximately preserve the original typographical layout and punctuation of the lyric sheets.)

WOMEN.

fuck is womens money / we pay with our bodies / there's no purity in our love / no beauty / just bribery / it's all the fucking same / we make soldiers with our submission / wars with our isolation / fuck is womens money / we pay with our bodies / there's no purity in motherhood / no beauty / just bribery / it's all the fucking same / we are all slaves to sexual histories / our awareness of whoredom can be a release / war is mens money / they pay with their bodies / there's no purity in that game / only blood, death & bribery / it's still the fucking same / but we've all got the power / don't just stand there and take submission on the strength of fear /

FIGHT WAR, NOT WARS/

I should describe the vocal delivery and aural property, the very qualities that are most patently absent in a written discourse, the very qualities that demonstrate most effectively the vibrancy and energy of Crass. The piece is spoken – almost intensely shouted – by an English woman with a northern accent, the addressees ('we') being all other women; men ('they') are excluded. The voice is set against a musical backdrop of arhythmic white noise/guitar distortion/indistinct radio sounds. It's not a punk song at all – musically, it's too stark and uncompromising – but what it takes from punk are the extramusical aspects: its DIY aesthetic, independent distribution, typographical layout, flaunted otherness, taboo language. . . . One thing to note in particular is the connection of what we might call a negative or dystopian criticism – patriarchy, capitalism, war – with a utopian moment or desire: 'we've all got the power / don't just stand there and take submission on the strength of fear'. The situation described in the song is found in the present, the past ('slaves to sexual histories') and the future ('we make soldiers'); the system is complete and, to date, closed. The piece ends with vocalist Virginia Creeper (aka Joy de Vivre) quoting the refrain (the entire lyrics, actually) of one of the other songs on the record: 'FIGHT WAR, NOT WARS'.[31]

As we've already seen, the texts of Crass were often self-referential. An auto-critical discourse is inscribed within their cultural productions, seen in a late piece from *Yes Sir, I Will* in which the lyrics deal with a retrospective critique of their own strategies and positions.

> Words sometimes don't seem to mean much;
> Of anyone we've used more than most.
> Feelings from the heart that have been distorted and mocked,
> Thrown around in the spectacle, the grand social circus. . . .
>
> We didn't expect to find ourselves playing this part,
> We were concerned with ideas, not rock and roll,
> But we can't avoid that arena,
> It's become a part of us even if we don't understand it.
>
> In attempts to moderate they ask why we don't write love songs.
> What is it that we sing then?
> Our love of life is total, everything we do is an expression of that,
> Everything that we write is a love song. . . .
>
> Critics say that it's just punk rock or that we're just naive anarchists.
> They hope to discredit us with their labels and definitions. . . .
> We've had problems from self-appointed Gods from Bishops to MPs.
> They've tried to ban our records
> Saying that we're a threat to decent society.
> Fuck them. I hope we are.

The piece is delivered in an overtly dialogic manner, two lead voices, male and female, operating in a loose kind of unison. The univocal focus of most rock music is subverted, suggesting a practice of solidarity. This interdependence is accentuated because reference to the lyric sheet is essential: words won't be recognized, let alone understood, by only listening to the music (the words are that shouted and garbled in delivery, and there are too many of them to fit the music). Surprisingly for a band so concerned with the message of the text, lyric clarity is not a priority. This is deliberate: 'There's a certain advantage in not hearing all the words. People don't switch off,' they've explained.[32] Any effort, with the lyrics, at rhyme and scansion is long gone. Though Crass describe *Yes Sir, I Will* elsewhere as 'an impassioned scream' the message of which is 'loud and clear',[33] the piece is partly concerned with Crass's sense of exhaustion in political and cultural activity. Interestingly, this is expressed both through the lyrics ('Words sometimes don't seem to mean much; / Of anyone we've used more than most') *and* through the form of the recording: *Yes Sir, I Will* is an album comprising a continuous 40-minute live studio recording. The listener experiences and shares the performers' exhaustion as voices crack, the beat wanders, energy flags and returns. There are no individually titled songs, but blocks of musical and lyrical text. This is in sharp contrast to the early Crass, where pieces (even if recorded live in the studio) were short and fast in that speedy punk style. One of the situations explored on *Yes Sir, I Will* is the challenge to maintain the energy level and the righteousness of the critique through a non-stop recording of an entire album, as in the same way the challenge outside the studio was to maintain the energy of radical cultural activity for years on end. It's surely an indication of the sophistication of Crass's cultural practice that their discourse includes formal musical aspects as well as the more standard lyric/textual ones (that is, it's not 'just punk rock'). Surprisingly maybe, Penny Rimbaud points the listener towards connections with classical composition in the structure of Crass's music:

> We composed in the classical way, using atmospheres and development . . . it sounds ridiculous, but if you knew Britten, you would hear a lot of Britten in our stuff. A lot of the chord sequences are very beautiful dissonances. I even thought at one stage of sending some of our records to Peter Pears, and saying, you might not like it, but you inspired this.

I like the way even here, on this recording, at their most tired and self-analytical, that Crass keep up the defiance ('Fuck them. I hope we are' 'a threat to decent society').

For a rather less sympathetic view of Crass's musical practice it's worth turning to a contemporary, 1979 review of *Stations of the Crass* by Graham Lock in *New Musical Express.*

CRASS: TOO MUDDLED, TOO LATE

Crass, as you probably know, are a group of intensely sincere people who live in a communal house near Epping, daub London's underground with provocative graffiti and make independent hard-core punk records which advocate anarchy, peace and freedom. . . .

My view is that Crass have backed themselves into a corner, casting off potential allies with an abusive ferocity that has me wondering how they can accuse others of divisive tactics. The music press, RAR [Rock Against Racism], bands with record deals – all are written off in a series of aggressively hostile songs with no less venom than Crass expend on more obvious targets like religion and the monarchy. The fact that these groupings include many people with aims similar to their own seems to have escaped Crass. The line appears to be that all tactics must be identical to theirs or be wrong. . . .

'Punk was once an answer' they claim on 'White Punks on Hope', already idealizing and distorting the past in an archetypically regressive manner. Punk was a gesture, a fart in the face of authority – it was never an *answer*. At best, it was a beginning, opening up possibilities which people are still exploring in a variety of ways. It seems a good thing to me: the more inroads into the heart of the beast (read music biz) the better. But Crass seem to want a mass return to the simplistic sloganizing and song structures of early punk. They want to turn back the clock and start again. . . .

[T]hey restrict themselves to basic punk noise. Why? Why do Steve Ignorant's gabbled, sneering harangues dominate the album to the point of relentless monotony? Why do Crass write lyrics which Tony Parsons acutely, if a little unkindly, characterized as 'Gumbie-activism' when in conversation their political analyses are so much more sophisticated? . . .

Stations of the Crass is a double album, containing nearly 40 tracks, and sells at £3 per copy. Of which £1 goes to recuperating costs, 70p to the band, 30p to the distributors (Rough Trade) and £1 to the retailer (or £1.50 if you're Virgin Records and think you can get away with selling the album for £3.50). . . .

Lock makes a number of valid points, especially about Crass's relations with other political and campaign groups (though it wouldn't be anarchist if it didn't involve a quick split!), and possibly about their musical limitations, though I've tried to show above that Crass don't offer only 'the simplistic sloganizing and song structures of early punk'. I'd argue that Lock misreads the quotation 'Punk was once an answer', seeing *answer* as meaning 'solution' rather than as 'response'; the complete couplet is 'Punk was once an answer to years of crap/A way of saying no where we'd always said yep'. Punk was a response to 'crap' music; that's what it 'once' was, say Crass. Doesn't that 'once' suggest that it isn't and wasn't so fixed or static as Lock suggests? Neither does Lock do justice to the complexity of Crass's textuality as a whole – by which I include the *bricolage* of performance and visual graphics. As we've seen, one of Crass's considered strategies is precisely the contradiction between musical impact and quieter personal rhetoric. On the sleeve of *Stations of the Cross* there is a powerful (and for once understated) visual statement about cultural and imperial hegemony. Juxtaposed are two similar visual images below the word TRADITIONS. These show the backs of two women – one a bather from an oil painting, the other a victim of a nuclear bomb. Dates and names are supplied: J.A.D. INGRES 1828 and HIROSHIMA 1945. Ingres painted 'poeticized Oriental scenes providing an excuse for voluptuous nudes'[34] – Crass's record sleeve invites the viewer/listener to consider connections between the worlds of high art and global politics as versions of orientalism, in Edward Said's use of the term, and between representations of women and modes of violence as patriarchal narratives. This does not read like 'gumbie-activism' to me, but rather, as Pete Wright wrote, 'The way we do handouts, record covers, etc smacks of care and diy.'

Still, at least it was a review in the national music press. In analyses of punk culture and social engagement Crass are more noticeable by their absence. Offering a tense merging of political and cultural activity, Crass have been placed outside the critical framework – possibly because their process of self-marginalization was so successful that it sited them outside critical and historical discourse. Of course, Crass's audience themselves may have had little interest in recuperating them for discursive purposes. That's the old punk authenticity / street credibility hurdle Crass did more to maintain than ever to challenge. Intersections are conflicting, though. Their cultural forms were sited in the social, even as they marginalized themselves. They were avowed critics of the dominant repressive totalizing narratives of the state, patriarchy, religion, of the standard revolutionary left, even as they offered their own cultural and textual *bricolage* of micro-narratives that was intended to function in a totalizing manner. The spectacle, the moment, of Crass, even as they proclaimed their radical vision with a sometimes overwhelming (or is it just embarrassing?) intensity, includes the knowledge of its own failure through their sell-by-date slogan. Further, there was a reluctance to historicize: Crass's is a curiously (and, frankly, in anarchist circles, refreshingly) autonomous anarchism, free-standing of history. There's little reference throughout to the anarchist tradition of thought, to those heroic and dead achievers such as Proudhon, Bakunin, Kropotkin, Malatesta that regularly turn up in anarchist discourse. This makes for an awkward combination of ahistorical arrogance and a more positively opportunistic construction of anarchism around the newness, the perceived radical difference of punk. In a piece of creative prose called 'The Pig's Head Controversy. The Aesthetics of Anarchism' on the sleeve of *Yes Sir, I Will*, someone explains:

> I too could quote you voices from history, but they are the voices of the dead. Marx. Christ. Freud. (Swirling rhetoric from the tomb.) I seek my own explanations, exhilarated by my own presence upon this living earth.

The anarchist subject – from Max Stirner all the way up to Crass – proclaims that '[t]here is no authority but yourself'.[35] For Crass the micro-perspective of focusing on the individual subject has been both their strength, as we've seen, but also one of their greatest potential weaknesses. How do you move beyond the call to simply be yourself? Take away the radical rhetoric and cultural practice and what's the response to the charge that anarcho-punk is merely a form of 'prosaic laissez-faire individuality', as Simon Reynolds puts it?[36] Crass discuss the problem: 'The what, where and why of our anger needed explaining, as did our idea of "self".'[37] An effort to achieve this was made with 1984's *Acts of Love (Fifty Songs to my Other Self)*, poems set to music by Penny Rimbaud and sung by Eve Libertine. Unfortunately, this large quantity of variable haiku-like fragments hovers over rather than addressing the issue, one central to anarchist tradition, directly.[38] However, even if Crass's 'idea of "self"' is never adequately explained, in a way to make this observation is to miss their achievement. Graham Lock's review of *Stations of the Cross* offered his own view of punk as 'opening up possibilities'; I'd suggest that Crass's project, rather than global transformation and the construction of a new human subjectivity, is a more local and achievable one. That is, the effort to *keep possibilities open* through the cultural milieu of punk.

Setting aside their communistic lifestyle, there's a contradiction between the peaceful, egalitarian state espoused by Crass and the apocalyptic, masculinist cultural practice that expresses and explores that desire. For Crass, is the term *anarcho-pacifism* itself the source of the splitness of their cultural and political strategies? Is the anarchism the down side of a laudable pacifist belief? Or is it that the shock tactics of their anarchism are the material side that balances the potential Christian pacifist tradition? Or are Crass teasing out these tensions, foregrounding uncomfortable contradictions we (or at least other anarchists) might rather leave alone? In the brief history/autocritique that accompanies *Best Before . . . 1984*, they write: 'The ambiguity of our attitudes was beginning to disturb us. . . . Were we being destroyed by our own paradoxes?'

> After seven years on the road we had become the very thing that we were attacking. We had found a platform for our ideas, but somewhere along the line we had lost our insight. . . . We had become bitter where once we had been joyful, pessimistic where once optimism had been our cause.

Internal contradictions combined with external circumstances to pressurize the margin further, so that even the most precious principle of Crass – pacifism – was under question. Rimbaud:

> [The Falklands War] and the miners was the end of another era of direct energy, the direction had to be changed. What happened with us is we became so fucking angry that we didn't know what to do with our anger, we started to split in what we felt should happen. Half the band supported the pacifist line, and half supported direct and if necessary violent action. It was a confusing time for us and I think a lot of our records show that, inadvertently. We couldn't maintain the front. . . . I think the sourness of our final works leaves a dirty taste in the mouth.

You can sense the desperation in a 1984 single like 'Nagasaki is Yesterday's Dogend', each section of which opens with the shouted word 'ATTENTION', punctuated by breaks in the music. For a Crass piece, there's a surprising amount of silence. The piece concludes with a succession of short shouted sentences, directly invoking action, uprising, accompanied by a distorted music the drumbeat of which breaks down, resulting in a rare rejection of harmonic and rhythmic discipline. For the Crass of rhetoric and propaganda, in periods of state war and internal clampdown 'words are no longer enough', people no longer have the cosy luxury of taking the time to 'make your own fucking minds up': the optimism of 'ideas again', of Pete Wright's letter from 1979, has been replaced – erased even?

> ATTENTION. Stand up and fight. Choose life or
> destruction, love or hate. You cannot have both
> and survive. Go forward. Get out in the streets. Down
> the sewers. Snap the rules. Creep through the net.
> Fuck their diseased system. The words are no longer
> enough. The information has been given. The lies have
> been exposed. Choose your path. It's time to fucking
> act. No time to be nice. It's time to fucking act.

However, don't we need to question whether Crass's largely utopian anarchism (all those early 'smiling faces ready and willing to create an alternative') is actually negated to some extent by their quite dystopian cultural practice? How far were they caught up in the aggression of their own rhetoric – musical, textual and visual? Is there a sense in which their disgust with the machinations of the capitalist and militarist state comes to dominate all else, and becomes a figure, if not of desire, then of fascination? While they insist that 'Everything that we write is a love song,' the bewildered listener may be thinking that it doesn't much sound like it. Or is it that you have to search for the love in a Crass text? For all their relentless challenge, direct language, visual bombardment of good taste, and their focus on the extreme manifestations and effects of war, death, patriarchy, religion, maybe the utopian element Crass offer is that implicit belief in a different, a better other, and in the positive possibilities of cultural practice: there is a truth (of some sort) and people can be convinced of it. This utopian reading is qualified, though, through a scepticism signalled by the dissonant music and dystopian visual imagery employed. Crass themselves suggest retrospectively that

> The true effect of our work is not to be found within the confines of rock 'n' roll, but in the radicalized minds of thousands of young people throughout the world. From the Gates of Greenham to the Berlin Wall, from the Stop The City

actions to underground gigs in Poland, our particular brand of anarcho-pacifism, now almost synonymous with punk, has made itself known.[39]

After punk, after Crass, the possibilities are open again; the cultures of resistance are gathering pace, a generation is re-energized by youth and by the sheer thrill of new music and culture. Small wonders have grand repercussions.

4

EVEREEEBODEEE'S FREEE; OR,

CAUSING A PUBLIC NEW SENSE?

RAVE (COUNTER)CULTURE

The venue was the Roundhouse. . . . The posters went up, in a scattered fashion, around the autumnal city. 'All Night Rave' they proclaimed. Back in 1961 at the Beaulieu Jazz Festival . . . some mild disorder had occurred amongst teenagers inflamed by the wild sounds of terrible trad bands. The *Daily Mail* had proclaimed that a new and ugly word had entered the English language, 'raver'. That Saturday, 15 October, five years later, the ravers had come home to roost, this time accompanied by Strip Trip, Soft Machine, a steel band, and Pink Floyd. . . . It didn't even start until 11 p.m. How the ravers were to find their way out of Chalk Farm and into their bedsits would also be a challenge worthy of the do-it-yourself times into which the metropolitans were moving.

Nigel Fountain on the launch party of *International Times* in 1966[1]

If the ravers came home to roost in 1966 five years after some mild disorder, what on earth have they done during the proclaimed Second Summer of Love in 1988, and in the years beyond? The 'do-it-yourself times' have spread over about three decades by now. Not until the expansion of rave culture,[2] though, has the counterculture so explicitly harked back to the sixties. One of the fundamental questions with this is the degree to which such reference is parodic or critical, or both. If it's mainly parodic, it's difficult to take rave culture seriously as constituting a political project; if it's critical, the reference back in time isn't simply nostalgia or *mode retro*, but a way of using a clearly politicized past to engage with a difficult present situation. The rewriting of the sixties in the late eighties and early nineties is a cultural act I constantly return to in this chapter. Why? Because the sixties (either authentically or in terms of its own retro-spective reconstruction, or for a mix of the two) was an epochal period of political and social action by many youth and other people in Britain and elsewhere. The '"freakified" youth . . . exploring new aspects of selfhood'[3] we associate with that period – whether British, American, French – must feel they're part of some collective acid flashback as they look and listen around them twenty-five and thirty years on. If aspects of sixties youth – music, style, drugs, language, attitude – are being recontex-tualized in the nineties, then I want to interrogate one central question, which rave culture itself revolves around: where are the politics? We've touched on the problem of the political engagement of counterculture before, particularly with the East Anglian fairs, those atavistic sites of temporary pleasure. Can the same accusation, of hedonism being favoured over engagement, justifiably be levelled at raves, the cel-ebrated temporary autonomous zone becoming ever more temporary, to the extent that it's ephemeral even?

To answer that question the origins of rave culture need to be traced, since these indicate what rave culture is, or what it says it is. (These may not always be the same thing: rave frequently offers a sophisticated and knowledgeable discourse about itself in the context of countercultural action – how valid is this? Does rave simply talk a good struggle, as it were? On the other hand, maybe I'm too easily led to take the dis-course at face value in the case of counterculture more generally, because that's what I want to believe.) The main sources of rave disperse and collide swiftly, sometimes sur-prisingly: post-disco dance music from the USA, the Mediterranean island of Ibiza, the north-western post-industrial city of Manchester, a general sixties and early seventies nostalgia, and the movable feasts of squatted warehouse parties that mushroomed in Britain in the mid- to late eighties. I want briefly to look more closely at some of these.

According to Antonio Melechi:

Pop analysts failed to theorize the actual origins of Acid House in the contem-porary space in which it was born, at the degree zero of popular culture: the package holiday. . . . [T]he British experience of Acid House belongs [here], attempting to relive the jouissance of the Mediterranean holiday in the pleasures of dance, music and drugs.[4]

'The re-staging of Balearic memories over metropolitan weekends'[5] occurred on the dance floors of British clubs in the late 1980s, focusing on the London club Shoom in

1988. Where punk had rejected such obvious pleasure a decade before, with the Sex Pistols singing 'I don't want a holiday in the sun', youth hedonism was now back, with a vengeance. A fortnight's holiday in the sun became packed into a single weekend – then the next weekend and the next. Tanned youth queuing up in dreary London streets to get into the club, to get out of it, dance floor as beach, beachwear as night-club garb in British winter – why not?[6] The British parody themselves abroad on package tours – why wouldn't sharp youth offer a parody of themselves as parodies abroad when they get home? In Ibiza the Balearic Beat took dance rhythms and mixed them with eclectic tracks to produce an intriguing and fresh sound on the dance floor, which British DJs and audiences were quick to pick up on and take home. There's a greater significance to the package destination though: Ibiza itself is a site of historical resonance for counterculture. Going on the hippy trail, for instance, often meant returning via Ibiza; alternatively, that might be as far as you actually got. Kristian Russell elaborates on its significance: 'Ibiza certainly has a drug history, as it was a hippy island during the 60s and 70s (as were Kos and Crete, for example) and they still house a large contingent of original and new hippy communities.'[7] Here is one of those perhaps surprising connections between generations of counterculture, that a European melting pot of pleasure and dance suddenly offers a throwback to an earlier international moment in youth experience. Like a palimpsest: examine the surface, look through the paper, see or feel the sixties underneath, half-erased, half-rewritten. Showing some historical awareness, rave culture quickly proclaimed 1988 the 'Second Summer of Love' – this time more clearly located in Britain than in 1967 America – though it's worth noting that, as Antonio Melechi observes:

> While club culture purists insist that '88 was the one and only 'Summer of Love', it was, in many ways, merely an inkling of what was to happen in '89, as raves became a crossroads where unlikely subcultures (football, Indie and traveller, amongst others) would meet.[8]

For Kristian Russell such an unlikely meeting of subcultures is itself 'reviving a San Franciscan ideal of 1966, in the "gathering of tribes" – young, old and differing youth factions. Youth had fragmented in the aftermath of 70s punk, but was now beginning to reunite in the light of some severe sociopolitical developments.'[9]

The North of England was one area that suffered from such sociopolitical severity. Though Balearic Beat replaced any remnant – even memory – of other regional popular musics like Mersey Beat, none the less the North-west of England still had its contribution to make. It's possible to identify again a cultural politics of the provinces, of regional self-identity, with rave:

> 'Scallydelia' (in both Liverpool and Manchester) was a challenge from the North to the North/South cultural and financial divide – the traditional notion of the working class North and the richer, middle class South. London's Acid House might have accepted the ethic of anti-hip, but both Liverpool and Manchester were still very competitive – very hip-orientated. This clash had also occurred in the 60s and 70s, when Merseybeat and Northern Soul respectively, momentarily challenged London for supremacy in the music industry.[10]

Unsurprisingly perhaps, bearing in mind that he's based at Manchester Metropolitan University, legal and cultural critic Steve Redhead emphasizes the links of the new music with Manchester/Madchester. The still much-neglected Northern Soul scene, based around all-nighters that drew crowds of dancers from all over Britain to Wigan Casino and Locarno in the seventies, is influential here. An unspectacular dance sub-culture rooted partly in the mod scene from the sixties, Northern Soul took an appreciation of contemporary African-American music and expressed it in the form of dance. Indeed, amphetamine-aided dance marathons attended by the cognoscenti in their superwide bags with superhigh waistbands, ignored or dismissed by more *serious* pop music fans,[11] were a significant underground precursor to the northern impetus of rave culture. This is identifiable in the eruption of the squatted ware-house party scene around the Lancashire town of Blackburn in the late eighties. Dance venues like the Empire in Morecambe switched almost overnight from Northern Soul to acid house and kept their audiences. With the Happy Mondays, Manchester became Madchester: maybe baggy clothes and all-nighters had never really gone away in the North-west. 'Scallies' (baggy style, originally from Liverpool) and 'perries' (after Fred Perry casual clothes, originally from Manchester) are unspec-tacular or unoppositional youth styles located within the rave scene which clearly problematize a straightforward reading of subculture as opposition, or of rave culture as justifiably being located within a narrative of countercultural tradition. As Steve Redhead argues, the baggy style of the Madchester rave scene, like the earlier Northern Soul scene, is part of 'a long and complex history of a casual youth style which is impervious to analysis with the aid of the orthodox tools of contemporary subcultural theory', which interprets style innovation in terms of social resistance.[12] To return to my original question, the issue with rave is precisely this: can it be located in terms of social engagement, as contributing to a culture of resistance?

I've already suggested one political angle, that of a cultural politics of the provinces, one working against a London-centred internationalism and perceived privilege. Another is found in the warehouse parties that contributed to the development of rave culture. These usually illegal events took place in squatted buildings in towns and cities, were publicized by word of mouth in the right pubs, were attended by the usual mix of hedonists, students, politicos, and other youth. Sometimes you paid for entry to some down-at-heel type who'd shortly be a minor hero of Thatcherism; others were free in the unrecognized spirit of the sort of things Alan Beam et al. had thrown at the Meat Roxy in London in 1974.[13] Here rave culture illustrates its debt to the festival scene, becoming a new autonomous zone distinguishable by being that much more temporary than those that had gone before.

The Cauldron, 29 September 1984
Post-pub night-time, a vacant shop premises, perfect squatted setting with its huge hall of curved ceiling and peeling paints, a grand sweeping staircase that does need to be swept, one male toilet bowl that blocks and is inevitably broken by 3 a.m. mayhem, and, the final touch, a high balcony for the quiet dopesmokers and resters, from where they can peer and piss and spit and sit. All the young punks drunks and drugheads stand around, dance a little, look at each other by devious means so there's no danger of showing respect or appreciation of others' modes or dresses. The blasting generator-powered music sounds like it will run out of fuel long after it has run out of ideas.[14]

Technoculture

One of the classic texts of the American counterculture of the sixties is Theodore Roszak's *The Making of a Counter Culture*. Its subtitle indicates its argument: *Reflections on the Technocratic Society and Its Youthful Opposition*. For Roszak, one of the counterculture's defining features is that it was constructed in opposition to what he calls the 'technocracy', literally government by technology, symbolized by anything from the military–industrial complex to nuclear power to the war machine in Vietnam to one-dimensional corporate man (sometimes woman). The project of the people of the counterculture in the sixties was an effort 'to fight their way free of technocratic entrapment'.[15] Of course, this distinction is itself based on a false premiss – the sixties, with its new (to the majority) drugs like LSD and its developments of music through amplification and studio instrumentation, was itself predicated to an extent on technological innovation and exploration. None the less, Roszak raises a pivotal issue, and distrust of technology – of mega-technology anyway – has pervaded all countercultural moments since, as seen in anything from the peace camps to a common DIY ethos in cultural production to an implicit or explicit eco-concern. Rave culture in the nineties, on the other hand, is frequently defined from within and without as a discourse of technocelebration: rather than rejecting, it embraces technology, from the mobile phone onwards. Indeed, one of its music forms is called – techno. For Kristian Russell rave culture can be seen as, in fact, '100% technology'.[16] Similarly, for Douglas Rushkoff rave revolves around technological innovation and celebration:

> . . . a giant, illegal party – a 'rave' where thousands of celebrants took psychedelics, danced to the blips of computer-generated music, and discussed the ways in which reality itself would soon conform to their own hallucinatory projections. No big deal. Bohemians have talked this way for years, even centuries.[17]

Except that by his own argument, they haven't, or at least they haven't in this context of production, where drugs, music, visual images are manufactured and inspired by innovative computer technology. In his book Rushkoff even goes so far as to coin a new name for this brave new world, Cyberia, 'a very new sort of turf – the territory of digital information'.[18] If we saw the mythical or mystical end of the New Age spectrum with travelling communities, with rave culture we access its hardware store. Rushkoff offers a Learyesque paean to the E-generated utopia of a technoculture that opens minds and bridges generation gaps in an almost religious way:

> Psychedelics can provide a shamanic experience for any adventurous consumer. This experience leads users to treat the accepted reality as an arbitrary one, and to envision the possibilities of a world unfettered by obsolete thought systems, institutions, and neuroses. Meanwhile, the cybernetic experience empowers people of all ages to explore a new, digital landscape.[19]

Technoshamanism or technosham?

Technocultural features of rave include music and drugs. A dance music of technology is one of its central thrusts. Surprisingly perhaps for such an uncompromising music, rave originates with that antagonist of punk rock – seventies disco music – moving into eighties electronic hi-energy dance backed by drum machines. With greater mediation and experimentation, dance music has fragmented into any number of eclectic styles and labels. Rushkoff describes the bewildering range:

> There's 'bleep', which samples from the sounds of the earliest Pong games to extremely high-tech telephone connection and modem signals. New York house, or 'garage' sound, is more bluesy and the most soulful; it uses many piano samples and depends on mostly black female singers. There's also 'headstrong' house, for the hardest of headbangers; 'techno', from Detroit; 'dub', coined from [William] Gibson's *Neuromancer* for Reggae-influenced house; 'progressive', which combines styles; and 'new beat', from northern Europe. Less intense versions of house include 'deep' house, with more space on the top layers and a generally airier sound, and 'ambient' house, which has no real rhythm at all but simply fills the space with breathy textures of sound.[20]

This recent largely American description was itself rapidly out of date. It's been overtaken by other developments like jungle, a heavier black sound with reggae/ragga influences and intense percussive elements, or drum 'n' bass. Jungle in particular was demonized even within the club scene: rooted alongside hardcore in the scene of 1990–91, it quickly became associated with a folk devil narrative of crack cocaine and guns, at least until its successful commercialization in the mid-nineties. For Mary Anna Wright, jungle is interesting in part because 'it doesn't lie: there's none of the "Everything's gonna be alright" stuff in the lyrics'.[21] Others read their music in different ways. For instance, Mark is a leading member of Spiral Tribe, one of the main free festival/rave affiliations in the early nineties in Britain and abroad. He offers the provocative line that, by virtue of the accessibility of its production and its mass roots audience, 'Techno is folk music. Never has folk music been so accessible or so loud.'[22]

The newcomer to rave may be blasted away by the inability to root his or her expectations of popular music in perceiving lyric or melody or in gazing at a performance – there are very few words, almost none whatsoever in a verse/chorus structure, melody is absent too in the normal register, there is almost never a stage focus as in the presence of a live band. Rhythm, counted in beats per minute, is relentless, generally in a pumping 4/4 time. As the commentary of the TV documentary *Rave New World* put it, 'machines rewrote the rules of Western popular music. For the first time in its history, lyrics, melody and a human voice were stripped away and the music was dominated by what machines were good at: repeating rhythmic patterns that could go on and on.'[23] Does the lack of lyrics inherently constitute a lack of any discursive possibility or social involvement? No: instrumental be-bop or free jazz never prevented African-American jazz musicians from contributing to the civil rights movement, for instance. Yet musicologist Philip Tagg hears interesting things going on in rave, as in its penchant for the Phrygian mode, one more usually associated with flamenco guitar or Turkish reed improvisations. Tagg even concludes that 'rave music – especially techno – differs so basically from rock and roll . . . that old models for explaining how popular music interacts with society may need radical revision'.[24] There is no lyric to sing along with or think about, no predictable chord progression to recognize with a smile, no melody to hum or be irritated by, no live band to see and shout at – Tagg's certainly got a point, the negative side of which is seen in the results of a survey of ravers' attitudes carried out by music psychologist Mitch Waterman. He found that

> They [ravers] don't want things with a lot of content – I don't mean content in the sense that it's empty, I mean content in the sense that they have to think about things and understand in any conscious or aware manner. If the music in these sorts of clubs had lyrics, the responses would be nothing like those that we found.[25]

Certain drugs have commonly been associated with different subcultures over the years – speed with mods and punks, acid and cannabis with hippies, for instance[26] – but it's in rave culture that drugs seem to be most centrally placed, and one drug in particular: Ecstasy. Both ravers themselves and reporters and critics on the scene emphasize the centrality of E, whether to praise or demonize it. Both its sixties forerunner acid (LSD: lysergic-acid-dyethylamide) and Ecstasy (MDMA: methylene-dioxy-meth-amphetamine) were synthesized in the laboratories of pharmaceutical companies in the early twentieth century. In fact, MDMA was patented as early as 1912, thirty-odd years before Albert Hoffmann synthesized LSD-25. The underground versions of these drugs of the sixties and nineties vary. Whereas acid commonly comes in the form of tabs, tiny squares of paper impregnated with a dose of the drug and printed with some sort of identifying image – a fly agaric mushroom, Donald Duck, a bolt of lightning, and so on – Ecstasy often comes in the form of pills of varying colour, with embossed motifs such as birds on one side and, like aspirin, a fracture line for ease of halving on the other. Psychedelic effects are used in the visual culture of rave, in its computer-generated graphics on the flyers that advertise events,[27] and at raves themselves: both the colour coding of dancefloor lighting with beats per minute (yellow = a cool 116 bpm, red = an energetic 144 bpm[28]) and, more important, the mutating abstract images generated by computer programmes on giant screens around the dancing areas. It's surely a significant aspect of the rewrite of the sixties that the use of a new hallucinogenic (or at least psychoactive) designer drug[29] is widespread – it's at least as surprising as the fact that the term 'acid' itself survives (as in 'acid house', or in the shouts of 'Acieed!' across the country that puzzled older people in the late eighties). Harry Shapiro suggests that 'The very word "acid" sounded hard and dangerous, a corrosive element in society' in the sixties; ecstasy on the other hand is a state of being, and the word sounds altogether more uplifting, certainly less corrosive.[30] Acid and Ecstasy, LSD and MDMA – the parallels across the decades are self-evident (and thus most in need of unpacking).

Ecstasy seems to combine the effects of acid and speed in a more empathic package: mild hallucinations, plenty of energy and an urge to be friendly are all noted by ravers on E. (Other ravers say that, with the loud upbeat dance music, psychedelic visual images and joyous crowds at raves, there's no need for chemical stimulation anyway.) A raver explains the drug-related effects of rave music's repetition: 'You sort of lose track and the rhythm is very important in enabling you to lose track because it's something that moves your body, it's not something that you have to concentrate on. You have to click into it and get into the groove and the pattern and relax with it, and that is this incredible feeling.'[31] Mary Anna Wright connects E, the music and the crowd as part of a holistic, and even utopian, experience:

> DJs control the music and take the dancers on a journey over a night – not just one record – build up, peak and slow down like movements in a symphony. The music is used as a tool to create a rush – music is a powerful tool in trance induction. Your mind and body respond to the subtlety, but it does help if you know what to look for – a learned experience, which is why if you've taken an E you know when the music will make you rush.[32]

However, much of the media scare over raves and the earlier acid house was as a result of a number of deaths of young people in house clubs and raves, all of which

Designer drug flyer, 1995.

were blamed on Ecstasy. Estimates of these numbers fluctuate wildly: a television programme *Rave New World* concludes with the sobering statement that around twenty-five people die every year in Britain from the search for the feeling described by the raver above; the *Guardian* in October 1994 reported sixty deaths a year from designer drugs (of which Ecstasy is but one) in the Strathclyde region of Scotland alone; the *Guardian* in November 1995 reported an estimated total of 52 deaths from Ecstasy since 1985. Yet, as Philip Tagg points out, 'MDMA-related death at rave clubs is connected with dehydration, insufficient ventilation, over-crowding and excessive body temperature'[33] – usually, anyway, and it's for these reasons that resources such as adequate water supplies and ambient chill-out areas are common to raves now. Monthly dance magazines like *Eternity* include reports on the health issues, such as describing bad batches of Ecstasy, or naming clubs that turn off tap water in the toilets in order to increase drink sales.

Not all designer drugs that play a part in rave culture are illegal. Technology has also been used to produce legal agents of 'personal neurochemical adjustment', as it's put by those in the know. These are called 'smart drugs', and in the United States the technoculture scene has led to Smart Bars, where smart drugs and drinks are sold that don't break the law but that apparently do still give a hit. Some are based on healthy fruit drinks, others are concentrated or chemically refined versions of the kinds of nutrients, stimulants and proteins previously found mainly in health shops. Others look elsewhere in the world for their designer drug inspiration. In Britain the *qat* plant is imported from Ethiopia, originally for the traditional social chewing by Somali men. Ravers can buy a drink including *qat* made by a company called Cybertoniks, which claims that it's a great legal way of getting high. The Herbal High Company markets Herbal Ecstasy, described thus in a publicity leaflet:

A revolutionary organic alternative to MDMA. The effects of herbal ecstasy beyond smart drug capacity include: euphoric stimulation, highly increased energy levels, tingly skin sensations, enhanced sensory processing, increased sexual sensations, mood elevations. Developed by a team of master herbalists from around the world from these rare varieties of tropical plants: Tibetan Ma Huang, Wild Brazilian Guarana, Indonesian Wild Fo-Ti-Tieng, Chinese Black Gingseng, Russian Gotu-Kola, German Wild Ginko Biloba, Chinese Green Tea Extract, Rou Gui . . . .

Legal or illegal, exotically organic or pharmaceutical – that's still the aim, to get high.

Don't make a point, make a feeling!

The lyrics all emphasize the sound 'eee'. 'Evereeebodeee's freee', drones one vocal, in pleeesing gleeeful breeezes, winding their way onto the extreeemely wide smiles of dancing boys and girls. It's just the E!

Douglas Rushkoff, *Cyberia*[34]

. . . rock, as a forum for teenage rebellion, has been completely replaced by House. Indeed, with rock artists supporting worthy political causes, it seems that much of rock has been *accepted* and absorbed by the establishment. . . . Meanwhile, the government and the police are determined to bury the House scene, branding Acid House raves as harmful to this nation's youth. What could be more rock 'n' roll?

Bobby Gillespie, singer with indie band Primal Scream[35]

Does rave culture really belong in this book? The above quotations indicate two ways of looking at it. Rushkoff reads rave as the 'gleeeful' narcissistic hedonism of the 'E-generation', for whom 'revolution has become E-volution', Gillespie locates it more clearly as the latest instance in the long line of youth resistance through popular music. Possibly in an apt manner, bearing in mind the digital nature of technoculture, my approach to rave is still binary, the zero or one of self-indulgence or social engagement. For myself, I'm having problems with the idea that the focus of rave culture – dance – is somehow oppositional *per se*. On the other hand, if, say, the simple act of wearing a flower in your hair can provoke the ire of a government, then why shouldn't a huge youth movement, in control of itself and of its own spaces and entertainment, be considered subversive?

Hillegonda Rietveld argues against an oppositional reading of the rave scene; like others who have studied rave at the Manchester Institute of Popular Culture, she sees rave fitting a new, postmodern approach to youth subcultures, one wedded less to resistance and more to decontextualized pleasure. As DJ Aztek puts it below, 'Don't make a point, make a feeling.' By Rietveld's reading, rave's Second Summer of Love in 1988 refers back to 1967 not in order to maintain or rebuild oppositional impulses, but as an indication of the lack of development of activity: 'a countercultural inertia (although using the signs of a counterculture) could be identified. It is therefore possible to argue that a (political) critique was never posed.'

> Rather than creating a spectacle of resistance or 'alternative' patterns of living, the rave offered a release from day to day realities, a temporary escapist disappearance like the weekend or holiday. It was never felt that a critical distance was necessary.[36]

As rave exploded in the late 1980s, with tickets at £25 and Ecstasy at £20 a throw, 'The free market dream of Margaret Thatcher and the New Right, the unrestrained mode of consumption supported by credit cards and an entrepreneurial spirit, was taken to its ultimate limit.'[37] Was it a coincidence that the Second Summer of Love happened a decade into Conservative rule in Britain? Certainly the rapid commercialization of the rave scene is viewed as suspiciously tainted, as the deradicalized indulgence of Thatcher's children. DJ Terry Farley describes 'the sort of yuppie, city whizzkid, "I've got a vodaphone and a Porsche, let's have a party" mentality' of the times.[38] Rietveld argues though that such a mentality doesn't necessarily signal the victory of the New Right within youth culture, but signals rather 'a complete disappearance of the value of money'.[39] Well, maybe – though it's worth recalling that an argument around the rejection of the value of money can also explain the restrained spending of, say, mod subculture in the sixties, long before Thatcherism: 'A mod would spend three weeks' wages having vents put in or taken out of jackets, lapels widened or narrowed, knowing that three weeks later something else would be "in", and mods would rather stay at home than be seen out in last week's fashion.'[40] Does rave represent the return of *youth* to youth culture? Stuart Cosgrove argues that the pleasures of rave 'come not from resistance but from surrender'.[41] The problem with the rave scene is precisely its hedonism, its focus on the simple activity and pleasure of dance.[42] Or is this a problem only for a writer/academic needing to make rave fit the orthodoxy of his argument of a tradition of resistance? If rave is another temporary autonomous zone, where's the autonomy in a twenty-five-quid ticket for a night's dancing? For Steve Redhead such unashamed indulgence is the very factor that defines rave's 'politics of pleasure, a hedonism (in hard times) – a pleasure for its own sake in times when moral regulation of youth is pervasive and deep economic recession is rife'.[43]

Sarah Thornton argues that one feature rave has maintained from the tradition of subculture is its obsessive concern with authenticity, precisely the view that the place of *real* rave is the underground. Thus the effort of real ravers lies not in challenging the assumptions and practices of majority culture but rather in maintaining rave's exclusiveness. Thornton says that 'selling out means *selling* to *out*siders. . . . [Rave culture's] main antagonists are not the police who *imprison*, but the media who continually threaten to *release* their cultural knowledge to other groups.'[44] It's increasingly difficult to hold this line of argument, following the succession of laws introduced or employed to curb the perceived excesses of rave culture – the Licensing Act 1988, the Entertainments (Increased Penalties) Act 1990, and, most notoriously, the Criminal Justice and Public Order Act 1994, for instance. None the less, is there an elite/elitist cognoscenti within rave culture whose aim is to maintain its underground status? Not simply the club purists who recognize the seemingly endless variations in the music, its (for outsiders) bewildering range of names and styles. (Of course, the point of the range may precisely be that it bewilders outsiders.) Is it more an exclusiveness that may be at odds with any wider countercultural or oppositional framework? Or is this exclusiveness rave culture's distinct contribution to countercultural strategy, one of disappearance? It's this point that Antonio Melechi explores:

> If, as [Dick] Hebdige suggests, the politics of youth since the fifties have been principally enacted through a spectacle of style and body, the invisibility which the Acid House subculture has attempted to attain (by escaping traditional sites of surveillance and mapping a new sphere of sound) moves to a new order of politics and resistance.[45]

Here is a variation on the theme of dropping out versus being pushed out which I talked about in connection with New Age travellers, though a distinction is clearly made by traveller Jeremy of the Levellers. For him, travellers *live* the alternative, do not merely have an alternative-type occasional lifestyle: 'the friction between the ravers and travellers has ruined things a bit. For them it's a night's anarchy then you go home; for the travellers they have to live there and suffer the consequences.'[46] Critic Dave Hesmondhalgh observes that 'there is little evidence of social collectivism in the institutions of rave and dance music culture, in spite of a discourse of love and unity amongst its insiders'.[47] So why is rave different? *Because it says it is.* By this argument, counterculture no longer consists of actually doing anything, but entirely of talking about it, of discoursing it through. Rave as a repetition of the sixties without critical distance? Rave as the triumph of countercultural discourse over the effort to engage – over any effort to engage? Douglas Rushkoff, his own rhetoric suitably overblown, writes heroically that 'The mission of the cyberian counterculture of the 1990s, armed with new technologies, familiar with cyberspace and daring enough to explore unmapped realms of consciousness, is to rechoose reality consciously and purposefully.' The comparison in terms of significance Rushkoff makes betrays the poverty of his argument: 'the aesthetics, inventions, and attitudes of the cyberians will become as difficult to ignore as the automatic teller machine and MTV'.[48] The system of capital and American cultural imperialism – very revolutionary. . . . Is *this* the triumph of the technological counterculture?

Yet a politics of rave can be located. Ravers constantly emphasize the considered democratic status of house events, particularly in relation to popular music tradition more generally. Hesmondhalgh summarizes the arguments:

> A number of features of contemporary dance culture are commonly invoked as representing its rejection of the dominant modes of musical organization and consumption: its lack of an established star system; the fact that much of the music is issued without information about performers; that it is often consumed in clubs where, instead of facing performers on a stage, dancers face each other.[49]

Globetrotting DJs working for very large fees might raise their eyebrows at claims of the lack of a star system, but none the less a democratizing impulse is further identified in the technology and its use in creative processes: 'Anything is up for grabs – street sounds can be turned into music, frames of television into art.'[50] Music sampling enables producers and musicians not only to extract from earlier recordings – the postmodern plundering of pop – but also to expand the possibilities of music. Philip Tagg explains the politics of music technology:

> The sampler allows the composition to interact with the world outside its own discourse, not in the usual way of including lyrics to concretize some idea that is not necessarily primarily musical, but by incorporating not-necessarily musical sounds *into* the musical discourse, thus broadening the concept of what music can and cannot be on a highly popular basis.[51]

Also looking at the sampler, Kristian Russell offers the idea that 'Maybe Acid House was reviving the old punk ethic of 1977, that anyone could produce music because there were cheap opportunities?'[52] Both Tagg and Russell focus on the cultural politics of sampling in contemporary dance music, Tagg to construct a new politics from a new form of music, Russell to suggest that the new music echoes the ideology of an earlier subculture. And some, like American techno-hippy Michael Lane, do contextualize arguments about music production within the grander narrative of countercultural traditions more generally:

> The whole Summer of Love – what is that but an inclusive gathering? What is the beat generation but an inclusive thing? What is gay rights but saying, 'Hey, they're equal to us'? What is the digital revolution? – everybody can play together. And this really represents the high point of that because all the different tribes come together: tribal, technology . . .[53]

One of the spaces of the dance scene side of rave – the club – is presented as libertarian utopian space, packed with transformative possibility. In his characteristic hyperbolic style, Rushkoff places Ecstasy at the centre of transformation: 'E turns a room of normal, paranoid nightclubbers into a teaming mass of ecstatic Global Villagers.'[54] Even the nocturnal preference of ravers itself is seen by some as part of their rejection of majority culture. As one explains: 'You share the same space physically as that society [of majority culture], but you're actually moving into a different dimension by shifting through the hours.'[55]

But it's in the rewrite of the sixties and the extension of the free festival ethos, 'executed with updated hardware',[56] that rave's strongest claims to countercultural activity lie. It's no coincidence that one of the first book-length texts on rave culture, *E For*

Ecstasy, was put together by Nicholas Saunders in 1993. Until then, Saunders was perhaps best known by those with long memories as the person behind the very first *Alternative London* book, which was published in 1970, a key text of the counterculture packed with information about subjects from health food to communes to drugs. In the 1995 update of the rave book *Ecstasy and the Dance Culture*, Saunders describes the way in which the twin features of Ecstasy and dance remind him of the old days:

> I felt symptoms familiar from taking LSD in the sixties . . . a kind of uplifting religious experience of unity that I have felt only once before . . . I felt much younger, almost reborn.[57]

Fraser Clark, another sixties veteran of psychedelia, clearly sees house as the continuation of countercultural possibility, the rediscovery of (possibly questionable) alternative histories:

> A kid grows up in a Christian culture and thinks he's probably the only one questioning these ideas. When he comes to house . . . he suddenly realizes he's got a whole alternative history. He might get into UFOs or whatever there is – drugs, witches, it's all in there.[58]

Kristian Russell goes further, connecting the late eighties and the sixties, to argue that 'the political opinion [of rave] might not have been expressed as consciously as the "yippie" [Abbie Hoffman's Youth International Party] movement of the late sixties, but it certainly ended with a conscious political demonstration, carrying the slogan "Freedom for the right to party". Could one not compare that provocative expression by youth to the anti-Vietnam and student protests of 1968?'[59] Let's see – in the sixties there were international demonstrations against the international power and wars of capitalism, against the maintenance of its brutal inequalities around the globe, for the rights of workers across Europe, in collaboration with students, to overthrow the state and its repressive apparatus. In the late eighties and early nineties a few disparate groups of British youth come together to demonstrate for the right to carry on getting out of their heads and dancing to weird music at weekends. Are these really so glibly comparable? Can action and engagement be claimed simply by repeating the rhetoric? Of course, we'll see later, with the Criminal Justice Act, how almost the entirety of rave culture was inadvertently politicized by the legislation of an inept government, but even then the motivation can be seen as a narcissistic one: change the dance laws first, and *then* let's have a better world. (More worrying: change the dance laws and then *there will be* a better world.) Rushkoff offers an even wilder analysis of the politics of rave and other technoculture:

> Using media 'viruses' politically inclined cyberians launch into the datasphere, at lightning speed, potent ideas that openly challenge hypocritical and illogical social structures, thus rendering them powerless.[60]

Wow. That was easy, wasn't it. Through the computerized magic of Cyberia the total power of problematic social structures is erased. By challenging the relevant information network society itself is changed utterly. Just like that. Plainly what hippies and punks and generations of other subcultural political activists have missed is the overwhelming subversive potential of technology. They thought you had actually to change the world, when by American Rushkoff's reading all you have to do is change the computer disk. What energy was wasted!

But it's not all so straightforwardly dismissable. Outdoor raves or free parties, at which part of the process is the construction of a new space, one constructed uniquely for the event, have more in common with the free festivals and fairs I've already discussed.[61] Long-time festival services worker Don Aitken wrote in 1990: 'The "scare" about Acid House parties gives new relevance to a comment made by a commercial festival promoter in 1972: "festivals . . . represent a temporary urban excursion into the countryside. . . . There is undoubtedly an influential and vociferous minority of residents who are totally opposed to the presence of large numbers of young people in their midst for even a limited time."'[62] Don Aitken still holds this opinion; in a recent letter he confirms his belief that 'the root of the hostility which has so successfully been created against festivals, travellers, raves, etc. etc. is that the upper-middle class who now control the countryside of at least southern England are determined that the problems of the inner cities should stay in the inner cities and not turn up on their own doorsteps'. Because of 'the often semi-illegal, cooperative way in which raves are organized', Philip Tagg asks if 'it is going too far to hypothesize that rave music prefigures new forms of collective consciousness?'[63] My answer is that there is nothing particularly new about the collective consciousness or cooperative organization of rave culture, when seen in the context of the free festival circuit. Indeed, one of the problems with rave – a bit like with punk, and maybe with all youth movements – is its stress on its newness and difference. Groups and sound systems like Spiral Tribe, Circus Normal, Bedlam, DIY have been involved in putting on rave events as an update of the free festival, with much the same motivation of opposition and creativity behind them. These rave events are generally compressed in time[64] – lasting a long night rather than a long weekend or solstice week – but with the familiar use of squatting as challenge to rural land ownership, some drugs-selling to finance things, some moving around the country, that the festival and related traveller scene displayed:

> The point of Circus Normal was to provide an environment for creativity, whatever form it takes. We'd provide generators, electricity, sound equipment, a roof, so anyone who wants to do anything can do it: bands, circus performers, jugglers, clowns, tightrope walkers, anything. We do raves now as well which is why we get in all this trouble. . . . Times change and things take on a different shape and form but what we're doing, tribal festivals, have been happening for centuries.[65]

The pinnacle of the festival/rave crossover to date was undoubtedly reached at Castlemorton Common in Hereford and Worcester in May 1992. For eight days anything from twenty to forty thousand people camped to enjoy free music and entertainment in the single biggest countercultural gathering since what became the last Stonehenge Free Festival in 1984. In fact, the Castlemorton megarave happened because the authorities were determined that the annual Avon Free Festival first held in 1988 wasn't going to happen that year: Castlemorton was literally a displaced hippy event. The Avon Free was itself a response to the prohibition of Stonehenge, so rave culture at Castlemorton can be clearly traced back to the earlier free festival movement in Britain. John of Bristol Free Information Network, organizers of the Avon Free, explains the festival/traveller/rave crossover encapsulated by Castlemorton:

> Getting to free festivals had become difficult for travellers and punters alike since 1985. . . . [T]he arrival of ravers at festivals throughout the circuit in 1990 was a welcome boost to the scene (especially I feel for travellers who were trying to make a living from the festival circuit). . . . In 1992 the Beltane festival happened at Lechlade at the beginning of May. This was a huge event of rave and festival

Traveller/rave crossover at Castlemorton Common, 1992.

involving about 10,000 people. Spiral Tribe had been doing the free festival circuit throughout '91 and them and Bedlam were both involved at Lechlade. . . . So the stage was set for Castlemorton with travellers and ravers both looking forward to it and the Avon and Somerset constabulary more determined than ever to stop it. The convoy pulled away very slowly northwards led by a 1940s or '50s tractor. It was easy to imagine this convoy stretching 30 or 40 miles from the A46 to Castlemorton Common. It was actually more like a 35-mile traffic jam. We

Nineties youth experience the free festival spirit at Castlemorton Common, 1992.

finally arrived at about 9.30 p.m. The site was quite linear which meant the main drag [route through the site] was constantly blocked. Spiral Tribe, Bedlam and the main stage were near the main drag and so constantly packed. DIY and a smaller stage were further back and slightly mellower. It was possible to get away to the hills around the common, where the views of the site and the countryside were breathtaking. Every evening, from these hills, you could see long lines of car headlights snaking their way to the festival.[66]

When she reached Castlemorton, Mary Anna Wright was confronted by a policeman whose only words were 'First turning on the right, love, you can't miss it.' She describes the sheer variety of people at the scene:

> There were loads of impromptu cafés being set up and everywhere smelt of veggie curry, wood smoke and summer. There were thousands of Travellers, many more so than there were ravers. Even this early on a lot of them seemed to have overdone the acid and Special Brew. People were wearing all sorts of clothes. The travellers in army-surplus stuff, some had their 'festi-gear' on – mad psychedelic patterns, lots of fun-fur and over the top stuff. There were a few club queens, they looked distinctly out of place trying to scramble through mud without getting their designer lycra dirty. Then there were the festi-ravers, veterans of this kind of event, heavy duty trainers, lots of layers of clothes, practical sportswear.[67]

DJ Aztek, then with Bedlam, later with Spiral Tribe, describes a set he played at Castlemorton. Note – like classical Indian ragas, different ones played at different times of the day – the relation of music, hour and crowd feeling.

> . . . at sunrise, people were tired and needed a change. So I started off with House, happy Techno and uplifting Trance, building and bringing up the tempo and content of the trax. Six hours later I finished, playing hard Euro, Detroit Techno Trance and Acid. This is what I mean by creating moods and atmosphere through music. I think too many DJs have too much attitude. They come on the decks and try to make some sort of point. Don't make a point, make a feeling.[68]

Actually, not everyone did enjoy it: tensions between the 24-hour rave sound systems and more traditional festival-goers as well as local villagers (the ones who weren't partying, anyway) eventually led to some heated arguments about turning the music off for a while. Bedlam did; the Spirals refused ('Our attitude is, "Make some fucking noise"'): they were charged with causing a public nuisance, though 'We prefer to call it causing a public new sense.'[69]

So even such brief events as squatted or outdoor raves can create problems for their own constituents, as traveller Jeremy of the Levellers noted earlier: free festivals over

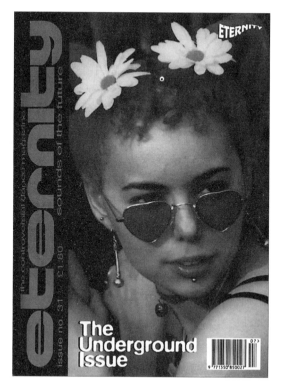

Sounds of the future echo the past: the 1990s embraces the spirit of the 1960s underground.

the decades have shown that self-policing can be a haphazard affair. In order to survive with such unlicensed events more recently, especially under the Criminal Justice and Public Order Act 1994, organizers have had to pull their acts together, not merely to rely on the energy and cheek of old. Diplo, of West Country free party organizers Sunnyside, explains the scenario in a special 'underground issue' of the dance magazine *Eternity*. By mid-summer 1995 Sunnyside had thrown four free all-night dance parties, maintaining the spirit of the urban free festival, learning from the confiscation of sound systems and from arrests suffered by earlier free organizations like Spiral Tribe and Bedlam.

THIS IS THE SOUND OF THE UNDERGROUND . . . 1995 STYLE How the fuck, I hear you saying, they didn't get busted? Well, here's how.

The venue is on public land, and it's indoors, it's away from local residents and it has land for car parking. Crucial! This is squattable property, put up your section 6's and take up temporary residence. Make it safe and clean. When the police come, inform them of your status, show them stewards, fire extinguishers and a first aid kit. If possible get St John's Ambulance/student nurses to attend. Sort out your power; don't steal it. Provide toilet areas. Have some lawyers ready, know your rights and show the coppers your good intentions. Don't sell beer – that's what seems to worry them most – no pennies for their masters I suppose. Provide free water . . . [and] a café, chill out area for rest, tea, coffee, food.[70]

Perhaps the single most impressive outcome from the free party scene in Britain is the efforts of the Exodus Collective, based in Luton, Bedfordshire. Taking their name from the Bob Marley song, Exodus form a new movement of the people in the early nineties, one that originates in something as mundane as a sound system. In Luton (a town

DIY culture moves from entertainment to community, 'massive and passive', celebrated in DIY magazine Squall.

known until Exodus largely for its airport and car factory) black and white youth pull their energies and imaginations together to create their own entertainment, then lifestyle, community, network of campaigns and events. In the words of *Squall: The Magazine for Sorted Itinerants*, the Exodus Collective began

> . . . after the discovery, in a Luton garage, of three unused speaker boxes. These boxes were fixed up, taken to a nearby forest and set up to create the first Exodus party [in June 1992], drawing a couple of hundred people. Three years down the line and the Exodus Collective hold regular FREE dances, attracting around 6,000 people from the area.[71]

Exodus blend a black-and-white rasta rhetoric with nineties dance music. The flags and banners that decorate their free parties indoors remind me of the radical proclamatory DIY ethos of Crass gigs, and this echo of the late seventies to early eighties is strengthened by the use of reggae music and quotations. However, the Exodus Collective move beyond much of what punk – or indeed rave culture – has attempted. There's an emphasis on the collective, on the community involvement, on the social issues that hedonistic youth cultures, even cultures of resistance, ignore too easily.

> [A]nother sight . . . stands out proud and anomalous to Luton's nylon carpet landscape. It is HAZ [Housing Action Zone] Manor, formerly a derelict old people's home and now a thriving community and housing co-op. . . . [U]nder construction are a gym, a community room, forty bedrooms, a massive kitchen, an allotment and a repair/storage room for the prize possessions – the speakers that pump up the dance. . . . Exodus have also reconstructed a derelict farm into a city farm open to the public and an atrophying town into a place where you can dream and see those dreams realised.

THE STORY OF

EXODUS

A MOVEMENT OF JAH PEOPLE

Documented and presented by

SQUALL

the magazine for sorted itinerants

Extracts from **SQUALL** issues 8 and 9. The story of EXODUS continues in SQUALL 10 and also issue 11 (due out Sept 95).

As Exodus member Dread Bigs put it, 'it's not just a party, get a crowd then they disappear. It's more, much more than that.' 'Community regeneration – massive and passive' is their goal, which means anything from repairing derelict buildings for housing to ensuring adequate health and stewarding provision at their free raves, from the constructive channelling of Luton youth's anger to having the flexibility and persistence to make use of squatting or of official applications depending on each situation. Exodus have gradually won round the support or at least grudging respect of the local council – though the initial story of the authorities' response to their activities seems like one of shameful incompetence at best, wilful vilification and harassment at worst. There is dark talk of an alleged Masonic conspiracy between local police chiefs, the local press and representatives of the brewery whose weekend profits dry up with every free party.[72] Certainly, numerous charges have been made and dropped against members of Exodus, police evidence has been ruled inadmissible or found unreliable in court. Sympathetic police officers have been moved to other jobs, and in one instance an officer actually burst into tears in the middle of a raid when asked by Exodus to justify his actions. On New Year's Eve 1993, the Exodus party in preparation at Long Meadow Farm was raided and around forty members were arrested. When would-be party-goers discovered this later there was a mass demonstration of several thousand outside the central police station, demanding the release of the Exodus people and the return of the sound system, both of which duly happened. From such local support with the springboard of contemporary dance culture, the Exodus Collective have created an impressive, self-reliant, politically conscious party scene and community. Nicholas Saunders describes an Exodus experience in a quarry in May 1995:

> We parked at the top and all 3,000 of us found our way down in complete darkness except for a few flares while the truck drove down to the bottom and a team set up the equipment, then the music started and we danced. . . . As the sky lightened and dawn broke, the cliffs were topped by silhouetted figures dancing. And behind the dancers on top of the army truck with the red star stood a man in loose overalls waving an Exodus banner: it looked just like a scene from an old Soviet poster, the happy workers celebrating their victory over oppression, a magic atmosphere that carried on until midday.[73]

The Spirit of Albion lives on, it just has a relentless backbeat behind it nowadays.

5

DIRECT ACTION OF THE NEW PROTEST: ECO-RADS ON THE ROAD

[B]y adopting direct action as a form of politics, we . . . look to ourselves as a source of change. . . . Therefore the key to the political significance of the . . . campaign lies less in the immediate aims of stopping the road and in the immediate costs we have incurred for capital and the state (although these are great achievements and great encouragement to others), and more in our *creation of a climate of autonomy, disobedience and resistance.* . . . Thus, this life of permanent struggle is simultaneously a *negative* act (stopping the road etc.) and a *positive pointer* to the kind of social relation that could be: . . . a community of resistance.

John, of the radical political theory magazine *Aufheben*

The direct action movement is the most potent popular force of the 1990s, yet it has one fundamental and potentially fatal weakness. So far it has been largely responsive. The Government proposes a road or a bill and the movement opposes it: the Department of Transport and the Home Office have set the direct action agenda. Political change does not take place until the opponents of government fight for what they're for, rather than simply for what they're against.

George Monbiot, land rights campaigner[1]

Previous chapters dealt with politics through pleasure or lifestyle, politics as expressed and disseminated through the culture of music or event, politics even ill-defined but revolving around some kind of desire for autonomy, politics as general resistance to dominant culture. Much of the rest of *Senseless Acts of Beauty* deals with the politics of direct action, in which resistance moves beyond the show (the demonstration) of protest or the expression of opposition to the considered and sustained obstruction of what's seen as socially or politically objectionable. In this chapter I examine the extraordinary surge of direct action in the 1990s – looking in particular at anti-road protests – and trace the origins and developments of apparently new campaigns in relation to what we can surely begin to see as a significant tradition of largely youth-oriented cultures of resistance from the 1960s and early 1970s on.

The sheer popularity and widespread nature of street protest and direct action emanating from single-issue campaigns is in part a response to a lack of confidence in – or even a rejection of – parliamentary democracy, a result of approaching two decades of what's effectively been one-party rule in Britain. Furthermore, it's possible that nineties direct action was kick-started by the nationwide uprising around the Poll Tax, from Scotland southwards, the Trafalgar Square riot of 1990, the tax's successful scrapping (or modification). Indeed, the radicalizing effect of the Poll Tax legislation was twofold. The Poll Tax both appealed to a wide constituency in terms of the campaign against it – that is to say, it mobilized massive numbers in opposition to it – and, ironically, it contributed to people's disillusionment with parliamentary politics by virtue of its perceived connection of tax paying and voting rights. Direct action is a response not only to disillusionment with parliament, but also to what's been seen as the lack of success of established pressure groups. The importing of radical environmental ideas and strategies like those of Earth First! from the USA is one clear symptom of this.[2] Earth Firster Iain Donald notes that 'grassroots activists see the use of conventional methods of protest such as legal challenges as not only ineffectual and often expensive, but playing "their" game by "their" rules'[3] – hence they dismiss the easily contained politics of conventional protest in preference for the perception (sometimes illusion?) of the authentic, the real, the direct and undiluted – the action itself.[4] *Guardian* journalist John Vidal has written of a 'green hole' being filled in the early 1990s by direct action protest, superseding both established (or moribund) international environmental campaign organizations and official inquiries. Former Twyford Down campaigner Emma Must patiently explains why opposing voices have felt let down by official channels for dialogue: in the nineties 'there have been 146 public inquiries into trunk roads and on only five occasions has the inspector found against the government. So it is no wonder that people end up in trees.'[5]

It should be remembered that direct action is not in itself in any way a new strategy – picking as an arbitrary historical starting point, say the Chartists, we can move through the suffragettes to the 1926 General Strike to the anti-nuclear-bomb Direct Action Committee, each on a national scale. Or we can trace an alternative social history

Eco-rads Earth First! offer an apocalyptic ultimatum: Do or Die.

through direct action, with perhaps surprising results – such as ramblers' mass trespasses in the 1930s, or the Squatters Movement of 1946, organized largely by ex-servicemen to claim empty army and airforce barracks for homeless families,[6] or the road protest of November 1971, when five hundred cyclists held a 'bike-in' in Cambridge in a forerunner of the 1990s Critical Mass anti-car bicycle demonstrations. I particularly like the story of the woman taken to court in May 1972 for painting a zebra crossing on the road at night in a spot where the council had failed to provide one.[7] She would have been at home in Claremont Road. As we begin to see, direct action is not new even in the areas in which it has most recently appeared, specifically anti-roads[8] and animal rights campaigns. Perhaps the most publicly identifiable direct action groups in recent years have been those demanding animal rights. It's arguable that groups like hunt saboteurs or the Animal Liberation Front (ALF) were responsible for keeping animal rights on the agenda prior to the eruption of protest in relation to live animal exports and veal crates in 1994–95.

These two groups illustrate well the range and the problem of definition of the term *direct action* itself within a single issue: basically sabs confront and irritate through their direct presence at events, while the ALF attacks property with varying degrees of clandestine violence, and has moved towards a more clearly 'terroristic' structure and activity. Thus the very term *direct action* has a broad frame of reference, whose one common denominator is, as April Carter points out, that its activists have 'abandoned the processes of discreet lobbying in the corridors of power'.[9]

> The central methods of direct action comprise . . . the tactics evolved within the labour movement – strikes, go-slows and boycotts; and the more recent forms of physical obstruction and intervention – sit-ins and trespassing. A third category is that of civil disobedience: deliberately breaking laws considered unjust. . . . Another historical form of direct action is non-cooperation with the state, for example, through tax refusal, or in the more radical form of draft resistance.

This explanation from 1973 is useful, but also outdated. Ever since the peace camps, direct action has developed physical obstruction and intervention to combine an oppositional impulse with a positive effort at community organization. The aim is to produce the kind of situation witnessed by John of *Aufheben* at Claremont Road in east London, 'a community of resistance', a form of communal protest honed from the jumble of lived experience and space. The significance of culture, of 'creative resistance' at Claremont Road is explained by 'artist activist' John Jordan:

> The Campaign is a non-stop performance. . . . Non-Violent Direct Action is performance where the poetic and pragmatic join hands. The sight of a fragile figure silhouetted against a blue sky, perched dangerously high, on a crane that has stopped work for the day, is both beautiful and functional. NVDA is deeply theatrical and fundamentally political.[10]

Another road protest offers another version of direct action. Steff of the Dongas Tribe from Twyford Down views the strategy of withdrawal or refusal as itself a central creative act: 'the most effective direct action you can do is pull yourself out of being a part of that problem, as much as you possibly can'.[11]

'Turn on, tune in and lock on': DIY magazine POD *champions direct 'in yer face' action.*

Of course, we've already seen that pleasure and direct action can be intertwined political strategies – in anything from squatting a building or a monument for a free festival, to living at the nomadic margins of the social, to attending a musical–political event such as a Crass gig or an Exodus free party. More specifically, in the grandly titled book *The Philosophy of Punk*, Craig O'Hara constructs a direct action mentality for punk, echoing Mikhail Bakunin's anarchist maxim that 'the urge to destroy is also a creative urge':

> Destruction of property is not only seen as a way to make a political statement, but many Punks advocate it as a way to have fun as well. Punks have taken a similar view to that used by groups such as Earth First! regarding direct action. Monkey-wrenching and trying to subvert the system are regarded as primary parts of Punk.[12]

For O'Hara many of the current actions in animal rights activism and environmentalism have roots of sorts in punk; his argument is helped by the fact that his largely American translation of punk seems to originate in the mid-eighties. This may be a questionable retrospective construction, but it does illustrate the way in which direct action is seen to be something worth talking about, worth claiming a hand in today. While making efforts to distinguish between eighties/nineties punks and anyone else's sixties hippies, O'Hara's punks none the less tread similar ground: 'The ideas and actions which we have come to identify with Native Americans (whether rightfully or not) are much more of an influencing factor on the Punk philosophy . . . the Punk community is attempting to foster a biocentric philosophy in response to environmental concerns.'[13]

Yet in the 1990s cultures of resistance are not the preserve only of the disenfranchised or disaffected, such as O'Hara's philosophical punk-hippies. Constantly commented on is the presence of the respectable (rather than the dropout) middle class of Britain, and the efforts of direct action campaigners to develop and maintain links with local communities. The nationwide upsurge in protest against live animal exports in Britain in 1994–95 was accompanied by frequent and initially curious references by older people involved to the Second World War and its sense of collective energy and belief. In a collection of writings by protesters against the export of live animals in one Sussex port, *The Siege of Shoreham*, for instance, there is even a piece called 'The Dunkirk Spirit is Alive and Well, Living in Shoreham'. Another protester writes of early-morning alarms to meet the animal trucks: 'A hasty coffee and a cold wash and it's off to the front line. A bit like Army days.' A third, employing Churchillian rhetoric, writes: 'We will "fight" in Parliament, we will "fight" on the media, and we will "fight" along the sea front, until we overcome!' Brighton vicar Dominic Walker describes the protests against live animal exports in his domain.

> Ordinary people take to the streets, clashes take place with the police, people march and sing, they write poems and prayers, there are tears and laughter, hopes and disappointments, there is friendship and division, tempers and passions flare and arrests take place, the press gives both support and criticism, people are injured or even killed but still the message spreads, and slowly but surely the issues are heard.[14]

Such 'ordinary people' and more experienced activists form coalitions that are viewed less than positively by the government. The then roads minister Robert Key described the anti-roads campaign at Solsbury Hill near Bath as organized by a 'tiny minority' backed by a 'weird alliance between the rich, famous and influential'.[15] As we see below unlikely alliances have been formed between the travellers-style road protesters Dongas Tribe and the respectable inhabitants of Hampshire,[16] and between other eco-rads and the propertied classes of leafy Wanstead in London. Alexandra Plows suggests that, for the Dongas, such a set of alliances is itself part of the project, so that direct action resistance can also liberate protesters from the older framework which is viewed as inadequate now:

> The answer [is] to move from [one] definition/classification to another, . . . or to try to avoid total definition altogether, leaving room for growth and movement of thought and the possibility of unity and cooperation with other groups,

ideologies, etc. (This happened within the roads protest movement, with inter-activity between establishment environmental groups and direct activists such as Earth Firsters, between Travellers and 'NIMBY' Tories, etc.)[17]

Donga Alex here echoes the thoughts of André Gorz in 1973, writing about the limitations of the traditional left/right framework for resistance to auto-culture:

> The spread of the private car has displaced mass transportation and altered city planning in such a way that it transfers to the car functions which its own spread has made necessary. An ideological ('cultural') revolution would be needed to break this circle. Obviously this is not to be expected from the ruling class (either right or left).[18]

The sense of shock as street protests, barricades, long-term camps spread through Britain, down the lane, outside your school or estate, at your scenic sleepy little port, can be compared with Anthony Esler's shock and surprise at local expressions of counterculture on university campuses and towns in the USA a couple of decades previously:

> A barricade, in the streets of 1970 America! . . . I saw the red flag of revolution and the black flag of anarchy planted defiantly on the jagged ramparts. I had taught it all often enough to college history classes – I had never dreamed of seeing it. In Paris, in the Revolution of 1830, or 1848, or 1871. Or 1968, for that matter: barricades were somehow *natural* in Paris. But in Evanston, Illinois – *now?*[19]

The shock goes further though – it's not simply that people see the signs of direct action around them, but that they suddenly recognize themselves there, too, or feel their sympathies going out to protesters, are politicized by the first curse from a visored policeman's mouth. Debbie of United Systems, a free party organization that also opposes the Criminal Justice Act, recently expressed her own shock about con-temporary British politics – using the US sixties as her reference point: where Esler locates protest and repression largely in the history of nineteenth-century Europe, she locates them in turn in her childhood memories of news broadcasts of the kind of scenes from the USA that Esler writes of. As she put it to me, 'I thought the protesters on the TV then were these extraordinary people, and never thought that one day in England I'd be putting myself through that kind of hassle, least of all to stand up for something as mundane as the right to have a dance!' There's also a kind of rewriting of Englishness (sometimes Britishness) here: the different language of Albion, from fairs and history, shouts out again. It's identifiable in older protesters' references to the 'Dunkirk Spirit', and even in the slight and at the same time huge shift of the British love of animals and pets into round-the-clock blockades of sea and airports. The English Dongas see themselves as 'indigenous Englanders', recovering and celebrating the pre-Christian traditions of the land. (New Protesters often have a better grasp of ancient history than of what happened only ten or twenty years ago.) Journalist Linda Grant has felt this, too:

> There is a sense of a reclaiming of Englishness, a harking back to the radical protest movements of the English Civil War, the Diggers and the Levellers. . . . At some protests one spies the extraordinary sight of the Union Jack, wrenched away at last from the hands of the British National Party and reworked as a Union Jill in rainbow colours.[20]

The nineties Levellers are a New Age traveller band; the land rights activists of the nineties called New Age Diggers hark back to the English Civil War, but also to Sid Rawle's Hyde Park Diggers of the sixties. Another instance of alternative traditions being consciously explored and constructed was seen in May 1995, at the height of the patriotic nostalgia trip of the fiftieth anniversary of VE (Victory in Europe) Day in the Second World War. While Vera Lynn sang to massed troops and members of Parliament in London, a group of three hundred activists held a pagan party at Stonehenge. This first major appearance of alternative types within the stones for over a decade marked the tenth anniversary of the Beanfield – and it drew attention to the dangers of the Criminal Justice Act by reminding people of the social freedoms British working people had fought for half a century earlier.

Dongas on the Down

For some New Age travellers and their cultural representatives such as the Levellers, the road is a special space that somehow encapsulates the sense of freedom they seek, a Beat event without end. More recently, roads have been constructed (*sic*) as site of all that's wrong with Britain, a single-issue campaign that's not single-issue at all. The anti-roads movement embraces issues of land ownership, environmentalism, health and pollution, technology, big business, regional and self-empowerment and self-development, the power of the law itself. For travellers until the 1990s the road was perceived as a solution of sorts, a way out; more recently this notion has been challenged, so that the road – or rather, roads in the plural – are seen as part of the problem.

Jo Waterworth recalls the rationale and the problems of the travellers' strategy of living resistance at Rainbow Fields Village at Molesworth in 1984–85:

> We tried practically to stop [the cruise missile base] by living on the land, taking Peace Camps one stage further. It was really exciting front-line stuff at the time, although the practicalities of mud and winter and endless disagreements took their toll and we ended up just sort of getting on with life as best we could. Also made many efforts to get on with the local communities, but again some people didn't care, some kids shoplifted regularly – so many types of people that everyone tends to get lumped together with the lowest common denominator, frustrating for the nice middle-class greenies. Rainbow Village West, those of us who stuck together after Greenlands into '86, very much saw ourselves as the acceptable face of travellers, mainly families with children, and into it for the ideology more than the refugee mentality (once we'd got over the Beanfield trashing).[21]

A decade on, the travelling camp is used as a long-term protest strategy by eco-radicals, focused primarily, at least in its beginnings, on road protest. One of the earliest, perhaps the first, certainly the best-known, was the culmination of the campaign against the M3 motorway extension at Twyford Down in Hampshire. Here in 1992 a new acceptable face of travellers, the Dongas Tribe, emerged.

The final section of the M3 motorway from London to the port of Southampton was a campaign issue for twenty years before the arrival – more accurately, the on-site invention, apparently from nowhere – of the Dongas Tribe in 1992. Locals had protested against the extension of the M3 over Twyford Down, south-east of Winchester, with the help of the national group Friends of the Earth and the large local campaign group the Twyford Down Association. The land for the road was supplied by

Winchester College, the public school which had been left it in trust for future generations of schoolchildren. (This contributed a degree of class antagonism to the campaign, more so when it was realized that the new road would shift car pollution further away from the highly privileged pupils of the college.) In return, the college – rather than, say, the general public – would later effectively be gifted the land of the old road, the A33 bypass, by the Department of Transport. Where the hills of the South Downs end was an extremely well-protected landscape by official designation: one Site of Special Scientific Interest, an Area of Outstanding Natural Beauty, two Scheduled Ancient Monuments. None the less, inexorably, 'Work finally began on the [River Itchen] watermeadows in February 1992, and the bulldozers were met with massive resistance from all sorts of people. Young Earth First! activists were joined by 70-year-old lifelong Tory voters.'[22] Following in the footsteps of the nascent Earth First! direct action eco-radical group, the Dongas came into being in around March 1992.

> [A] group of people arrived in ones and twos on Twyford Down near Winchester and stayed to defend it from being destroyed by the M3 motorway. While most of us were already keen environmentalists, craftworkers and herbalists, living full-time outdoors in a communal situation, cooking on fires, building simple but snug shelters was new.[23]

The very term Dongas Tribe derives from the landscape the tribe came together at the camp to preserve, Dongas being a Matebele name originally adopted in the nineteenth century by Winchester College teachers for the medieval pathways that criss-cross the Downs. One form of route, ancient, local, and on a human scale, is deliberately pitted against a newer, invasive one – a motorway to the Continent.

The Dongas were young people, and many were new to direct action political campaigning. One, Becca Lush, told me, 'We didn't know what the fuck we were doing, only that we *were* doing *something*.' Earth First! inspired their early actions; both groups can be seen as a clear response to the deep dissatisfaction felt with the established environmental pressure groups of the time. It's fair to say that the Dongas were created in reaction not only to the government's road-building programme but also to the perceived inadequacies of mainstream environmental pressure groups. This sense of youthful impatience, even arrogance, is voiced and justified by Laugh of the Dongas:

Well obviously, you know, the Earth was still being fucked about and fucked up and nothing was happening, they weren't doing anything new, they weren't solving the problem, obviously, because it was still going on, like, so something had to be done stronger than that.[24]

Donga Alex (Alexandra Plows) retrospectively considers their antecedents:

Perhaps our most direct ideological links are with the environmental movements of the late sixties, seventies and eighties; for example, CND, Greenpeace and the Greenham Women's Movement all used creative action for a global cause. Our tactics were also influenced by Earth First!; tree-sitting, climbing on machinery to stop it moving, etc.[25]

The role of travelling in Donga action should not be overlooked: Sam and Steff were New Age travellers prior to camping up on the hill in the spring and summer of 1992, and, as we'll see, travelling became a central feature of their later Dongas identity as they went on the Freedom Trail. On occasion there's been friction between the idealistic Dongas and other travellers, particularly the 'lunch out' element (see below), an issue that came up at Claremont Road in east London, too. Other road protesters too are judged to lack the holistic aspect of Donga lifestyle and protest. In a short piece originally written for distribution at camps, Donga Alex calls such protesters 'ego-warriors': 'many of these people (mostly young men) are first up the bulldozer but nowhere in sight when the porridge pot needs cleaning'.[26] Even their calling themselves a 'tribe' signals the Dongas' interest in what they see as the more sympathetic approach to the land taken by tribal and travelling societies, such as some Native Americans. Here the Dongas echo what has been going on in Tipi Valley in Wales since the mid-seventies. Donga Alex makes grander claims, though.

We are a tribe in far more than name. We have a collective purpose and a cultural identity as the nomadic indigenous peoples of Britain – we have formulated our own customs, mythology, style of dress, beliefs and are evolving our own language.[27]

I asked Alex to elaborate on this last point: it seems that the simple linguistic invention claimed by the Dongas consists of two categories. The first involves the embracing of standard New Age travellers' slang, such as 'tat' for possessions and 'lunch out' referring to someone who contributes nothing at camp. However, Alex explains:

> The second category interests me most as it is based on a number of made-up words and verbal signals. For example a made-up word like 'gablonga!' could mean hello/welcome or be used when a bottle of mead is passed round the fire. People approaching the camp from a distance signal their presence by a call of 'eeyip!' – not only can we determine that a visitor is friendly, but we can distinguish different people's calls. . . . Sitting on top of a CAT 245 [bulldozer] we would signal the arrival of police/security and potential danger by ululating – 'ayayayayaya!' – which helped to mentally strengthen us while undermining the confidence of these often violent men.[28]

There is a definite Donga lifestyle, which is closely related to the Dongas' actions and protests. The homology between lifestyle and politics is fundamental: 'our lifestyle was addressing the root cause of the problem'.[29] For example, their mundane yet practical micro approach to environmental respect is evident 'every time we shit in the earth where it becomes fertilizer and do not flush it out to the sea where it becomes a poison'. The Dongas are an amazing mixture of the wildly New Age (Sam: 'if you play music around a stone circle . . . you do have this aura of really powerful energy with you and everything you do from there on becomes really magical'[30]) and the eminently and stubbornly practical (as with the huge kick-start they gave road protest). Donga Alex calls this 'practical paganism', but 'political paganism' is possibly more accurate. Their camp defences before Yellow Wednesday consisted of things like a ditch dug in the shape of a dragon, with crystals for eyes and fire torches in its nose, decorated barricades, small packets of information tied to fences, even spells. This tension between New Age and material, between otherworldly and practical, was evident on occasion at the various Twyford camps. The Dongas learned as they lived as they campaigned, which meant that there were equal measures of impulsiveness, innocence and action not only during the early days on camp but also in their resistance strategies.[31] These sought to combine direct action with their occasional temporary alternative of a deeply passive and pacifist approach, partly through the simple and less confrontational aim of building camp numbers up. Such thoughts were quickly jettisoned in the wake of Yellow Wednesday, as the power of the state and its new associates displayed itself openly, and with the realization that it was indeed the state that Dongas action was challenging. There is a strand of spirituality and ritual in Dongas experience, which taps into the usual diverse New Age sources such as Celtic myth, stone circles, world music and drumming, equinox and solstice celebrations. There is a Dongas Play – featuring dragons. (Donga Alex recalls an official site report from October 1992 which recorded that 'work was stopped by six people dressed as a dragon'.) Dragon good, CAT 245 bad. A frequent criticism put at the Dongas is their atavism, which is viewed by critics as regression. Alex explains:

> Any attempt to protest against the destructive effects of e.g. road-building is open to the criticism that protesters are 'anti-progress' (progress defined as the latest technological advance rather than environmental or even economic sustainability). Any ideology which looks back to the past for an interpretation is seen as 'regressive'.[32]

Some of the Dongas try to overcome this problem by taking issue with the dominant linear concept of time, arguing instead for a cyclical concept, one that follows the earthly, seasonal and bodily cycles. Hence they have developed rituals and festivals celebrating the seasons. There is also evident a millenarian perspective, much tinged by current New Age thought: 'Donga people feel that the awareness process is speeding up, a necessary response triggered by the fact that we are also moving towards ecological disaster and the possible extinction of our species at an alarming rate,' Alex writes.

Iain Donald describes the situation at Winchester in 1992, as seen by the people who would become the Dongas: 'Friends of the Earth and the Twyford Down Association were following the conventional lines of protest, lobbying and organizing legal challenges.'[33] The birth of the Dongas Tribe was a spontaneous response to the final stage of the road-building programme, partly inspired by the direct action protest of a few local Greenham Common veterans against the first damage to the Itchen Navigation waterway in early 1992. What began as Earth First! and led to Dongas direct action – squatting the very land to be dug up for the motorway, using their own bodies as the focus of resistance – had infamous consequences. Yellow Wednesday, 9 December 1992, was a pivotal moment in the road protest movement: 'for the first time in roads protest security guards (Group 4) were hired to ensure that the contractors finally got past our defences (a hawthorn hedge, a ditch in the shape of a dragon . . .)'.[34] For some time before Yellow Wednesday, the start of the three-day battle, the Dongas and the road security people had been living in their separate

The lunar anniversary of Yellow Wednesday is an opportunity to celebrate and develop resistance, Twyford Down, 1993.

camps almost literally side by side – electric lighting and caravan on one side, canvas and dancing round the fire on the other. Relations were quite amiable during this period, the phoney war. On Yellow Wednesday the first of the ritual confrontations that would spread up and down the land took place: the yellow-jacketed private security guards waded in with sometimes shocking violence to clear protesters from the site. As with the anti-M77 confrontation in Pollok, Glasgow, three years later, some guards were themselves so shocked by their side's violence against protesters that they resigned: in fact, thirty-two quit in the first two days of the battle at Twyford. (At the M11 in London and the M77 in Glasgow, former security guards joined the protesters.) It would take two years for at least some private guards to be told to wear identification numbers on their jackets, something all police have to do as a matter of course (except when they cover them up or rip them off). John Vidal recalls the aftermath of Yellow Wednesday:

> The powerful modern image of private money hand in hand with the machinery of state together rolling over the economically weakest to appropriate common resources was given perfect expression. The subtext for environmentally aware youth was obvious: to the list of oppressed people in Latin America, Indonesia and elsewhere, add the English.[35]

Group 4 security quickly became known by eco-radicals as Grope 4 following accusations of sexual harassment during the eviction of female protesters. Media environmentalist David Bellamy reportedly said he'd never seen anything like it in twenty years of campaigning at home and abroad.[36]

Yet, as Donga Alex notes, 'this appears to have been the catalyst needed to boost a flagging environmental movement with its hands largely tied by, for example, charitable status or centralized control over policy'.[37] The second day of the battle became known as 'Black Thursday' due to the very large police presence, and on this day the contractors began to clear the woods at the bottom. These few days could be seen as effectively the beginning of the end for the M3 protest, although it's fair to say that the publicity surrounding Yellow Wednesday generated new interest in the protest through into 1993. This became the period when most delay to construction was caused, and the protesters' effective new weapon of causing financial pain through delay and security costs was first seen. Following Yellow Wednesday, most of the Dongas regrouped at a camp near Salisbury, both devastated and frightened by the state's reaction to their protest at Twyford. They were in turn evicted from several other sites. A tiny group splintered off, determined to maintain the protest's presence as near as possible to the M3 site. A small camp set up at Plague Pits Valley, only a few hundred yards away, consisting of the odd Donga and other protesters. With New Age humour they called themselves Camelot Earth First! The main Dongas camp returned in late February 1993. Later again, Dongas would be evicted from here and set up different camps at Bushfields, a disused army barracks some distance from the Down. From occupying the land, tactics shifted to the peaceful obstruction of site work, obstructing specifically the digging of the mile-long cut through the Downs. Here the chalk landscape offered its own visual contribution to the protest, with much-reproduced images of a gaping white wound cut across it, 'so horrific, so visible, so palpable', as Jonathon Porritt writes.[38] Resonant of white cliffs, the protest successfully tapped into an alternative version of England, Blake's green and pleasant land.[39] There is landscape art at the Vale of the White Horse, at the white man at Cerne Abbas – here at Twyford Down in the last decade of the millennium there was the white wound.

Bail conditions were used by courts to keep protesters away, effectively infringing their right to peaceful protest. From March 1993 onwards Dongas and other protesters were bailed following police arrest on condition that they stayed away from the site. Becca Lush picks up the story as Dongas forced the authorities' hand:

One Saturday morning, when asked to leave the site, we refused and were arrested. We were refused bail and held for 49 hours. . . . On Monday we went to the court and told them that we would accept no bail conditions. If they put us on bail [conditions] not to protest we would break them again and again until they had to imprison us. The magistrates granted unconditional bail and after that no one else was given bail conditions.[40]

The Bailey Bridge action by Twyford Down Road Alert!, Dongas and others of May 1993 was one of the biggest actions, certainly in terms of numbers arrested and in terms of the sheer amount of fear and excitement experienced by the protesters:

> . . . over 200 people burst through lines of police, security, and razor wire to occupy a temporary bridge for the bulldozers that was due to be laid over the existing road. 300 police reinforcements in riot gear had to be called to remove the protesters which took most of the night.[41]

Erecting the bridge over the existing motorway to facilitate contractors meant closing the motorway temporarily and also involved a huge security operation. Protesters heard whispers and rumours in the weeks leading up to what was called Operation Market Garden, and they planned their action in response – Operation Greenfly. In spite of planning over several weeks, perhaps they weren't quite aware of the enormity of their task, and a mere quarter of an hour before the action was due to start the protesters were still having a meeting to discuss (and argue about) whether it should go ahead, was it not too dangerous, was the security not intimidatingly overwhelming, and so on. Eventually a voice rose saying something like 'We said we were going to take it, let's fucking do it!' and the mood changed from vacillation to determination. The landscape of the Down played its part: protesters' faces were smeared with chalk and charcoal, hundreds of black-and-white-camouflaged faces carrying dragons, beating drums, trooping down the hill. The police thought they would be coming from another direction and were in disarray. Using techniques they'd been practising, small groups of protesters rolled through and pushed aside the banks of wire, and the bridge was taken. As dusk fell Road Alert!, Dongas, Earth Firsters and others were drumming on the bridge, the sounds echoing round the valley, the action itself already sure of its place in road protest history and in Dongas mythology.

In 1995 Emma Must, a young veteran of Twyford Down, was awarded a Goldman Environmental Foundation award of $75,000 and named an international 'environmental hero' in recognition of the achievement of the Twyford Down campaign in raising the profile of environmental concern over road building in Britain. Must used the money to further expand the activities of the sister organization to Road Alert!,

Alarm UK, which is an alliance of 250 anti-road community groups in Britain. Though not specifically one of the Dongas, Must was a local woman who had played on the Downs as a child. Along with Dongas Becca and Phil, amongst others, she became one of the Twyford Seven who were jailed in 1993 for breaking an injunction preventing them from entering the site or disrupting work – despite an appeal judge stating in court that the protest was part of an 'honourable tradition' of dissent. (In order to name some of the protesters mentioned in the injunction, the Department of Transport somehow received details about people who had been arrested *but not charged.* This information was apparently confidential to Hampshire police. Other names on the indictment included those of animals whose habitat would be destroyed by the road, taken from protesters' placards! The government, ever careful with tax-payers' money, hired private detectives to undertake surveillance of Dongas and other protesters.) Legal costs alone for proceedings arising from the Twyford Down protests are put at £465,000, which the government initially tried to claim from the protesters. In fact the entire bill approached £3.5 million, though when it sought to sue a number of protesters for this sum the Department of Transport was forced into a humiliating retreat, which culminated in the demand being reduced to £1,000 from each protester, a figure itself halved in court. Very few of the people named in this injunction for costs have actually paid their £500.

What has happened to the Dongas since the failure of the M3 campaign? Donga Alex describes the versatility of their post-Twyford actions:

> The Tribe itself has grown and diversified in that time with some people now working full-time in the grassroots protest movement which has sprung up, or in related areas such as tree-planting and permaculture. A small group continues to live a nomadic lifestyle, moving from hillfort to hillfort with horses, donkeys and handmade carts to transport personal and communal possessions. We remain in close contact and meet up often at major seasonal celebrations and feel bound together through our experiences and shared vision.[42]

But what am I doing writing about 'failure'? Alex again:

> The actions of the Donga Tribe at Twyford Down established direct action against roads as part of protest culture, and inspired action against many forms of destructive development, from logging firms to quarries. Our peaceful protest

Two years after the Dongas Tribe forms, road protest grows and grows: mass trespass at Twyford Down, 1994.

and the establishment's violent reaction to it has triggered a response from a broad section of society.[43]

Or, as she put it elsewhere in more New Age language, 'the Earth Dragon, awoken at Twyford, is now at large in the land'.[44] Ecology writer Simon Fairlie goes further, pinpointing the significance of the Dongas' embracing of direct action: 'The Dongas have put the entire spectrum of the British environmental movement to shame; their conviction has exposed the hypocrisy of pragmatism.'[45] It's likely that, though the Down was lost as the road was completed in late 1994, the resistance first raised there contributed to the government's U-turn on a road to be built through the ancient Oxleas Wood in London – a major achievement for anti-roads campaigners which signalled the government's recently manufactured concern about environmental impact translating for once into actions.

So, some of the Dongas became a tribe in a more nomadic manner altogether: they travelled from hillfort to hillfort on pushbike or horsedrawn cart, a living, fluid group of politicized travellers, whose each encampment was viewed by themselves as statement and evidence of deep ecological protest and example. This was called the Freedom Trail, and it started in the late summer of 1994 with their first camp at Ham Hill in Somerset, a site partly chosen because of the campaign potential around reclaiming old tracks and trails again – an issue harking back to the original source of their name. That winter the Dongas' Freedom Trail moved through the West Country, celebrating the winter solstice at Cerne Abbas and the summer solstice at a stone circle on Dartmoor. Other Dongas have become more involved in environmental direct action organizations such as Road Alert! and Alarm UK. Phil, Becca Lush and Emma Must took this second route, and are concerned in their protest to develop links with local communities: Dongas ideals are far removed from the perceived hedonism and pose of youth subcultures, seeking instead an uncompromisingly engaged and situated attitude. For instance, Tinker's Bubble in Somerset was a traditional gypsy stopping place bought by radical environmentalists and New Age travellers – including some from Twyford Down – as a permanent facility. A small Dongas action at Tinker's Bubble protested against the felling of a mature tree, and Dongas have withdrawn their support and presence from the area, and from people who might otherwise be thought to be among their closest allies. There is a clear concern to maintain their radical edge through the strategy of direct action on the land itself. Quarries are the sites for Dongas actions for two reasons: because of the industrial damage to the land *and* because materials produced are used as hardcore for building – roads. Dongas are rightly and righteously proud of their widely perceived status as founders of road protest, and in relation to this they claim responsibility for the extraordinary upsurge in direct action politics seen in the 1990s in Britain. Whether such a claim is entirely justified is debatable – none the less, there's no doubt that the actions, the style, even the strangely different name of the Dongas significantly crystallized and popularized the road protest movement in particular and direct action protest in general during the early nineties.

In a fascinating development – all the more so for their apparent ignorance of the precedents – Dongas in the nineties have revived the tradition of the fairs, something like the East Anglian fairs, especially the early fairs such as Barsham and Bungay Horse Fair. This was achieved in the summer of 1994 with the revival of Tan Hill Fayre, near Avebury in Wiltshire. The strategy is precisely that of twenty years before: an old chartered fair is brought to life again, constructed as question about the notion of 'progress', as opportunity to sell local crafts, as celebration of the ancient and mystical (the stones at Avebury), as connection with the nomadic lifestyle, as temporary space of difference and autonomy. Tan Hill Fayre had last been held in 1932, by then more of a sheep fair, with some horse dealing between local gypsies. Dongas and their sympathizers put together a small event on the old fair site, now land owned by two different farmers, and over an early August weekend in 1994 up to 150 people turned up. In effect, this was a mini-scale squatted free festival, but one that passed off without trouble, due to the small scale, the fact that it was reviving a local custom which led to a sympathetic reception by people in the area, and of course because the Dongas themselves were committed to it being a responsible statement as well as event (and they cleared up all the litter). Their motivation is clear from the written text included in the flyer for the 1995 event:

TRIBAL GATHERING

All folk welcome to join the growing tribe living in benders on the hillforts, backways & woodlands of Wessex . . . travelling by foot, horse, donkey, bicycle & handcart, reclaiming our stolen countryside, the right to live together tribally and celebrate the seasons! . . . Dongas forever!

In 1995 the Dongas tried to repeat the Tan Hill Fayre, but low-key police intervention,[46] coupled with a well-spread – who by? – rumour that 30,000 people were going to turn up, prevented it. One farmer – a local historian? – expressed familiar sentiments about the first group of thirty Dongas and other travellers, their horses and carts: 'All this business about the ancient festival and charter rights is rubbish. It is just an excuse for a hippie gathering. This is private land and we want them moved on.'[47] The horses were moved from the fair site on Tan Hill to a drove on nearby Knapp Hill. Dongas energy made the police move off, I'm told, and the fair went ahead on its new site. Culture of resistance pays tribute to culture of resistance: the Albion Fairs of the late 1970s, intended as moving feasts across the summer countryside, are reinvented with an explicit environmental slant by the Dongas in the 1990s.[48] Iain Donald, one of the organizers, explains this and the Dongas Tribe's motives for the revival of Tan Hill Fayre, which was first discussed by him and Donga Steff at a site on the Ridgeway in Wiltshire in 1993. His letter also indicates the Dongas' post-Twyford awareness of the need positively to offer something, rather than merely to react to negative events.

We considered the resumption of these traditional gatherings as important for re-energizing these sacred sites, for getting people back on the old trackways to celebrate the land and the changing seasons, to get people away from their TVs and out of their houses and cars and into contact with the land, which in return would lead to an increase in respect for their rural environment. Would people allow Twyford-style destruction to their local hill if they had a more regular contact and a greater spiritual respect for it?[49]

As Steff himself put it, 'if you're living on the hill then it's everything, it's 360 degrees around you, it's every direction you walk in, you're always on the hill'.[50]

Dongas have come to position themselves at the other extreme to the technocultural celebration of the rave scene, whether in Alex's dig in 'Practical Paganism' at the way 'we hurtle down the highway to destruction clutching our mobile phone' – that symbol of yuppie rave organization – or in the fact that, when Spiral Tribe turned up at the Dongas camp at Bushfields to throw a free party in their benefit to celebrate Beltane in May 1993, the Dongas refused to allow it. (For once, the Spirals relented; the rave did happen at Bushfields, but not at the Dongas open air camp, rather in a building removed from it up the hill, thus reducing the noise and disturbance.) The Dongas suggest here that amplified music is part of the problem not the solution. We shouldn't overlook the fact that this is itself the conscious development of a holistic position – in earlier times, such as at the Torpedo Town Festival in August 1992, Dongas had leafleted a Spiral Tribe event with details about their actions. Donga Alex was at Castlemorton a few months before events at Twyford Down. Although professing to 'quite like rave (wind-powered these days . . .)', her more recent holistic position sees such earlier happenings as 'typified by young people on dodgy chemicals who leave their rubbish and literally crap all over the place'.[51] The flyer for the first Tan Hill Fayre stresses 'All acoustic music'. The more recent Dongas hark back not only to the pre-industrial past but also to what Andrew Ross, discussing New Age culture and beliefs more generally, calls 'the romantic disavowal of modern technology that was all too common in countercultural literature and thought' of the sixties.[52] On the one hand, the Dongas are open to criticism that they, like other New Age groups Ross looks at, simply indulge their 'atavistic taste for supernaturalism'[53] through their emphasis on ancient myth and ritual, dragons and hill forts. On the other – like the insistent libertarian politics you can't avoid when reading the swirls of symbol in William Blake – the Dongas constantly root their actions, their living, in the contemporary social and political sphere. Donga Brian expresses the current position of the Freedom Trail Dongas, as well as that of 1990s direct action activists up and down the country:

A lot of people assume that the Dongas Tribe is just about protesting, and it's not really true. Protesting is not a way of life, but your way of life can be a protest.[54]

'We are more possible than you can powerfully imagine': Wanstonia, Leytonstonia and other independent free states of Britain

At Twyford they weren't really connecting it. It was nice fluffy landscapes and not about houses and people and their communities. The M11 has made roads into the issue it should have been.

No M11 Link protester[55]

In the case of the direct action protest against the construction through London of a link to the M11 motorway, homes, roads and the environment are all connected. The etymology of the word *ecology* is apt here: one of its roots is the Greek word *oikos*, meaning 'habitat' or 'house'. From the pastoral beauty of the South Downs, road protest spread to embrace urban concerns.[56] Already in the early seventies, André Gorz describes the impact of the car on urban space: 'The car has made the big city uninhabitable. It has made it stinking, noisy, suffocating, dusty . . . cars have killed the city.' But Gorz also began to feel (will?) an alternative: now, ironically, 'After killing the city, the car is killing the car.'[57] Gorz sees the possibility of the car turning in on itself, consuming itself, as its rhetoric of individual freedom and speed is replaced by its social reality of pollution, death and, worst of all, for we allow the car industry to cope with these first two awful facts with surprising ease, the nightmare of contemporary existence, *slowness*. (The point of the M11 link road is to cut seven or eight minutes from commuters' driving time into central London.)

Planning blight, the gradual decay of an area proposed for development of demolition, has a long history in east London. Patrick Field writes that 'Long-term residents of Leyton and Leytonstone will tell you about shops that closed in the fifties because the Link Road was coming.' Such blight had an up side, too: gentrification bypassed the blighted streets, and 'As well as architectural authenticity the side roads in the Link Road corridor became a preservation area for legendary East London life.'[58] An article in the Earth First! magazine *Do or Die* called 'News From the Autonomous Zones' describes the situation:

> The area threatened by the Link Road comprises two very different localities. At the eastern end of the route is Wanstead, a reasonably affluent, conservative leafy-green London suburb. To the west are Leyton and Leytonstone, areas of high-density urban housing, built at the turn of the century, but badly neglected ever since the proposal for the Link Road first blighted the area forty years ago.[59]

As at Twyford Down, when the latest campaign began there was already strongly established opposition to the road, in the form of local committees, presentations to official inquiries, and so on. Some of this opposition had employed direct action, too, such as the disruption of public inquiries by a long-term vociferous campaign group. However, in September 1993 contractors moved in to Wanstead with their bulldozers to begin clearing trees along the proposed route. This led to the first sustained direct action of the No M11 Link Campaign: the first squat in Wanstead, in a roofless house at 110 Eastern Avenue, and six weeks of obstruction of the tree-clearing operation by local protesters and a small number of experienced eco-rads. A chestnut tree (later capitalized and given a definite article) at George Green in Wanstead suddenly became the focus for protesters and increasing numbers of locals when they realized that it was to be cut down to make way for a cut-and-cover road tunnel under the park of George Green. The protection of the Chestnut Tree in the park came quickly to symbolize what was under threat from the road: residents' health, their past, nature more generally, even simply an effective local voice. Through November and early December 1993 the Chestnut Tree functioned as new impetus and the focal point – a tree house and a bender appeared, and each evening locals, squatters, schoolchildren, the odd Donga from Twyford would gather round the campfire for chat and campaign. After a letter was delivered by the local postman to the tree itself, campaign solicitors argued in court that 'the tree-house should be formally recognized as a "dwelling"'. This duly happened, with the result that the authorities 'now had to apply for a court order to evict the tree dwellers from their new "home"' – causing further delay. However, in the early morning of Tuesday, 7 December the familiar and inevitable happened: several hundred police arrived with full equipment to claim back the land and the Chestnut Tree. This may have been the first time a cherry-picker – a high-hoist hydraulic platform – was used to reach and lower protesters from on high. The sight of such an operation – and its widespread reporting in the media – reflected badly on the Department of Transport, signalled its seemingly inflexible approach to the community. The local lollipop woman (a worker whose place of work is a road) said after being sacked for attending a ceremony at the ancient Chestnut Tree of Wanstonia while wearing her uniform: 'All life is politics – if you step out of line.'

A number of large Edwardian houses were next in line for demolition, on Cambridge Park Road. Two were still lived in by long-term residents, and these became the heart of the Independent Free Area of Wanstonia, born on 9 January 1994, the inspired result of a long session in a pub between a campaign solicitor and a Donga. Wanstonia was picked up by the media as self-consciously constructed and was declared in part to refer back to the anti-bureaucracy little England of the 1950s Ealing comedy *Passport to Pimlico*. Wanstonia printed its own passports, its flag was the Union Jill. This seriously parodic unilateral declaration of independence set the tone for much of the rest of the No M11 Link Campaign: Situationist-inspired humour and art and an emphasis on alternative English social and cultural practices (as with the politicized echo of Ealing) became paramount features of daily life for protesters. Wanstonia was evicted on Ash Wednesday 1994, renamed Bash Wednesday by some of those on the receiving end of things.

'The M11 campaign as a whole has largely been this sequence of evictions, each one of which has broadened the campaign and been a spur forcing us to think up fresh ideas,' explains protester Phil McLeish.[60] The focus of the campaign moved farther into London along the line of the planned route. A bender site in which protesters lived was set up in old gardens and waste ground at the rear of Fillebrooke Road, signalling a nomadic tradition and the continuing concern with the destruction of living spaces all around. The seemingly temporary living space of the bender showed a surprising solidarity with the previously considered permanence of bricks and mortar. The bender site, and the old yew tree in it, were the short-lived heart of Leytonstonia, decorated with a kerbhenge, a replica of Stonehenge made with torn-up kerbstones. (Some talked of the significance of the names Leyton and Leytonstone, of their relation to ley lines more generally, as though this might explain the energy of the protest sites. A brickhenge was made at Claremont Road, halfway between Leyton and Leytonstone; again art and countercultural reference were created from the waste

The 'activist aesthetes' of Claremont Road, east London celebrate their utopian possibility: not the end, merely the end of the beginning.

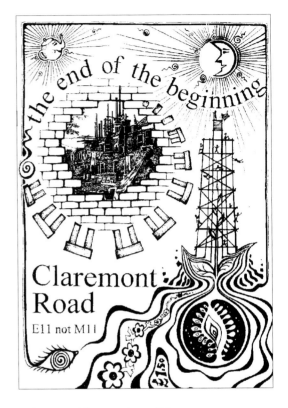

products of destruction.) 'Particularly after the bender site was trashed, Claremont Road became the centre of the campaign. . . . In concentrating on Claremont Road, we gradually moved into a siege situation where defence became the overriding priority, although irregular actions on site continue[d].'[61]

The idea of direct action as performance was seen at its most vibrant in the squatted row of terraces at Claremont Road, which gained much of its impetus from the artwork it produced. The relative density of artists in the local population was, ironically, partly due to the link road: houses that had been compulsorily purchased over the years were released to housing associations which encouraged artist communities by providing short-term low-rent accommodation. This short street was squatted and blocked off to prevent any vehicles entering it; it was an effort to reclaim a safe public place. Armchairs on the road blurred the distinction of internal and external space, and more: the project was 'the turning of the street itself into a "living room" by using the furniture, carpets, fittings and other objects from some of the houses . . . to make actual rooms on the street'.[62] There were two cafés, an information centre and an exhibition area, the Art House. In the Art House coinage was painted onto the enamel of a sink: money going down the drain. The street itself was full of public art, a chessboard painted on the road, hubcaps as pawns, traffic cones and broken hoovers as other pieces. Sculptures in the road were also barricades. A car was 'pedestrianized': chopped in two with each half placed on opposite sides of the road, painted and joined by the black and white stripes of a pedestrian crossing. Another car sprouted plants, had RUST IN PEACE on its side. Walls were painted with bright slogans and murals, including a daisy chain the length of the terrace. Installations vied with rubbish for attention. Above the street there was strong netting, an aerial walkway from tree to roof. A scaffolding tower built on a roof reached up into the air, described by Claremont Road residents variously as a critical parody of the Canary Wharf tower, an update of Tatlin's unbuilt monument to the Russian Revolution, a NASA rocket launcher for other campaigns. It was also a landmark visible for miles and an effective obstruction to bailiffs when the eviction finally took place – in all these interpretations of a single piece of resistance culture can be seen the wealth of these new versions of what John Jordan calls 'activist aesthetics'.[63]

Campaigners and sympathetic visitors to Claremont Road – like much of the culture of resistance before the nineties, though possibly more so – view and respect alternative histories and possibilities of Britain to those put forward by majority culture. Utopian space created in the present reaches back and forward in time; the temporary autonomous zone puts down roots. This can be sentimentalized as well as politicized:

> Claremont Road also contained in its being something that was very much the 'essence' of London, the London that is always struggling to break through modern economic restraints: 'old' Mick with his 'no compromise' East End spirit in the face of impossible odds, the jazz musicians and street party pulling all and sundry to the street on a Sunday, . . . the tolerance (London's unique quality as a city) of mixing different groups, individuals and cultures, the humorous publicity stunts grabbing the headlines . . .[64]

Regular Sunday parties began to attract people other than strict environmentalists, including, following the July 1994 national demonstration in London against the Criminal Justice Bill, ravers, and a less welcome element of 'lunch outs' which severely tested the tolerance praised above.

> Although some people in the No M11 campaign have argued that the new people didn't seem to be here because of the fight against the road, it was already apparent to many of us that our struggle was about far more than the road anyway. The road itself obviously raised issues that didn't fit neatly into the 'environmental issues' category: housing, the issue of protest itself, etc. But in taking over Claremont Road it became increasingly clear that the struggle was about a whole way (or ways) of life. Thus for many of the new people coming onto the street, the issue was the Criminal Justice Bill – an attack on non-mainstream ways of life. Claremont Road was a free space . . .

NVDA as performance? Activist–musician at Claremont Road.

In an uncomfortable irony, the protest which had done so much to dodge eviction had itself on occasion to fall back on a similar tactic: some 'lunch outs' were evicted from the free space of Claremont Road. The effort talked about here – to take a single-issue campaign beyond its self-imposed limitations in a sustained manner – was termed by one protester 'polysemic dissent', by another a 'life of permanent struggle'.[65] By this stage there was a definite split, both geographical and political or tactical, between the No M11 Link campaigns of Wanstead and Leytonstone. As one protester wrote at the time, 'Some of the Wanstead residents feel disappointed that the perceived Donga ethos of earlier times has been replaced by the dominance of a harder edged attitude. . . . The campaign has become more proletarianized in many ways. This conflicts with the middle-class pacifism, nature-loving environmentalism and educated-dropout character that used to predominate.'[66] In fairness, Wanstead residents did attempt to organize their own direct action site to protect Bush Wood, but contractors moved in in September 1994 and prevented it.

At the end of November 1994, the eviction of Claremont Road that all had been waiting and preparing for finally came. Tip-offs led to protesters having time to finalize what they had been working towards for months, and a phone tree whereby each protester alerted by phone called others spread the word and brought people onto the street, or onto streets as near as possible to the officially closed-off areas. 'Knowing that the future is rubble gave us the strength to approach the eviction as a game. . . . Barricades, bunkers, towers, nets, tree houses, lock-ons, the tunnel . . . all energy stored and stockpiled for that final moment, everything tuned for maximum intensity during that one hundred hour explosion.'[67] Two hundred bailiffs, seven hundred police and four hundred security guards arrived to carry out the eviction, or just to stand around and intimidate. For four more days Claremont Road obstructed the M11 link road, from the first protesters encountered, apparently nonchalantly lying on mattresses in the road until police tried to remove them and found arms buried into the tarmac and concrete, to the very last protester on the greasy-poled scaffolding tower one hundred feet in the air.[68]

From the M3 and the M11 campaigns, direct action against the government's road-building programme for the 1990s has mushroomed. A local beauty spot, Cinder Path Woods in Cuerden Valley, 'made the mistake of growing in the path of the £142 million 12 mile M65–M61 link road in Lancashire'.[69] On the edge of Chorley near Preston, a derelict house near the woods was squatted and turned into an 'eco-police station', complete with blue-and-white check livery on its walls. Developing tactics from the Chestnut Tree at Wanstonia, and from the tree sitting of Earth First!, other protesters lived in the trees of Cuerden Valley. The dramatic difference offered by protesters at Cuerdenia, as some called it,[70] grabbed the imagination: people actually living in trees in the wood, away from the ground, dramatized the effort to visualize alternatives. While the Department of Transport and the contractors maintained the same old bulldozing mentality, inspirational youth were literally reaching for the skies in a dynamic illustration of possibility. The way in which the road protest direct action campaigns across Britain have been in part a display of imagination to put the authorities to shame was captured here at Cuerdenia, having initially been given voice by the protest in east London: 'We are more possible than you can powerfully imagine' was the slogan. Following the clearing of Cuerdenia, activist attention turned to a site further inland on the route of the M65, nearer Blackburn, where a row of houses was squatted at Darwen. In the spring of 1995, Stanworth Valley became the location of the most elaborate treehouse community yet, the Cosmic Tree Village, with over thirty tree houses and 4 kilometres of aerial walkways.[71] Helen Prescott makes some surprising connections:

> The recent campaigns of Wanstonia against the M11 extension and Cuerden Valley, near Preston, in opposition to the M65, have shown a penchant for living in trees. . . . After the Toxteth riots in 1981, in Liverpool, Michael Heseltine was appointed Minister for Merseyside. On a trip to Liverpool, he told people to 'plant more trees' but he didn't expect that people could end up living in them! He was subsequently given the nickname 'Tarzan'![72]

The anachronistically titled Under-Sheriff of Lancashire was responsible for overseeing evictions at the M65 protest tree house camps. He was called home one day to find activists squatting a tree house he had in his own garden! All tree houses are equal, but some are more equal than others.[73]

In Scotland massive local opposition to the extension of an urban motorway, the M77, led to the formation of new protest camps, proclaimed Pollok Free State, featuring the now familiar scenes of camp fires, benders, banners, outdoor kitchens, schoolchildren mixing play and protest, and so on. This was on the south side of Glasgow – a birthplace of the Anti Poll Tax Federation, with a city centre cut in two by the M8 – and rose up as a response to the proposed destruction of protected land at Pollok Estate, the city's largest open space. The alliance at Pollok was between experienced eco-rads and local working-class communities, an achievement not even matched at the M11 Link campaign which, when it shifted from prosperous Wanstead to Leytonstone, was unable to maintain its close local contact. There have been a number of strange lapses in the law at Pollok: for instance, though there was a public inquiry, it's been argued that no environmental impact assessment was carried out (European law demands one); a Tory MP (the junior minister for a nearby constituency) who wielded an axe handle at protesters was not imprisoned. The Pollok

Free State Declaration of Independence explained that 'we face no choice but to separate and determine our own future'. More recently, the vogue at anti-road camps has been for tunnels, a kind of Tolkien Goes Radical: at the A30 protest camps in Devon, calls went out for steel pipes and cement as well as for more protesters, and a hill fort was built using the very trees felled by contractors. Tree houses, 'twigloos', benders and tunnels: a politicized retreat into the pleasure sites of childhood, a Dongas-style technophobic withdrawal from the modern world, but one that's rooted in the real: the Devon camps partly exist to disseminate information and tactics, and are dubbed 'the university of road protesting'.[74]

The Free States of Britain are having a revival as a result of the government's road-building programme, yet, working back through this book and the decades, we witness them as a recurring feature: Pollok Free State, Cuerdenia, Leytonstonia, Wanstonia, Avalonia, Albion Free State . . . I'm reminded of one of Hakim Bey's celebratory and heroic definitions of the Temporary Autonomous Zone: 'The TAZ is like . . . a guerrilla operation which liberates an area (of land, of time, of imagination) and then dissolves itself to re-form elsewhere/elsewhen.'[75] Maybe Bey ignores the possibility or desirability of permanent effectiveness, of transformation rather than simply transgression, yet when the underground history of such TAZs in Britain is traced, they begin to look as though they contain a little more transgressive constancy.[76] Writing about free festivals, I discussed the Albion Free State Meat Roxy events in west London that Alan Beam describes from the early seventies. (Free love slogan: EVERYONE'S YOUR MATE IN ALBION FREE STATE.) A series of urban squatted events which 'unbelievably . . . lasted throughout the summer, about 14 Saturdays in all', these began really to develop with mock passports, Albion postage stamps and Albion Free State joke £50 notes. During double election year 1974, Albion Free State produced 'a kind of Alternative Society election manifesto' which included this clause:

> (8) It's not hard to dent the old system. Everyone can do their bit. Even symbolic gestures help. For instance, *bicycle rickshaws* instead of cars. Or digging up the fast lane of your local motorway for *allotments*.[77]

Twenty years on and it's happening. In 1994 in Lancashire, M65 protesters turned up early one morning with a surprise from Greenpeace: a multicoloured road digger which began digging up the current construction work. In an inspired Situ-style reversal, security men found themselves doing the digger-diving, trying to halt the

Situ-inspired reversal: turning an icon of road-building against the industry, Cuerden Valley, 1994.

machinery, as one of the road-building industry's icons was turned against the industry itself.

The Albion Free State was itself a variant on the Orange Free State, the deliberate and provocative proclaiming of autonomy for a zone, the ironic flaunting of power where none exists, by the Kabouter movement in Holland in 1970. This in turn was a revival of some of the social and cultural strategies of the Provos in Holland in 1965–67, with their efforts to construct a 'counter-society'. Sadie Plant notes of the Kabouters in their self-proclaimed autonomous zone of Orange Free State, 'They produced alternative plans and imaginative reforms for every area of Dutch life, many of which prefigured the demands of the later green movement.'[78] As the Kabouters explained:

> the new society will have to make the most of its knowledge of sabotage techniques to hasten the transition from an authoritarian and dirty society to an anti-authoritarian and clean one. In fact, the existence of an autonomous, new community in the heart of the old order is the most effective sabotage.

The Provos themselves, a group of politico-cultural activists, sought to provoke the Dutch authorities with a series of 'white plans', the best-known of which became the White Bicycle Plan, which has since been attempted in many cities.

> The Provos announced in a leaflet that white bicycles would be left unlocked throughout the city for use by the general population. The prototype of this 'free communal transport' was presented to the press and public on 28 July 1965. . . . The plan proved an enormous success as a 'provocation against capitalist private property' and 'the car monster', but failed as a social experiment. The police, horrified at the implications of communal property being left on the streets, impounded any bicycle that they found unattended and unlocked.[79]

These free states and autonomous zones illustrate the historical tradition of resistance culture, connecting road protest, the urban space, the environment and a cheeky challenge to business interests and authority generally. The direct action of eco-rads from the Dongas to the artist-activists at Claremont Road and beyond frequently provokes such daft reactions from the authorities as that of Dutch police impounding white bicycles – but more important it seeks to 'generate imagined alternatives' on social and environmental issues.[80] The 'free states' up and down Britain, the self-styled 'tribes' of travellers and protesters, are the latest in the line of living, indeed thriving, cultures of resistance, ones that offer their resistance through direct action.

6

CAUGHT IN THE ACT

In October, I announced the most comprehensive package of measures to tackle
crime ever announced by a Home Secretary. The measures rest on some basic,
common-sense principles: that protecting the public is the first job of Government,
that criminals should be held responsible for their actions and that the police, who
are in the forefront of the fight against crime, should be given the powers which they
need to catch criminals. Those are the principles in which the Government believe.

Michael Howard, Home Secretary, 11 January 1994

The Criminal Justice and Public Order Act 1994, talked of so proudly by Michael
Howard, followed a short Criminal Justice Act 1987, a major Criminal Justice Act
1988 (originally one, these were split because of a general election), a Criminal Justice
Act 1991 dealing with sentencing policy, and a Criminal Justice Act 1993 intended to
correct the widely anticipated problems of the 1991 Act. As the solicitor James
Morton, author of Butterworths' *Guide to the Criminal Justice and Public Order Act 1994*,
puts it in his introduction, rather than crime, '[p]erhaps one thing out of control was
the legislative process' itself.[1] In fairness though, maybe Mr Howard is right to be
proud of his Act, generally known simply as the Criminal Justice Act, since its 172 sections constitute an extremely wide-ranging set of police and judiciary powers to deal
with everything from combating terrorist actions to raising the fines for dredging
shellfish, from recognition of the offence of male rape to reducing the number of travellers' vehicles allowed to park up on a piece of land. It was precisely the inclusive
breadth of the government's proposals that enabled the Labour opposition to abstain
in Parliament, rather than organize against them (this was left to the unelected
chamber of the House of Lords). Labour effectively overlooked the Act's blatantly
repressive aspects, sidestepping the awkward issue of standing up for people's rights.

Michael Mansfield QC has described the Criminal Justice Act as 'the most draconian act this government has put through', adding, 'The democratic right to demonstrate in this country is going down the chute. . . . For the Labour Party to abstain on this bill, when they should be opposing it, is obnoxious.'[2] As in the sixties, it appears to be Tweedledee and Tweedledum all over again.

This chapter focuses on the repressive aspects of the Criminal Justice Act, and on the massive nationwide opposition to it, which has often taken the form of direct action. This has ranged from the mobilization of established and new national organizations and demonstrations to endless small local events – gigs, trespasses, leaflet distributions. The irony is of course that, while the Act has aimed to snuff out many of the events and groups that constitute the culture of resistance in Britain, its effect to date has been quite the opposite: to encourage new and to revitalize older campaigns and actions.

Britain is good at subculture, at cultures of resistance. When the economy's gone to pot, the Empire's a bad memory, the Commonwealth is fragmenting, the special relationship with America is turning sour, the European Union is leaving us behind on the station platform – you *know* that we can still hold our heads high in the subculture style stakes. Teds, mods, skinheads, punks, crusties, ravers, jungle, you name it, the youth flourishes its imagination, takes it seriously, the fashion and music industries take it even more seriously.[3] Such vitality can partly be explained by the energizing plurality of regionalisms and nationalisms in these small islands, by the antagonistic awareness of class distinctions and blurrings, and is expressed through the sometimes amazing explosions of popular music innovation the place has. It may come as a shock then to observe that a tired democratic government of no imagination manages to produce something dauntingly new and different: it passes a massive piece of legislation that has the potential to make practically everyone in this whole book illegal.

In this context the Act is an extraordinary piece of writing: it's possible to trace most of the actions and groups of people I talk about through it. In many ways it's a parallel text to this one. *Senseless Acts of Beauty* and Part V in particular of the Criminal Justice Act tell the same story, if from radically different perspectives. Almost everyone I've contacted in researching this book has wanted – needed – at some stage to talk about the Act's ramifications. Occasionally, features of resistance culture are explicitly named in the Act – raves, for instance (twice). More commonly, a degree of exegesis is required to ascertain precisely what, in the general scheme of the Act and in its legalese, is being prohibited. Textual and contextual interpretation is necessary – decoding the Act to lay bare its powers. This decoding tells us that the Act's banning of trespassory assemblies on land or at a monument of historic or archaeological importance means that the illegality of the Stonehenge Free Festival is enshrined in law. (As if the Public Order Act 1986 hadn't done enough already.) It tells us that, when more than six vehicles parked together in a field without permission are specified in the Act, then the nomadic lifestyles of New Age travellers and gypsies alike are under threat from the law.[4] Though they are parallel texts, where I champion or analyse or criticize, Part V of the Act more brutally and more simply criminalizes. Where I seek to celebrate the spark of transgression, the Criminal Justice Act aims to snuff it out. On the other hand, to attempt a positive gloss, the Act implicitly offers the same argument as this book: that the counterculture of the 1960s cannot be simply dismissed via a narrative of failure, but has spawned generations of activists, cultures of resistance to the present day. The argument is clear and simple here: the culture of resistance must be having an effect, or else why legislate against it? Not only does Part V of the Criminal Justice Act impart a degree of proof to this book's argument about the current significance of cultures of resistance, ironically it also contributes further to their strength and vitality, as we'll see.

The criminalization of diversity

Over recent years a remarkable network has grown up of travellers, dance people, squatters, and protesters, especially road protesters. . . . It has grown up organically, people meeting and discovering common interests, goals and friendship networks. Travellers have marquees that are used at outdoor dances as well as free and commercial festivals. Dances take place at road protest sites. . . . [According to *POD* magazine,] 'The result has been a creative epicentre built on energy and idealism; a pooling of resources to create something out of nothing.'[5]

New powers will be at [police] disposal for dealing with public order such as raves, gatherings of new age travellers and mass trespass which can be a blight for individuals and local communities.

Michael Howard, 3 November 1994

It may be, or it ought to be, a surprise that the full title of the Act is rarely used, since the words that are dropped – 'and Public Order' – signify some of the most worrying changes in the law which it has introduced in fits and starts as different sections have come onto the statute books since November 1994. Part V of the Criminal Justice Act deals with the public order issues of 'collective trespass or nuisance on land'. Groups affected range from those specifically targeted by the law to those who could be affected by the breadth of the legislation, if police extend their application of it to its fullest (which is of course precisely one of the situations in which problems are most likely to arise). It's necessary briefly to look at the words on the page of the Act and at their implications for the cultural and political activists, groups of people and related movements that *Senseless Acts of Beauty* has traced. When Michael Howard rails against such people, he is conveniently forgetting that ravers, travellers and protesters/trespassers are individuals and themselves often live in local communities. In many cases, as we've seen over the years from any number of self-declared 'free states' to Tipi Valley in South Wales to Crass's Epping Forest commune to Rainbow Fields Village to the Exodus Collective near Luton to the Dongas on the Freedom Trail, they're doing something even more interesting – forming *new* communities. These aren't 'blights' – Tory rhetoric moving from notions of 'the enemy within' to the greater dehumanization of people as disease – they're sources of energy, vision, creativity. Howard's rhetoric is deliberate and considered – and dangerous, as Anne Bagehot, then gypsy liaison officer with Save The Children and later a worker for the Gypsy Council for Education, notes:

> Speaking as an individual, my personal view is that the phrase 'ethnic cleansing' is not over the top. People are talking about scum and wasters and riff raff. There's a hate campaign going on.[6]

Both New Age travellers and traditional gypsies come under attack in section 61, which reduces the number of vehicles permitted on an area of land from not more than twelve to not more than six. When requested, if they don't move on 'as soon as reasonably practicable', under section 62 vehicles may be seized and removed by any constable. Sections 77 to 80 give local authorities new powers to evict unauthorized campers from land, and, with twenty-four hours' notice, to remove vehicles themselves if need be. The legal definition of a vehicle includes 'any load carried by, and anything attached to, such a vehicle'. Nor is it necessary for a vehicle to have wheels. Property such as vehicles or sound equipment that is seized incurs charges – in other words, under section 67 evicted travellers may be given the privilege of paying to have their homes taken away from them:

> 67(4) Any authority shall be entitled to recover from a person from whom a vehicle has been seized such charges as may be prescribed in respect of the removal, retention, disposal and destruction of the vehicle by the authority.

Note the extra vindictive twist at the end there: if you're a traveller and the authority removes your vehicle and decides to destroy it because you didn't move off a piece of land in time – you get the bill for having your home smashed up. These powers are combined with the repeal of some provisions of the Caravan Sites Act 1968 – most notably, the obligation of local authorities to provide adequate sites for travellers – to produce another breathtakingly inept, offensive and worrying response to homes and homelessness in Britain.[7] The arrogance is astonishing: over a decade and a half, Conservative administrations produce some of the worst social conditions in terms of homelessness and poverty seen since the Second World War, then, as its crowning glory, the latest Tory government seeks to punish with harassment, fines and imprisonment anyone – everyone? – who devises their own solution to these conditions.

Another attack on the homeless – more accurately, on the otherwise homeless who have been able to organize their own solution to their situation – is found in the Act's shift of squatting from a private, civil concern to a public, criminal activity. Even Morton, usually moderate of language, describes the new legislation against squatters as 'a dog's dinner'.[8] When served with eviction notices, squatters now have twenty-four hours to pack their belongings, find somewhere else to live and leave the squatted premises. Once twenty-four hours are up, they may not return to those premises for one year. A day to leave, a year before you can return: a combination of deadlines which is itself punitive, regardless of any criminal proceedings and subsequent sentence. Further, landlords and property owners now have even greater powers to ensure that their properties are left empty and unused while people sleep in doorways and in boxes. As if all this isn't enough – a landlord's agent can now use violence to evict squatters: section 6 of the Criminal Law Act 1977 which penalizes violence by a person securing entry to squatted premises is in certain circumstances amended by the Criminal Justice Act. According to Liberty, 'Squatters' organizations fear that [section 72] heralds the sanctioning of vigilante bailiffs and licensed heavies.'[9] Squats are by their nature insecure living spaces – the front doors to almost all but the longest-surviving squat communities are notoriously flimsy barriers. The Criminal Justice Act adds further to the social insecurity of the homeless.

Rave culture bears the brunt of the Criminal Justice Act's focus on youth resistance and art. In *Ecstasy and the Dance Culture* Mary Anna Wright suggests that the media representation of the megarave or free festival at Castlemorton in May 1992 'was of a marauding invasion, and the public outrage sowed the seeds of the Criminal Justice Act'.[10] I'm not sure it's quite so straightforward, yet section headings of the Act include 'Powers to remove persons attending or preparing for a *rave*', and '*Raves*: powers to stop persons from proceeding'.[11] Numbers of people involved are stated obsessively in the Act. In relation to raves, 100 or more persons gathering on land in the open air (even if they have permission); two or more persons preparing the rave; ten or more waiting for it to begin; ten or more attending it; any single person reasonably considered by a police officer to be on his or her way to the rave – they're all potentially illegal if there is no official entertainment licence.

In an extraordinary passage, music is defined in sub-section 1(b) of section 63 of the Act as follows: '"music" includes sounds wholly or predominantly characterized by the emission of a succession of repetitive beats'. The verb 'includes' in this sentence is intended to signal that rave music *per se* is not under attack. If you believe that you're probably a Tory voter. It's a corny point to make, and one that may well not be legally accurate, but I can't help but be reminded of Josef Skvorecky's description of a set of Nazi regulations on jazz music in the 1940s.

1. Pieces in foxtrot rhythm (so-called swing) are not to exceed 20% of the repertoires of light orchestras and dance bands; . . .
3. as to tempo, . . . the pace must not exceed a certain degree of allegro, commensurate with the Aryan sense of discipline and moderation . . .;
4. so-called jazz compositions may contain at most 10% syncopation; the remainder must consist of a natural legato movement devoid of the hysterical rhythmic reverses characteristic of the music of the barbarian races and conducive to dark instincts . . .[12]

Pinpointed by this legislation are the rhythms of the music and the related action of dancing – common features of the Criminal Justice Act's treatment of rave culture, its beats and its free parties. There's an element of taste here – the Act has taste inscribed within it, disliking loud music, music that's long in duration, that's intended for dancing, that's not purely acoustic. I'd say there's no overt race agenda involved in Part V of the Act, and yet someone closer to the scene, like DJ Aztek, takes issue. For him there's a clear racist effect of the anti-rave sections of the Act: 'they are doing everything to stamp out dance parties, which have done more for racial togetherness . . . in this country than any government organization could ever do'.[13] Of course it should be noted that the Criminal Justice Act is not a total ban on rave culture, only a ban in certain circumstances, and does not apply to commercial, licensed events (that would be too much for the political party of free enterprise). Yet, for example, the Surrey constabulary has stated in the past that 'raves will not happen – illegal or otherwise', suggesting a dangerous precedent of police action against legal events. This was before the Act came into effect – what attitudes linger now?[14]

The short history of rave culture belies the fact that it has been subject to a number of legal obstructions intended to curtail its general popularity or specifically its noncommercial strands. In fact, it's not going too far to state that rave culture has been subject to a sustained assault by legislative forces. Legal obstructions have included both the employment of old, sometimes obscure by-laws, such as the Private Places and Entertainments Act, and the introduction of new legislation, such as the Licensing Act 1988, or the Entertainments (Increased Penalties) Act 1990, which increased the penalties for private entertainment for financial gain without a licence.[15] This was known as the Acid House Bill. The assault on rave culture has been far more sustained and focused than any on earlier subcultures of resistance. For instance punk in 1977, with the Sex Pistols' 'God Save the Queen' topping the charts in Jubilee Week itself, was a terrifically provocative cultural form and moment – but they didn't effectively pass a *law* against punk events or lifestyles. There's no law that names and potentially criminalizes a dominant type of popular music from the seventies, or the sixties for that matter – both moments when arguably there were clearer oppositional voices and positions than with rave. There are no laws from the seventies or the sixties that prohibit '"music" including sounds characterized by the emission of a succession of repetitive vocal sneers', or '"music" including sounds characterized by the emission of repetitive and lengthy guitar solos'. Possibly the introduction of powers to prohibit raves is in part a reaction to the strong links constantly made between raves and drug culture, particularly Ecstasy. (Though this distinction only works if one ignores the prevalence of LSD in the sixties.) The reaction is connected with reports of deaths associated with Ecstasy, the shock of young death on a dance floor, which is supposed to be a site of pleasure. It may also be a response to the underground nature of the early rave scene – the sense of disappearance I discussed with rave, of disappearance especially in comparison with the uncompromisingly spectacular nature of, say, punk. Rave culture grew and established itself without outsiders knowing about it, and maybe this has exaggerated its perceived danger. I've already discussed Wright's location of the origins of the anti-rave legislation in the Castlemorton megarave of 1992. Of course the blame can also be laid at the doors of an increasingly intransigent government and quiescent opposition. An illustration at hand comes from James Morton, who unwittingly demonstrates the success of the negative representation of rave, performing a neat slippage in his comments on the genesis of raves and official reactions to them:

> The police also saw raves as places where drugs were readily on sale, where protection was being imposed on organizers and, on occasions, where guns in some quantity could be found. What was once a fairly anarchic affair had become big and dangerous business.[16]

The objectivity and deliberate distancing of the first sentence ('The police also saw') as well as its several qualifications ('on occasions . . . could be found') are rejected by the second sentence in favour of the stance of 'hard fact': rave is now a 'dangerous business'. In his critical annotations on the Act Morton thus repeats uncritically the Establishment argument.

The legal assault on rave is not only sustained but also extreme. 'A succession of repetitive beats' is not a description of police behaviour at Windsor Free in 1974 or the Beanfield in 1985 or at Spiral Tribe's Easter free party in London in 1992.[17] It's the legal description of rave music, a form of music described in law so that in certain circumstances it can be outlawed. I'm in danger of becoming repetitive myself here – but is this not a quite extraordinary state of affairs? Talking with academics and students in the United States in 1994, for instance, I encountered astonishment when I explained that a form of popular music, listened and danced to by large numbers of young and not so young people in Britain, was in the process of being inscribed in legislation by the government. 'Are you seriously saying that there's a law being introduced which aims to target a type of pop music?' was a common response.[18] This isn't the banning of a single from a radio playlist, as has happened to everyone from Paul McCartney to the Sex Pistols, or the refusal to press or release a particular record, as with Crass's *The Feeding of the Five Thousand* – it's the singling out by name of a widespread youth event, style and dance form, and its potential prohibition. The attack on music extends to the equipment used to play it, also named and defined, in section 64: '"sound equipment" means equipment designed or adapted for amplifying music and any equipment suitable for use in connection with such equipment, and "music" has the same meaning as in section 63'. Like travellers' homes, sound systems can be destroyed and their owners charged for their destruction.

Much of the anti-rave legislation also applies to free festivals – partly because the free festival scene has been revitalized by rave culture, even moulded into its image: the free festivals of the nineties are arguably less celebrations and demonstrations of alternative values than (as at Castlemorton in 1992 or at the effort to repeat it in 1995 with the Mother free dance festival) mega- or mini-raves in themselves, with 24-hour sound systems and so on. However, parts of the Act seem more slanted towards ending the ongoing struggle around the biggest and best-known free festival in Britain, the Stonehenge Free, last held in 1984. As I've explained, sections 70 and on deal with mass trespass, and include the power to ban trespassory assemblies that are deemed potentially to damage important historic or archaeological monuments – like Stonehenge. Surely this curious situation is a worrying development – nationwide legislation to deal with a peculiarly specific and local event, one that has been successfully prohibited with existing laws for over a decade anyway?

Trespass is dealt with in other ways, too. Writer and activist George Monbiot views the new trespass laws as 'the greatest victory this decade' of the landed gentry and other major landowners. Monbiot continues:

> The new act is another act of enclosure, a further assertion of exclusive rights by those who claim to own the land. . . . The argument most often advanced by the Country Landowners' Association in favour of the Criminal Justice Act is that travellers damage hedges, fields and features of historical or scientific value. Yet, every year throughout the 1990s, country landowners have overseen the loss of 18,000 kilometres of hedgerow.[19]

The new offence of aggravated trespass is intended to criminalize the actions of hunt saboteurs, or, as one hunt sab described it to me, 'to defend the lifestyle of the

British aristocracy and their sad wannabee hangers-on'. (The first people charged under the three-day-old Act in November 1994 were hunt sabs, arrested during the Woodland Pytchley Hunt in Northamptonshire.) As James Morton puts it with understatement, 'section 68 was welcomed by Masters of Foxhounds and owners of pheasant shoots'.[20] Aggravated trespass differs from trespass in that the purpose of the trespassers is to deter, obstruct or disrupt the activities of other, so-called legitimate groups on the land. As targets of protest, these so called legitimate groups could include not only hunts, but also road builders and exporters of live animals, for instance. The worry of civil liberties groups is that the authorities have merely to identify a 'legitimate group' that they 'reasonably suspect' is likely to be deterred, obstructed or disrupted in order to employ this new law. There is clearly the potential here for there to be an attack on what Simon Fairlie calls the 'ultimate extra-legal resource – the right of public, peaceful protest upon the site'. Recalling the direct action origins of some of today's respectable campaign organizations, Fairlie continues:

> This right should not be underestimated. It has provided collateral for respectable bodies lobbying in the public interest. Many of the august defenders of the environment gained their initial impetus and their subsequent status from acts of trespass or worse. The Commons Preservation Society in 1866 ripped down enclosers' fences and thereby saved Berkhampstead Common, Epping Forest, the New Forest and many other landscapes we now take for granted. The society still exists as the Open Spaces Society, while several of its leading members went on to found the National Trust. Similarly, the Ramblers' Association owes its reputation, above all, to the famous mass trespass on the moors of Kinder Scout in 1932.[21]

There was a traditional, if erroneous, understanding that trespassers could not be prosecuted in criminal law. Trespass was seen as belonging to the civil realm in which personal rights are defendable by damages or injunctions, rather than in criminal law where the state can intervene with the ultimate deterrent of imprisonment. This understanding has largely disappeared with the Criminal Justice Act. The underlying fear of many people involved in protest and direct action in Britain is that the Act's extension of trespass laws may supply a final great catch-22, as British law goes into postmodern self-referential mode: protest against the Criminal Justice Act can be prohibited by the Criminal Justice Act. One scenario for such a situation is as follows. Trespassory assemblies can be prohibited on land to which the public has only limited access; 'limited' is defined in section 70 as including the sense 'restricted to use for a particular purpose (as in the case of a highway or road)'. So, a demonstration of more than twenty protesters on a public highway could be deemed a trespassory assembly and banned. The law is in danger of becoming a closed circle; we are in danger of becoming well and truly caught in the Act.

Kill the Bill! Or, Chill the Bill!

> Everything is inverted. The Criminal Justice Bill will make dancing a crime. But beating people over the head in order to break up a festival is called 'public order'. Travelling is a crime. But trashing someone's home, taking their vehicle and then destroying it, forcing children into care and parents into prison, this is called 'justice'. Wanting a roof over your head is a crime. But vigilantes with pickaxe handles smashing through your front door and laying waste all your possessions is called 'property rights'. Something is fundamentally wrong here.
>
> C.J. Stone[22]

Something is indeed fundamentally wrong – and yet for many this has had a galvanizing effect, increasing rather than diminishing the power of direct action protest both against the Act itself and in wider campaigns. It's arguable that, to date at least, the Criminal Justice Act has seriously backfired: intended to clamp down on the irritations of cultures of resistance from travellers to ravers to squatters and campaigners, it's had the opposite effect, of ensuring that people are aware of their rights and continue to use them and to interrogate the limits of the Act on the land and in the courts. James Morton tells of how, 'on the day the Act received Royal Assent, demonstrators against the widening of the M25 were joined by those demonstrating against the Act in a final gesture of solidarity'.[23] Clearly, that gesture was not the *final* one at all – on the contrary, it was the first against the Act (as opposed to the Bill), and the first of many. It's important to stress the solidarity, too: one effect of the Act has been instantly to unite previously disparate campaigns, to bring different single-issue protests together.

In the legal arena alone there's been opposition to the Act, some from police forces themselves, more through the courts. With the huge costs in financial and social terms of road protests, there was identifiable reluctance on the part of police to meet the ever-greater demands being made on them. Talking of the £500,000 bill for the eviction of three houses at Wanstonia in January 1994, Chief Superintendent Stuart Giblin commented: 'We end up being caught in the middle of conflicts and drawn away from our primary aim of preventing crime. We don't want to be divided from our local communities by this type of legislation.'[24] Other forces have shown varying degrees of inconsistency in the application of the law. Of course, this can be the situation with any new and complex Act, but it may be significant that not all police forces have embraced the new legislative provisions with enthusiasm. Some use their discretionary powers *not* to intervene: I've heard for instance that unofficial advice has been sought from and given by police in cities with thriving autonomy scenes as to suitable squatted sites for free parties. In other cases, people have been charged under existing laws, rather than with potentially more serious crimes under the Criminal Justice Act.

Sections of the Act have been subject to opposition in the courts, from a number of legal challenges on a local scale, in county courts for instance, up to challenges in the international legal arena. Particularly successful have been challenges to the new trespass laws. Druid King Arthur Uther Pendragon (that is his name, though the royal title is optional) was arrested near Stonehenge as he tried to celebrate the summer solstice in 1995. He was charged, under section 70 of the Criminal Justice Act, with forming a trespassory assembly inside the traditional four-mile exclusion zone set up by Wiltshire police around the stones each June. In an exquisite moment where New Age myth met modern legal rationality King Arthur took the oath in court on the sword of Excalibur. He challenged police evidence of the number of people on the road (more than twenty are needed to form a trespassory assembly) and of their connection with each other. While police said twenty-seven people were trespassing, King Arthur argued that this number was made up of everyone along the entire stretch of road, including legal observers, a TV crew and some partying Europeans. He was acquitted, in a test case that illustrated both the difficulties police have in using this law and the ill-considered nature of the legislation in the first place. In a second case in September 1995, New Age travellers in East Sussex challenged their local council's attempt to evict them from an unauthorized site at Crowborough. The judge in the High Court ruled that the authority erred in law, basing his judgment on the lack of proper enquiries undertaken by Wealden District Council into the welfare implications for the travellers of their eviction. The judge ruled that the circumstances of all individuals must be considered before eviction, and that people who move onto site after such evictions cannot themselves be evicted until their circumstances have also been looked at. If the information about those being evicted is inaccurate or outdated (a reasonable enough assumption in the fluid world of travellers' sites), the new law becomes, as one council representative described it, practically 'unworkable'. Again, the ruling leads back to the ill-considered nature of the legislation in the first place. It's likely that small challenges to the Act in local courts will continue as it becomes increasingly employed. In the longer term, the civil rights group Liberty is looking at the Criminal Justice Act in relation to articles of the European Convention on Human Rights (ECHR) and of the United Nations International Covenant on Civil and Political Rights (ICCPR). Britain is a signatory to both these agreements, and Liberty is exploring the possibility that the Act breaches aspects of either or both of them. The table below shows some of the activities and groups potentially criminalized by the Act and the articles that Liberty considers they are in possible breach of:

Civil rights responsibility breached by the Criminal Justice Act		
Peaceful protest	ECHR Article 11	Freedom of assembly
Travellers	ECHR Article 8	Privacy and family life
	ICCPR Article 2	Freedom from discrimination
	ICCPR Article 27	Cultural rights of minorities
Squatters	ECHR Article 6	Fair trial
	ECHR Protocol 1, Article 1	Peaceful enjoyment of possessions
Raves	ECHR Article 10	Freedom of assembly[25]

However, the focus of this book is less on legal arguments than on swellings of resistance from the grassroots, and not even the grassroots of the traditional left. As the underground magazine *Aufheben* notes, 'The struggles around the 1994 Criminal Justice Act are notable for their relative independence from the Labour Party and the left'[26] – they constitute a sign of the by-now-familiar autonomy of the New Protest and DIY culture. An incomplete project by activists in Leeds called Forgive Us Our Trespasses aimed to collate and distribute a register of nationwide actions against the Criminal Justice Bill. Catherine Muller of Leeds Earth First! explains that 'the idea was to compile statistics of exactly how many protests were going on and how many people were likely to be criminalized by the Bill becoming law, but we were unable to keep tabs on everyone because there was so much going on'.[27] Nevertheless from the partial work undertaken, Forgive Us Our Trespasses does give a sense of the sheer extent and variety of protest. For example, for the single month of May 1994, 52 events are listed, ranging from the national demonstration in London on May Day to anti-road protests at Cuerden Valley in Lancashire, Solsbury Hill near Bath, Wymondham in Norfolk, to the Amazon Festival women's camp at Menwith Hill US spy base in Yorkshire, to a protest against the closure of an unemployed workers' centre in Edinburgh. The point Forgive Us Our Trespasses sought to make was that all these events and others like them were potentially illegal under the trespass sections of the Bill.

A spectacular show of power and anger against the Criminal Justice Bill erupted at the third national demonstration against it in London on Sunday 9 October 1994. The events of that afternoon and evening echoed the Poll Tax riot around Trafalgar Square of a few years before, which graphically illustrated the nationwide unpopularity of an earlier Tory idea. The Poll Tax riot was a key moment in the successful campaign against the Poll Tax: could recent radical history repeat itself? (The Criminal Justice Act has been called 'the Poll Tax on Acid'.) The demonstration against the Bill was a peaceful march in a carnival atmosphere from the Embankment to Hyde Park. In allowing the march to happen in the first place, the Metropolitan Police insisted on following local by-laws and prohibiting any sound systems in Hyde Park itself, fearing, as one senior officer put it, that they 'would become a focal point for those intent on causing disorder'.[28] It's interesting that music and dance became the focus of the struggle on the day. Was the Met right in its judgement? Or was it misguided, even provocative, to ban music at a demonstration that was demonstrating against what it saw as the banning of music? With hindsight the prohibition of sound systems in the park was not a terribly intelligent strategy, becoming on the day a source of trouble rather than a means of its avoidance. Locked into their role, riot police had then to break up the challenge to their authority, which took the form of a lorry with some speakers pumping out dance music trying to make its way into the park. As one demonstrator saw it, 'if you are charged by a line of baton-wielding police for merely dancing in the street, you fight back'. Missiles are thrown, mounted charges retaliate, while thousands of protesters find themselves blocked in by police, unable to reach their coaches to return home. Protesters sitting around in the park are charged by horses, sporadic running battles spill out from the park, police reinforcements rush up Park Lane clearing the way, shops in Oxford Street are trashed, the green heart of the capital shakes with the righteous anger of the youth of the country. A group of protesters from Leeds witnessed the riot that evening from their coach, which was trapped by police lines as it tried to leave along Park Lane. Four were so shocked by police behaviour, and by subsequent media misrepresentations of the day, that they afterwards wrote and distributed a short leaflet about it.

> We are not attempting to gain any political capital from this event, we are just highly concerned as individuals that the truth of the events is, through the mass media, being distorted beyond recognition. . . . Erihk: 'At the end of the day, people were going anyway, but the gates were locked, and riot police were sent round the back, in the park, to herd the remaining people to the fence to face even more riot police. If you treated people in any public gathering like that, at a football match or even in a shopping centre, if you locked the doors and rounded them up into a small space with no exit using riot police, some dickhead will throw something at them. If they then charged in and seriously injured the people who just happened to be at the front, the crowd would get outraged, angry and increasingly violent, and there would be a riot. You could do that in any public gathering, any time, anywhere.'[29]

Possibly the October rally and riot are as interesting for the political infighting that occurred around them as they are for the wholehearted opposition they demonstrated to the Bill. They highlighted the tensions not only within the coalition opposing the Criminal Justice Act but also within the history of the New Protest and DIY culture more generally. On the one hand, Class War (ironically given a boost of energy by the Act after a moribund late eighties) distributed leaflets at the demonstration offering advice on how to attack police, and other demonstrators or stewards if need be: 'When throwing – throw well. It takes a bit of guts but if you have your hands on some ammo, move up front. Don't stand so far back that you are unable to reach our target. . . . If [stewards] get in the way, clout them.' On the other hand, Josh of Freedom Network announced from the stage to some booing his far more limited agenda of the Right to Party: 'the kind of revolution that I like is the one that goes round and round the record player'. Though keen to distance itself from older politics, the New Protest is hardly immune from the traditional pastime of the radical left, squabbling amongst its elements over strategies. The tension can be seen even in the slogans paraded at Hyde Park: 'Kill the Bill!' is enjoyed for its deliberate ambiguity by

Spikeys take advantage of the fluffies: (non-violent) direct action?

Class War and other confrontational radical groups, 'Chill the Bill!' is the variant preferred by the fluffies and ravers. While the first group wants the total overthrow of the system, the second wants merely the right to party restored. (Elsewhere John of *Aufheben* defines 'fluffy' as referring specifically to non-violence.[30]) A special issue of *Aufheben* entitled *Kill or Chill?* explores these contradictions, initially locating the discussions about strategy in the context of lifestyle:

> 'Keep it Fluffy' or 'Keep it Spikey'? 'Kill the Bill' or 'Chill the Bill'? . . . this contradiction exists . . . in the antagonism between the different components which make up the campaign, most famously between the media *bête noire* Class War and the media darlings in Freedom Network.[31]

Implicitly here for *Aufheben*, if Freedom Network is acceptable to the mass media, it must be doing something wrong. A stronger narrative of the anti-Bill coalition is given in the long-standing, class-centred *Counter Information*, a free newsheet produced in central Scotland. Number 41, published in the wake of the Hyde Park riot, leads on actions around the country against the Criminal Justice Bill.

> More depressing and dangerous is the unfortunate point that in most areas the Freedom Network and their newly found pacifist allies, mostly discovered in the 'hippyish' elements within the environmental scene and the festival/techno scene, are growing in numbers and influence. They encourage people to 'keep it fluffy' – join hands, sing songs, sit down and in some cases grass on 'violent agitators' to the cooperative boys in blue. Many of us thought with relief that libertarian politics had mostly rid itself of such naive and deadend ideology back in the mid-1980s, we must now struggle once again to destroy this bullshit, it's even more of a pain than the Socialist Workers' Party/Militant/Revolutionary Communist Party trying to sabotage/take over our activities. . . . In any confrontation watch out for these people – they are not on our side.[32]

That's some appeal for togetherness, for working on many fronts! Solidarity, yes, but not with Freedom Network, not with ravers, not with the organized left. Resist on all fronts, yes, but not with anyone who's doesn't follow our line!

Further imagination and defiance have followed in the wake of the bill becoming law. In an alternative kind of roof-top protest, protesters have appeared actually on the Houses of Parliament; hundreds turned up in the grounds of the Home Secretary's Kent house in order to throw an alternative garden party to let him know what they thought of his work; a mass trespass of Chequers, the Prime Minister's official country retreat, was attempted.

Opposition to the Criminal Justice Act has also resulted in longer-lasting developments. The Brighton-based group Justice? is one of a number that sprang apparently from nowhere in order to organize opposition to the Act. More accurately, a group of young people were sitting in a pub in Brighton one night in 1994, bemoaning the imminent legislation, when they decided to do something about it. Justice? was formed in April that year. Displaying a neat sense of irony, later in the year Justice? squatted a derelict courthouse in Brighton intended as a focus for the region's campaign against the Act. *Schnews*, the free weekly newspaper Justice? produces, takes up the story.

> In just three days the derelict 100-yr-old former magistrates office was transformed into a thriving community centre with café, meditation space, crèche and free entertainment for a free people. Over 1000 people came through the doors.[33]

Gibby from Justice? described the Courthouse experience as 'a 51-day rush, . . . a real focus, a coming together of the people'. *Aufheben*, however, critically points out that 'the Courthouse squat in Brighton fell between the stools of a centre for a "community of struggle" and a "community arts centre"'.

> Overtly political activities – like workshops held on the continental squatting movement, prisoner support and contradictions in the anti-roads movement, and meetings to discuss the group's activities and direction – competed for space with poetry readings, Tai Chi, massage, cinema, drumming workshops and art displays etc.[34]

What's the problem here? Is poetry not hardline enough for *Aufheben*? Don't the arts have a (central) role to play in the struggle to build and maintain a community?

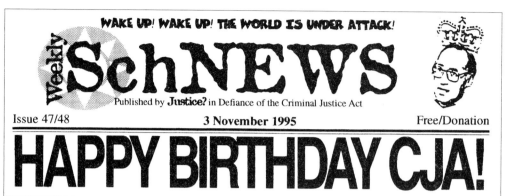

DIY culture tells the weekly news, Brighton, 1995.

Following the squatters' eviction in November the Courthouse remained derelict a year later, and the owners applied for permission to demolish the listed building. Justice? moved on to other premises, continued to produce *Schnews*, throw free parties, organize campaigns and demonstrations, run a telephone helpline, publish pamphlets and produce *The Book*, a directory detailing the national campaign against the Act, and *Schnews Reader*. While doing all that, Justice? activists also found time to help me with my research, mulling through their archive and contacts for information they thought I ought to have, reading and commenting on drafts. Actions, underground news, advice, support, creativity, thought, and lots of cheek – all this had been inspired by the Criminal Justice Act and was contributing to an impressively widespread culture of resistance. Early copies of *Schnews* included the following passage by the title, adapted from a 'Glossary of the Nineties' in the *Guardian*:

DISORGANIZATION *n.* An unstructured protest group of the mid-Nineties, without the leadership of a conventional organization. Want to join one of the loose coalitions such as Justice?, fighting road-building and criminal-justice laws? Don't expect to fill in an application form.

The Book was collated by Justice? activists from questionnaires sent around Britain, and produced and distributed with help from the Levellers, who as a band are based in Brighton. Each edition of *The Book* gives a snapshot indication of the scope of actions and groups involved against the Act, and is also a sign of faith on the part of the South Coast group themselves in their ambition – and indeed of the need – to move from local to national campaigning. The short foreword – titled 'FORWARD!' – illustrates their revised utopian propaganda-of-the-deed approach:

> [*The*] *Book* is symptomatic of a new awareness, a force of empathy, wit, vision and community spirit which has given a fresh sense of empowerment and freedom. The scapegoated have become united like never before. The old channels of protest and party politics are dead. DIY culture is creating homes and entertainment by the people for the people captured in the philosophy of Deeds Not Words. The Criminal Justice Act has, unintentionally, opened doors which can never be shut again. It has motivated the largest direct action movement in years.[35]

As described in one of their leaflets, a week in the life of Justice? goes something like this. The office is open Monday to Friday; Monday is for gardening at the Justice? allotments; Tuesday is a day off; Wednesday is for weekly meetings, ending up in the pub; Thursday is for putting *Schnews* together; Friday is printing and distribution day, followed by the pub; Saturday there's a street stall; Sunday is for chilling out. Actions and parties are fitted around these regular events. Justice? in Brighton is just one such centre of voluntary activity and resistance around the country: Freedom Network, Advance Party, Exodus, United Systems, Solidarity Centres, Arts Labs, there are many more. Springing from opposition to the Criminal Justice Act is an autonomous network outside parliamentary politics and largely outside Establishment pressure groups: this is DIY culture, not new by any means, but possibly bigger than ever before, taking its initial impetus from a single-issue campaign and rapidly expanding from there.

Actions against the Act have revived and simplified the whole notion of a politics of pleasure for large sections of British youth. Not only have there been campaigns, demonstrations, publications against it, but also there has been an extension of the 'Party and Protest' side of DIY culture, as a regular column in *Schnews* puts it. The government's legislative backfire maintains its spectacular nature as people around the country take the opportunity to have a good time *and* make a political statement. The point is of course that, with the Draconian laws now in place, the simple act of having a good time has been given a greater oppositional thrust. Merely reviving a fair or organizing a free party can strike a direct blow against the state's repressive

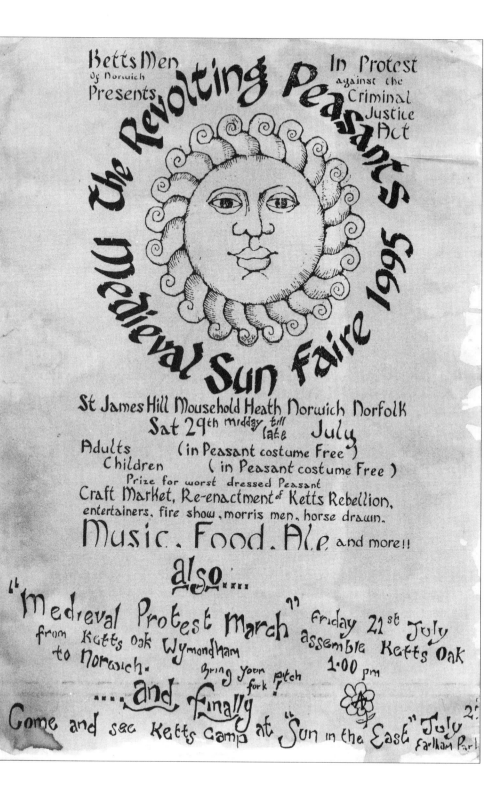

The revival of Fairs meets the anti-Criminal Justice Act coalition, Norwich, 1995.

apparatus. While this may sound melodramatic and self-important, it's actually – even unfortunately – frighteningly true.

July 25 1995 Mousehold Heath, Norwich
A tiny medieval-style fair, half-a-dozen tents and flags, three or four trucks and a couple of horses, a stage made from a horsedrawn wagon with two bales of straw and no electrics whatsoever, craft demonstrations by a flint knapper and an iron forger. Up on the viewpoint looking over to the buttresses of the cathedral is a mock gallows with a grey bespectacled and besuited hanging man representing the Criminal Justice Act. A mid-nineties fair directly engaging with political action – as the poster says: The Revolting Peasants Medieval Sun Faire In Protest Against The Criminal Justice Act. Here we have the return of fairs in East Anglia and elsewhere, some of which may be due to the crossover with the rave scene, drawing in a new generation. There's a keen sense of history in this too – it's not just a mock medieval fayre (Carry On England), all atavism and romance, like Barsham over twenty years ago. The main tent has a big display of texts people cluster around reading: a community history class pulling in the Peasants' Revolt of 1381, Kett's Rebellion of 1549, the Diggers of the English Revolution, and claiming events such as this small protest against the Criminal Justice Act as part of that tradition. (Curiously there's no mention of Captain Swing, the letters and riots of the 1830s.) The fair is the culmination of a week's marching and camping from Wymondham, where Robert Kett originally led the uprising, to Mousehold, where he had his famous camp of 20,000, and from where he captured Norwich, then England's second city. The iron forger is a traveller, works from a yellow flatback FG and lives in a chrome caravan – reversing the expectation that only gypsies not New Age travellers do that, as he tells me. Andy's from Yorkshire, but the sites are better in Norfolk and there are more people willing to buy and stock his wares here – pokers, firedogs, gates. He represents the next generation of travellers. As I drive round Norfolk these few weeks I see odd fields crammed with buses, commons sprinkled with wagons and horses. Travellers are gathering pace again, after the trials of the Beanfield and beyond, gathering energy. Fairs and travellers, organizing and living, standing up against the law.

I buy a copy of *Mixmag*, which calls itself 'the world's leading dance music and club culture magazine', in the summer of 1995. I expect the cover to show something like sunny smiling faces on a dancefloor, a snapshot of a feel-good temporary utopia in which young people with healthy bodies are having fun. In fact, the cover shows an altogether more intimidating form of choreography. It's like a shot from a miners' strike, a grainy black-and-white photo of a line of heavily armoured and heavily protected British riot police, faces visored, shields to the fore, pushing back out of the frame the devilish dancers and party-goers at a Sunday afternoon Rave Against the Machine in a London street. Here is one side of the extraordinary reality of the British government's attitude towards rave culture. Fortunately, the other side is a little more uplifting.

> When the government passed the CJA I am not entirely sure they were aware of what an enormous favour they were doing the underground free party scene. Put simply, the CJA has sorted out free parties in this country – BIG TIME! Every single weekend without fail since the enstatement of the Act, a huge party has gone [on] without interruption from the law, sometimes one, sometimes two, sometime seven sound systems. . . . It seems as though the CJA was just the kick up the arse that the scene needed.[36]

While DJ Weasel here celebrates the positive effect of the Act on free parties, Mary Anna Wright makes the further point that we are also witnessing 'the politicization of the scene with the Advance Party and United Systems voicing protests against the new laws and forging links with other groups affected'.[37] It seems that, if I had problems with the oppositional intent of rave culture in the late eighties and early nineties, the Criminal Justice Act has removed my grounds for concern, by dealing in so heavy-handed a way with the scene that it has been both energized and politicized.

United Systems in fact is an offshoot of the Advance Party, which was one of a number of groups set up to organize nationally against the Bill, with earlier origins in a Spiral Tribe information line for people interested in Spirals' raves of the early nineties. United Systems, which first came together around October 1993, is basically a collective of sound systems with a common purpose, to agitate against the Act through free parties. Its activities involve anything from advice and supply of sound and lighting equipment to DJs, to aiding with artwork and backdrops, to offering legal support and contact numbers in case of problems. A further illustration of the way in which the Act has galvanized cultures of resistance, is the fact that United Systems also liaises with groups such as road protesters and hunt saboteurs to organize and inform about regional celebrations, actions and benefits. Here we can see once more the widening of single-issue campaigns to take on board an entire raft of other oppositional interests. When I spoke to Debbie of United Systems in October 1995 she was unable to provide accurate information about one of my queries – since her files had been confiscated by police during a recent raid. The Criminal Justice Act is viewed by people involved in United Systems as the official admission of what had been going on for years anyway: a sustained and sometimes brutal effort to clamp down on the new music and its related underground scenes. Debbie describes the current attitude of the free party scene as 'hedonism with a purpose', the purpose being to resist the repressive aspects of the new legislation. However, this tends to overlook what she sees as the less conscious but still significant politics of earlier rave culture, with its emphasis on egalitarianism, and its non-racist and, in her view, surprisingly non-sexist attitudes. In these earlier attitudes lies the source of the anger and righteousness of rave culture's response to what it perceives as its criminalization in 1994. United Systems is a symptom of the grievance that rave culture feels today – but also a symptom of the sheer defiant energy of DIY culture more generally. UK plc cannot bear the mentality of 'do-it-for-free'. In the early seventies resistance was pitching a tent in the Queen's backyard; in the mid-nineties it's dancing under the stars at 180 bpm.

CONCLUSION; OR, WORK IN PROGRESS; OR, ET CETERA

Senseless Acts of Beauty set out to illustrate, analyse and celebrate the legacy of the sixties, whose student and worker uprisings, as Dick Hebdige put it, 'heralded the growing importance of cultural and identity politics, the politics of gender, race and sexuality, the ecology and autonomy movements'.[1] I'd also like to think that the book can be 'part of the project it has set out to examine', as another book on ways of life and cultures of resistance nicely put it.[2] These were the motivations I originally had in mind when I started. A further purpose of this book only became clear to me as I reached the end, though. Writing about direct action, the New Protest and DIY culture of the nineties, I've been surprised, maybe even disappointed, by the lack of historical awareness on the part of those involved. There's a slightly disturbing and insistent rhetoric of newness around, which sometimes veers on the dismissive. I hope that *Senseless Acts of Beauty* will act as a counter to that, will locate contemporary actions as part of a tradition, will offer the opportunity for dialogue between generations, styles of living, tactics, attitudes, musical tastes, and so on.

Looking back from 1983, when it was clear to all that the energy of the East Anglian fairs had begun to wane, performance artist Jill Bruce was one person who refused to be downhearted:

There are new people and I think this subtle relating of people, place and fair has gone, but it is not something to be nostalgic about, to regret or to strive to re-achieve. That was then. Now is now. Perhaps something will emerge that isn't fairs, another moment with a new purpose, and maybe a new awareness.[3]

Cosmo from *Justice?* voices one version of the new awareness Bruce tentatively hoped for, picks up the story from the next generation:

> In the eighties, a lot of people who were hacked off with the way we were living, or were just plain bored, got off their arses and did something about it. Free festivals, squat culture, the traveller movement and later Acid House parties pay testament to the energy and vision of people who decided it was now time to take their destinies into their own hands.[4]

In the nineties Glenn Jenkins of the Exodus Collective connects the mundane and the political when he states that 'every lick of paint, every word spoken, every dance put on, builds the positive'.[5] It's this continuing possibility of resistance, desire for alternatives and the expression of creativity since the sixties that I'm interested in celebrating. That's why I haven't got a conclusion, don't want one, don't believe there is one. *Senseless Acts of Beauty* is a work in progress in that the social and cultural challenges it's traced are ongoing, continual, changing. As *Justice?*'s *The Book* puts it, 'We are involved in celebration *as* a struggle.'[6]

Yet others would conclude things. Indeed, the real-world conclusion of this book, the end of the people and actions in it, is supposed to be Part V of the Criminal Justice Act. That's its purpose, to clamp down in the name of public order, to make Windsor Free and the Beanfield, the Convoy and Castlemorton, irrelevant events and ways of living located in the distant past. But, as Phil McLeish writes of the inspiring action at Claremont Road in east London:

> In seeking to criminalize such lifestyles the State has succeeded in politicizing them. No longer is dropping-out copping-out. . . . Youth-culture is now closer to radical politics than at any time since the days of punk. Squatters, travellers, ravers, activists – the common denominator of the movement is a demand for free space.[7]

The Criminal Justice Act has this neat new offence called 'damage to the land'. For travellers, festival-goers and ravers, for eco-rads extolling the virtues of the local/global connection, and for squatters providing their own solution to home-lessness when none is offered by the government, a criminal offence of 'damage to the land' is particularly offensive. By my reading, that land is Britain, and the damage is not done by but rather has been and is *drawn attention to* by – in no particular order! – the actions of the hippies and the punks, the constructors and defenders of Albion, the Dongas Tribe, United Systems, the citizens of Leytonstonia and Wanstonia, of Cuerdenia, the Tree Fairs, Road Alert!, Hyde Park or New Age Diggers, Greenham women, the Peace Convoy, the Quercus Tribe, hunt saboteurs, Undercurrents, Rainbow Collective, Crass, Sunnyside, the People's Free Festivals, Surfers Against Sewage – why not?, Poison Girls, the crusties and fluffies and spikeys, people at Shoreham and Brightlingsea, The Big Issue, New Squatland Yard, Earth First!, Spiral Tribe, Counter Information, AK Press, Bedlam, Green Deserts, Justice?, Freedom Network, Free Information Network, Class War, Exodus Collective, the good people of Pollok Free State, of Tipi Valley, Advance Party, DS4A, Reclaim the Streets, Rainbow Fields Villagers . . . et cetera, (utopian) et cetera, (autonomous) et cetera, (radical) et cetera, (musical) et cetera, (partying) et cetera . . .

NOTES

Introduction: the culture(s) of resistance

1. On the album *Anarchy*, London 1994.
2. Dave Hill, 'The New Righteous', *Observer*, Life Magazine, 12 February 1995, p. 20.
3. Theodore Roszak, *The Making of a Counter Culture: Reflections on the Technocratic Society and Its Youthful Opposition*, London 1970, p. 3.
4. Stuart Hall and Martin Jacques, eds, *New Times: The Changing Face of Politics in the 1990s*, London 1989, p. 14.
5. Anthony Esler, *Bombs, Beards and Barricades: 150 Years of Youth in Revolt*, New York 1971, pp. 7–8.
6. Esler, p. 303.
7. Elizabeth Nelson, *The British Counter-Culture, 1966–73: A Study of the Underground Press*, London 1989, p. ix.
8. Daniel A. Foss and Ralph W. Larkin, 'From "The Gates of Eden" to "Day of the Locust": An Analysis of the Dissident Youth Movement of the 1960s and Its Heirs of the Early 1970s – the Post-movement Groups', *Theory and Society*, vol. 3, no. 1, Spring 1976, p. 46.
9. Foss and Larkin, p. 60.
10. Richard Taylor and Colin Pritchard, *The Protest Makers: The British Nuclear Disarmament Movement of 1958–1965, Twenty Years On*, Oxford 1980, p. 110.
11. Quoted in Nelson, p. 123.
12. Penny Rimbaud, *The Last of the Hippies . . . An Hysterical Romance*, Glasgow 1982, p. 24. This is a reprint of some of the material originally included in a booklet called *A Series of Shock Slogans and Mindless Token Tantrums* accompanying the 1982 Crass record *Christ: The Album*.
13. Quoted in Douglas Rushkoff, *Cyberia: Life in the Trenches of Hyperspace*, London 1994, p. 185.
14. Stewart Home, *The Assault on Culture: Utopian Currents from Lettrisme to Class War*, Stirling 1991, p. 84.
15. Jon Savage, *England's Dreaming: Sex Pistols and Punk Rock*, London 1991, p. 195.
16. Sarah Thornton, 'Moral Panic, the Media, and British Rave Culture', in Andrew Ross and Tricia Rose, eds, *Microphone Fiends: Youth Music and Youth Culture*, London 1994, p. 177.
17. Quotations are from Lauren Langman, 'Dionysus – Child of Tomorrow: Notes on Post-industrial Youth', *Youth and Society*, vol. 3, pt 1, 1971–72, p. 83. The subsequent quotation is from p. 82.
18. Taken from an unpublished interview by Jon Savage with members of Crass in 1989. I am extremely grateful to Jon Savage for making this material available to me.

19. Thornton, p. 177.

20. Quoted in Rimbaud, *Last of the Hippies*, p. 8.

21. Hakim Bey, 'The Temporary Autonomous Zone', in *TAZ: The Temporary Autonomous Zone, Ontological Anarchy, Poetic Terrorism*, Brooklyn, NY 1991, p. 106.

22. Bey, p. 126.

23. A phrase borrowed from the introduction to another book of alternative histories: Ron Sakolsky and James Koehnline, eds, *Gone to Croatan: Origins of North American Dropout Culture*, Edinburgh 1993, p. 10.

1   The free festivals and Fairs of Albion

1. Quoted in Alan Beam, *Rehearsal for the Year 2000 (Drugs, Religions, Madness, Crime, Communes, Love, Visions, Festivals and Lunar Energy): The Rebirth of the Albion Free State (Known in the Dark Ages as England): Memoirs of a Male Midwife (1966–1976)*, London 1976, p. 160, emphasis in the original. Some of the material in this chapter is developed from ideas raised in a paper I gave at the sixth Utopian Studies Society annual meeting, which I organized at the University of Central Lancashire in March 1995. Many thanks to all who commented on it.

2. Quoted in Beam, *Rehearsal*, p. 205. Boveen was not the judge's real name: Beam's extraordinary memoirs make great use of pseudonyms, some less flattering than others. As 'Alan Beam' explains at the start: '"I" in these notes am nobody, or rather several characters rolled into one and improved by wish-fulfilment.' 'Alan has asked me to maintain the secrecy and, since half the other names in his and this book are pseudonymous anyway, I'm doing just that. Besides, Karen Eliot wouldn't have it any other way.

3. Beam, p. 161.

4. On the album *Space Oddity*, London 1970.

5. Daniel A. Foss and Ralph W. Larkin, 'From "The Gates of Eden" to "Day of the Locust": An Analysis of the Dissident Youth Movement of the 1960s and Its Heirs of the Early 1970s – the Post-movement Groups', *Theory and Society*, vol. 3, no. 1, Spring 1976, pp. 47–50.

6. Lauren Langman, 'Dionysus – Child of Tomorrow: Notes on Post-industrial Youth', *Youth and Society*, vol. 3, pt 1, 1971–72, p. 93.

7. On the album *The Best of Gil Scott-Heron*, New York 1984.

8. Quoted in Elizabeth Nelson, *The British Counter-Culture, 1966–73: A Study of the Underground Press*, London 1989, p. 101.

9. Nelson, p. 100.

10. Nigel Fountain, *Underground: The London Alternative Press, 1966–74*, London 1988, pp. 76–7.

11. Bruce Garrard, *The Alternative Sector: Notes on Green Philosophy, Politics and Economics*, Glastonbury 1994, pp. 14–15.

12. Though Phun City is described elsewhere as 'the first completely free festival' (Don Aitken, 'Twenty Years of Festivals', *Festival Eye*, Summer 1990, p. 18), I'm reluctant to press for its originary status: as well as the free one-day London park concerts, there were a number of smaller local free events which preceded it, such as the one organized by David Bowie that he sings about in 'Memory of a Free Festival'. Retreating from his first burst of fame in 1969, Bowie opened an arts lab in Beckenham, Kent. He 'organised a Free Festival down there, and the Mayor of Bromley came along together with the Chief of Police, and they all congratulated him on the way it was run' (George Tremlett, *The David Bowie Story*, London 1974, p. 73). In a move that suggests the temporary eclipse of musical judgement by cultural idealism, Bowie released the song as a double-A-sided single in June 1970. Phun City was, though, a national – and documented – event.

13. Fountain, p. 117.

14. For images of the early British festival scene, see Jeremy Sandford and Ron Reid, *Tomorrow's People*, London 1974.

15. Nelson, p. 98.

16. As reported in the *New Musical Express* of the time. See David Heslam, *The NME Rock 'n' Roll Years*, London 1992, p. 228.

17. Quoted from an anonymous single-sheet A4 leaflet, 'Free Festivals in England 1970–1978'. Crass, as often though supplying the most acute insider information on counterculture, draw attention to the problem of relying on fairy tale as oppositional narrative: 'a tradition in rock music that has become part of our way of life – the free festival. Free music, free space, free mind; at least that, like "once upon a time", is how the story goes.' Penny Rimbaud, *The Last of the Hippies . . . An Hysterical Romance*, Glasgow 1982, p. 5.

18. Beam, p. 165. The counterculture creates its own heroes in Romantic mode. Compare Alan Beam's description of Ubi with Penny Rimbaud's description of Phil Russell aka Wally Hope, instigator of the first Stonehenge Free Festival: 'Phil Hope was a smiling, bronzed, hippy warrior. His eyes were the colour of the blue skies he loved, his neatly cut hair was the gold of the sun that he worshipped. He was proud and upright, anarchistic and wild, pensive and poetic' (Rimbaud, p. 5). I hate to make this point, but – recalling the connections that have occasionally been made between 1960s counterculture, Fascism and Romanticism (see note 60) – the physical description here is surprisingly Aryan.

19. The ones I quote from being Alan Beam, Don Aitken and the 'Free Festivals' leaflet; others are rumour and the odd letter from people who remember.

20. Originally a free festival for one year (1971), Glastonbury Fayre survives in the 1990s catering to youth and the ageing idealists who want the freedom but not the danger. (Is that fair? Probably not: on several occasions in the eighties the harassed Peace Convoy was given a field by organizer Michael Eavis as a temporary haven.) For the 1995 Glastonbury Festival of Contemporary Performing Arts there were 65,000 tickets at £65 a throw, which sold out in record time. The underground theory magazine *Aufheben* has called Glastonbury 'the police-benefit festival', claiming that, '[a]lthough billed as a benefit for Greenpeace or CND, a far greater proportion of the takings goes directly to the police' (*Aufheben*, no. 4, Summer 1995, pp. 7, 26).

21. Rimbaud, p. 6. Wally Hope's story is told by Rimbaud in *The Last of the Hippies*, and by Bruce Garrard in 'The Legacy of Wally Hope' in *The Alternative Sector*. I didn't know until I began this book why I and thousands of others at the late 1970s Reading festivals would wander round late at night shouting 'Wally! Wally!' as though we'd lost a friend. Ignorant of the tribute I was paying, I'm glad I did it anyway.

22. Kevin Hetherington, 'Stonehenge and Its Festival: Spaces of Consumption', in Rob Shields, ed., *Lifestyle Shopping*, London 1992, p. 88.

23. Quoted in Michael Balfour, *Stonehenge and Its Mysteries*, London 1979, p. 171.

24. Rimbaud, p. 17; my emphasis.

25. A number of underground publications deal with aspects of the Stonehenge story, testaments to the continuing interest in it as a place and as an event. See for instance John Michell, *Stonehenge: Its History, Meaning, Festival, Unlawful Management, Police Riot '85 and Future Prospects*, second edition, London 1986. Photographer and Beanfield veteran Alan Lodge published a collection of photographs called *Stonehenge: Solstice Ritual* in 1987. The yearly struggle to re-establish the festival is described in a series of pamphlets from Unique Publications in Glastonbury, edited by Bruce Garrard and others. The events preceding the 1986 festival attempt are dealt with in a report by the National Council for Civil Liberties (now Liberty): *Stonehenge: A Report into the Civil Liberties Implication of the Events Relating to the Convoys of Summer 1985 and 1986*, London 1986. Newsletters from the national Stonehenge Campaign are well worth a read.

26. George Melly, *Revolt into Style: The Pop Arts in Britain*, Harmondsworth 1970, p. 119.

27. On *Bingo Master's Breakout EP*, London 1978.

28. I have several records on this label, mostly singles by Alternative TV bought in the late 1970s. It's only researching this book that I became aware of the possible reference in the label name, though: Phun City hippy festival of 1970 resituated to urban punk London in 1978.

29. Perry's punk fanzine *Sniffin' Glue* encapsulated the DIY ethos of punk, telling its readers 'don't be satisfied with what *we* write. Go out and start your own fanzines.' Another fanzine famously commanded, 'This is a chord, This is another, This is a third, NOW FORM A BAND.' (See Jon Savage, *England's Dreaming: Sex Pistols and Punk Rock*, London 1991, pp. 279–81). More recently, Perry has been sampled in the music of anarcho-band Chumbawumba, a neat tribute. As we'll see, DIY culture is a thriving way of life in the 1990s.

30. Alternative TV, 'How Much Longer'/'You Bastard'. London 1977.

31. On the album *What You See . . . Is What You Are*, London 1978.

32. Rimbaud, p. 5; my emphasis.

33. Beam, *Rehearsal*, p. 185.

34. Rimbaud, p. 11. I should make the point that, in their dealings with various cultures of resistance over the years, not all British police have jettisoned the right to the image of the fair-minded bobby. For instance, when generators failed one night, the stage at an early Stonehenge Free was lit up by police vehicle headlights. In the wake of the Battle of the Beanfield, one unidentified officer commented despairingly: 'I didn't join the police force to do that – what are they doing nicking women and children? What crime have they committed? There was no breach of the peace until we came on site' (quoted in *United You're Nicked: New Statesman and Society Criminal Justice and Public Order Bill Supplement*, London 1994, p. vi).

35. Rimbaud, p. 10.

36. Quoted in Rimbaud, p. 9.

37. *Pop Festivals: Advisory [Stevenson] Committee on Pop Festivals Report and Code of Practice*, London 1973, p. 8.

38. *Free Festivals: First Report of the Working Group on Pop Festivals*, London 1976, pp. 1 and 19.

39. Both of these touchingly utopian Department of Environment reports include an appendix on 'What to wear and what to take to a pop festival'! The final report, from 1978, is altogether less sunny: for instance, its title is *Pop Festivals and Their Problems*. It should also be noted that, while the Chief Constable of Thames Valley Police, one David Holdsworth, viewed it as 'a rather nasty, noisy, dirty, drug-infested Free Festival' (David Holdsworth, *The New Society: Development of Pop and 'Free' Festivals in the Thames Valley Police Area, 1972–1975*, p. 32), the government itself offered the alternative site for Windsor, the 1975 People's Free Festival at a disused airfield owned by the Department of Environment at Watchfield, Berkshire. Long-time festival welfare worker Don Aitken notes that 'Those who should share the credit for this are Roy Jenkins, the late Tony Crosland, Peter Melchett, and Canon Stephen Verney' (Aitken, p. 19). Michael Clarke's book *The Politics of Pop Festivals* (London 1982) tells the in-depth story of Windsor and the negotiations around the unique involvement of the government at Watchfield. A flavour of the Watchfield Free can be gleaned from the site letters produced at the festival by Freek Press, reprinted by the Suburban Guerillas at Zephyr Press in 1989.

40. I'm not sure this is accurate: France has also had a tradition of free festivals, and the autonomy movement in Italy in the seventies made sure that many festivals were free even if that wasn't what their organizers originally had in mind.

41. There is at least one British precedent, too. At the Weeley festival of rock music in Clacton in August 1971, gangs of Hell's Angels went on the rampage. Quickly pinpointing for revenge the Angels' central subcultural icon, a smart group of festival-goers trashed their bikes. I also have a personal recollection of Hell's Angels causing major trouble with other festival-goers at the Deeply Vale People's Free Festival in Lancashire some time in the late 1970s.

42. The description quoted here and below is taken from Rimbaud, p. 6.

43. 'Bikers Riot at Stonehenge', *New Musical Express*, 28 June 1980.

44. I'm told by Don Aitken, who has been involved in the festival scene since its beginnings, that the Battle of the Beanfield is now used in police training as a case study of how not to approach such a situation. So that's good, isn't it – something positive has come of it all. Personal letter, 18 April 1995.

45. Fiona Earle et al., *A Time to Travel? An Introduction to Britain's Newer Travellers*, Lyme Regis, Dorset 1994, p. 18.

46. Balfour, p. 177. And they were only fenced off from the public in 1978, an act which, incidentally, 'was contrary to a Deed of Gift made with the presentation of Stonehenge to the nation': Balfour, p. 168.

47. Don Aitken suggested another motivation to me: 'I think I first realised Stonehenge was doomed when (I think it was 1982) signs began to appear on the main drag advertising drugs in weight quantities. People weren't just buying drugs to take at the festival – they were coming specifically to buy drugs to take back home to distribute.' Aitken's term to describe the dealings within free festivals is 'anarcho-capitalism'. Personal letter, 18 April 1995.

48. Quoted in Nick Davies, 'Inquest on a Rural Riot', *Observer*, 9 June 1985, p. 3. Subsequent quotations are from this and a more quickly written piece, Tim Rayment and Maurice Chittenden, 'Stonehenge "Peace Convoy" in Pitched Battle with Police', *Sunday Times*, 2 June 1985, pp. 1 and 9.

49. Jay, quoted in Richard Lowe and William Shaw, *Travellers: Voices of the New Age Nomads*, London 1993, pp. 75–6.

50. I'm not being utopian here. In *The Enemy Within: MI5, Maxwell and the Scargill Affair* (London 1994) Seumas Milne writes: 'It has only gradually become apparent . . . how near the government came to defeat at the

hands of the striking miners in 1984' (pp. 15–16). In at least one critical meeting, iron Margaret Thatcher went 'wobbly'.

51. Milne, p. 20.

52. In a section headed 'More Law, Less Order', the National Council for Civil Liberties report on Stonehenge discusses the links between police tactics during the miners' strike and the events leading up to the Beanfield. The report concludes that 'The treatment of these travellers by the media, politicians and police shows how easily the civil liberties of an unpopular minority can be swept aside' (p. 37).

53. Nelson, p. 99.

54. Quoted in Richard Barnes, *The Sun in the East: Norfolk And Suffolk Fairs*, Kirstead, Norfolk 1983, p. 69. For much of the historical information, texts, images and reminiscences on the fairs, I am deeply indebted to Richard Barnes's book. Unless footnoted otherwise, all subsequent quotations about the Fairs in this section are taken from *Sun in the East*. Sandra Bell's self-help booklet, *Build Another Barsham: A Guide to Faire Making* (1975) includes information on everything from longdrops to public liability insurance, as well as some historical material.

55. See Bob Pegg's *Rites and Riots: Folk Customs of Britain and Europe* (Poole, Dorset 1981) for a run through some of the more spectacular surviving folkloric events. See E. Alan Jones's *Yorkshire Gypsy Fairs, Customs and Caravans 1885–1985* (Beverley, East Yorkshire 1986) for Appleby and other horse fairs. Clarke's *The Politics of Pop Festivals* deals in passing with the phenomenon of medieval fairs in the 1970s.

56. Alan Beam writes: 'I have heard it said that the immature hippies went to Windsor, the mature ones to Barsham. They coincided in 1974.' Personal letter, 2 May 1995.

57. Richard Barnes, personal letter, 7 April 1995.

58. Richard Barnes corrects me here: 'the true picture of site crews is one of stress and unenviable responsibilities – most people would rather leave the work to others and just groove. The ability and the equipment for putting on Fairs is still here and one forever hears the question "Aren't there any Fairs this year?" as if it was someone else's job to organise them.' Personal letter, 7 April 1995.

59. Beam, p. 138.

60. The common link between 1960s culture of resistance and early-nineteenth-century Romanticism can be read much less positively. Citing work on the connections between Nazism and Romanticism, Theodore Roszak also quotes playwright Arnold Wesker calling 1960s hippies 'pretty little fascists', and sketches an apocalyptic version of the counterculture with dark humour as 'a vision of rampant, antinomian mania, which in the name of permissiveness threatens to plunge us into a dark and savage age' (*The Making of a Counter Culture: Reflections on the Technocratic Society and Its Youthful Opposition*, London 1970, pp. 73–4).

61. Twenty years on, ragged beggars are no longer a summer fancy-dress routine; they're just an easy target for thugs and parliamentarians of all hues.

62. Though in fairness to the fairs, blaming the convoy for the deterioration of an insular scene was also a strategy of the free festival movement. George Firsoff of Free Information Network, a decentralized group which has distributed information about festivals over the years, writes: 'I feel let down by the Traveller movement. The Free Festival movement and the issue of religious access to Stonehenge . . . have been totally taken over in the media and the academic world by the issue of "Travellers". . . . Once upon a time, Free Festivals attracted thousands of young people from cities and I think that the main reason they stopped coming, and the festivals themselves died, is because the festivals and the Travellers' movement within it were unable and often unwilling to cope with the violence and banditry of a minority of their number, and *not* because of police harassment.' In Earle et al., p. 164.

63. Rimbaud, p. 16.

2   O life unlike to ours! Go for it! New Age travellers

1. Don Aitken, 'Twenty Years of Festivals', *Festival Eye*, Summer 1990, p. 19.
2. Brig Oubridge, 'Convoy Myth', *Festival Eye*, June 1986, p. 10.
3. Traveller Jo Waterworth wrote in a recent letter: 'When I first went "on the road" 82/83 the summer

started with a month at Stonehenge, where hopefully you made a fair amount of money, then you could choose between the eastern circuit – taking in the Norwich Free and any Albion Fairs and strawberry-picking interludes, usually ending with the Tree Fair – or the western circuit which covered the South-west, Wales and the Cumbrian Moon Fairs. . . . Generally which route to take was decided by the simple expedient of going in the opposite direction to the main convoy.' Personal letter, 6 July 1995.

4. Richard Barnes, *The Sun in the East: Norfolk and Suffolk Fairs*, Kirstead, Norfolk 1983, p. 95.

5. See for example Lionel Rose, *'Rogues and Vagabonds': Vagrant Underworld in Britain 1815–1985*, London 1988. Oubridge's short piece 'Convoy Myth' also offers this line.

6. Which, of course, contributed greatly to the problem of homelessness in the first place – by placing restrictions on the building of council housing, the imposition of increasingly Draconian benefits rules, the introduction of the sick joke of care in the community. . . . In Chapter 6 we'll see how the Criminal Justice Act 1994 extends such unsympathetic policies further still.

7. ADILKNO, *Cracking the Movement: Squatting beyond the Media*, translated by Laura Martz, Brooklyn, NY 1990, p. 8.

8. On the other hand, Tory policies could also insist on unemployed youth living nomadically. In December 1984, DHSS board-and-lodging allowance to unemployed people under twenty-six years of age was to be limited to periods of between two and eight weeks in any one district. 'Thereafter the claimant must move to another district to re-qualify. The object was to keep youngsters "on the move" looking for work. . . . To critics [these new regulations] smacked of a return in modern form to the old harassing approach to vagrants' (Rose, pp. 184–5).

9. Quoted in Richard Lowe and William Shaw, *Travellers: Voices of the New Age Nomads*, London 1993, a collection of first-person accounts of the lives of travellers, p. 56. In this chapter I refer frequently to the experiences of the interviewees in *Travellers*; all short quotations, unless otherwise annotated, are from this book.

10. Kevin Hetherington, 'Stonehenge and Its Festival: Spaces of Consumption', in Rob Shields, ed., *Lifestyle Shopping*, London 1992, p. 85. The experiences of earlier British homeless people are told in Steve Humphries and Pamela Gordon, *Forbidden Britain: Our Secret Past 1900–1960*, London 1994, pp. 190–1.

11. All three are quoted in Lowe and Shaw, pp. 240, 66, 162 respectively.

12. The narrator of the poem (published in 1853) exclaims, 'O life unlike to ours!' during his rapt description of the Oxford University dropout who 'roamed the world with that wild brotherhood'. Borrow's earlier *Lavengro* (1851), a novel partly about the Norfolk gypsy Ambrose Smith, takes its title from a gypsy term meaning 'philologist, lover of words, language, literature'. I suggested a link between New Age travellers and an alternative set of Victorian values first in a review of Lowe and Shaw, *Travellers* in *Anarchist Studies* vol. 2, no. 2, Autumn 1994, pp. 175–7.

13. For another look at this question see Fiona Earle et al., *A Time to Travel? An Introduction to Britain's Newer Travellers*, Lyme Regis, Dorset 1994, especially Chapter 6.

14. Quotations and information are from NCCL, *Stonehenge: A Report into the Civil Liberties Implications of the Events Relating to the Convoys of Summer 1985 and 1986*, London 1986, p. 35, emphasis added.

15. NCCL, p. 43.

16. Hetherington, p. 91.

17. Hetherington, p. 92; my emphasis.

18. Quoted in Lowe and Shaw, pp. 240–1.

19. Quoted in Ann Morgan and Bruce Garrard, *Travellers in Glastonbury*, Glastonbury 1989, p. 7.

20. See, for instance, *The Harmonic Convergence: Press Cuttings, August 1987*, Glastonbury 1987; Andrew Ross, *Strange Weather: Culture, Science and Technology in the Age of Limits*, London 1991, especially Chapter 1, 'New Age – a Kinder, Gentler Science?'

21. Ross, p. 15.

22. Stuart Hall, 'The Meaning of New Times', in Stuart Hall and Martin Jacques, eds, *New Times: The Changing Face of Politics in the 1990s*, London 1989, pp. 116–17; emphasis added.

23. Pat Kane, 'In Thrall to New Age Thrills', *Guardian*, section 2, 4 January 1995, p. 13.

24. Occult derives from the Latin verb *celere*, to conceal; culture – like cult – derives from *colere*, to cultivate.

25. Nigel Fountain, *Underground: The London Alternative Press, 1966–74*, London 1988, p. 215.

26. Ron Sakolsky, Preface to Ron Sakolsky and James Koehnline, eds, *Gone to Croatan: Origins of North American Dropout Culture*, Edinburgh 1993, p. 10.

27. Quoted in Lowe and Shaw, p. 229. A similar, though gendered, shock of opposition is described by Alison Young at Greenham Common Women's Peace Camp: 'On one side, the world of the base, with its miles of barbed and razor wire, grey concrete, watch towers, a hierarchy of uniformed soldiers. On the other side lies the encampment, a haphazard collection of tents, polythene, a disorganized chaos, colourful posters, diversely dressed women.' In Alison Young, *Femininity in Dissent*, London 1990, p. 36.

28. Bruce Garrard, *The Alternative Sector: Notes on Green Philosophy, Politics and Economics*, Glastonbury 1994, p. 27.

29. Patrick Whitefield, *Tipi Living*, Glastonbury 1987, 2nd edition, p. 3.

30. Derek Wall, 'Tepee Valley Left at Mercy of Big Chief Redwood', *Independent on Sunday*, 12 February 1995, p. 20.

31. Whitefield, pp. 17–18.

32. Quoted in Lowe and Shaw, p. 237. A bender is a DIY tent, built by shaping and fixing some flexible branches into a dome and covering the structure with a tarpaulin.

33. Dick Hebdige, 'Redeeming Witness: In the Tracks of the Homeless Vehicle Project', *Cultural Studies*, vol. 7, no. 2, May 1993, p. 175.

34. Quoted in *Creative Mind*, 1988, p. 2.

35. Traveller Alex, quoted in Lowe and Shaw, pp. 23–4.

36. NCCL, p. 4.

37. A little hesitantly, I'm using a footnote to justify the fact that I don't deal extensively with the more than twenty peace camps set up around Britain in the early eighties. I look at them here in relation solely to travellers. Greenham Common Women's Peace Camp in particular has been well documented and analysed. See for instance Alice Cook and Gwyn Kirk, *Greenham Women Everywhere: Dreams, Ideas and Actions from the Women's Peace Movement*, London 1983; Barbara Harford and Sarah Hopkins, eds, *Greenham Common: Women at the Wire*, London 1984; Young, *Femininity in Dissent*. There remains to be written a history of the wider peace camp movement.

38. Was Greenham Common a RAF or USAF air base? It was formally leased to USAF in 1968, though the sign at the gate maintained the pretence of RAF ownership, hence British control. Cook and Kirk have a swift answer in *Greenham Women Everywhere*: 'RAF Greenham Common is used by the US Air Force as part of a NATO agreement. At present, there is no obligation for the US government to obtain Britain's consent before firing missiles from Greenham Common. Hence the base is referred to in . . . [our] text as "USAF Greenham Common"' (p. 4).

39. Maybe *energized* is the wrong word: Jo Waterworth writes to me of the 'very strong and sometimes heavy male energy at the "Carnival". Many of the wimmin from the Main Gate hated their presence.' Personal letter, 6 July 1995.

40. Peter Gardner, *Medieval Brigands: Pictures in a Year of the 'Hippie' Convoy*, Bristol 1987, p. 5.

41. Both quoted in NCCL, pp. 9, 11.

42. Traveller Jay, quoted in Lowe and Shaw, pp. 75–76.

43. Bruce Garrard, ed., *The Green Collective: The Best from the Mailing, 1984*, Glastonbury 1986, pp. 27–8.

44. Bruce Garrard, *The Last Night of Rainbow Fields Village at Molesworth: An Account of the Eviction, February 5th–6th 1985*, Glastonbury 1986, revised edition, p. 8. Subsequent quotations from newspapers come from clippings reproduced in this booklet.

45. Prompted by Bruce Garrard, I'm happy to pass on this information: '(1) it took the MoD *3 months* to plan it, and (2) they spent more in that one night than CND's *entire annual budget!*' Personal letter, 28 June 1995.

46. Garrard, *Last Night*, p. 26.

47. The quotations that follow are taken from Morgan and Garrard.

48. The local police warned against the use of this tow truck. Other forces, though, have been experimenting with their own anti-traveller devices, such as the 'Stinger', a spiked metal belt laid across the road to prevent convoys or any vehicles moving by puncturing their tyres. *The Big Issue*, no. 82, 7 June 1994, p. 6.

49. Quoted in Bruce Garrard, ed., *The Green Collective: The Best From the Mailing, 1985*, Glastonbury 1986, p. 24.

50. Garrard, *Green Collective: The Best From the Mailing, 1985*, p. 21.

51. Bruce Garrard, ed., *The Children of the Rainbow Gathered in the Free State of Avalonia at the Christian Community of Greenlands Farm: The Other Side of the Story, July '85 to January '86*, Glastonbury 1986, p. 29.

52. On the album *Levelling the Land*, London 1991.

53. Quoted in Lowe and Shaw, p. 154.

54. Truck logos as images didn't start with the Levellers: earlier free festival favourites, based in a communal farm in Suffolk and travelling extensively during the early seventies, were the rock band/collective Global Village Trucking Company. Their eponymous album from 1976 features truck images on both cover and lyric sheet, signalling their affinity with travellers and festivals. More recently, at the bottom of every page of the book *A Time to Travel?* are line drawings of travellers and their vehicles, displaying the variety, the ingenuity of the lifestyle. The Levellers' DIY style extends to instrumentation: the violin 'was typically unconventional and eco-logically pure, "recycled" from three different broken violin bodies', while the guitarist used 'an old record player arm acting as pick-ups, as well as an amplifier acquired from the Revillos' (Colin Larkin, ed., *The Guinness Who's Who of Indie and New Wave Music*, Enfield 1992, p. 161).

55. ADILKNO, p. 237.

56. Young, pp. 55, 57.

57. Morgan and Garrard, p. 8.

58. Quoted in Richard Barnes, p. 100.

59. This and the following quotation are taken from Lowe and Shaw, pp. 53, 152 respectively.

60. There's a touch of apocalypse about travellers' vehicles and other living spaces, embracing an earlier, more dirty technology. It's a romantic movable feast that offers an instant mythology, through rejection, and which positions majority culture in total crisis. Older travellers think of the film of John Steinbeck's *The Grapes of Wrath*, younger ones of *Mad Max*. The New Age meets survivalist mentality? The familiar millenarian sense of an ending resonates deeply. Jo Waterworth: 'Survivalist mentality was strong, yes. I thought like that myself, too. We are the ones who know how to heal with herbs (strong among the women, that one), how to live without all the things that will soon be falling apart. A strong sense of the end of the "system" prevailed – how much prophecy and how much wishful thinking?' Personal letter, 6 July 1995.

61. See Peter Gardner's collection of photographs in *Medieval Brigands* and the photographs throughout Earle et al.'s *A Time to Travel?* for illustrations.

62. Earle et al., p. 55.

63. Both quotations are from Lowe and Shaw, pp. 106, 109.

64. Earle et al., pp. 67–8.

65. Lowe and Shaw: Lubi, pp. 51–2; Vic, p. 152; Harry, p. 188.

66. Gardner, p. 7.

67. Alan Beam, *Rehearsal for the Year 2000 (Drugs, Religions, Madness, Crime, Communes, Love, Visions, Festivals and Lunar Energy): The Rebirth of the Albion Free State (Known in the Dark Ages as England): Memoirs of a Male Midwife (1966–1976)*, London 1976, p. 160.

68. Document supplied in personal letter from Steve Staines, 21 September 1995.

69. Alan Dearling, in Earle et al., p. iv.

70. Both quotations are from Lowe and Shaw, pp. 96–7, 4.

71. Quoted in Lowe and Shaw, p. 239.

3 CRASS 621984 ANOK4U2

1. Bob Marley, 'Trenchtown Rock', on *African Herbsman*, London 1973; Patrik Fitzgerald, 'Make It Safe', on *Grubby Stories*, London 1979 (ellipses in the original).

2. A slightly later version of post-punk recuperation is offered in the anonymous republished punk text *The End Of Music* (Clydeside 1982): 'It has been necessary to create an image of "unemployed youth" which is then sold to unemployed youth as an identity. UB40 reproduced a UB40 as their first album cover, thus encouraging the unemployed to spend a portion of their pittance on a symbol of their own misery' (p. 2). In *The Most Radical Gesture: The Situationist International in a Postmodern Age* (London 1992) Sadie Plant raises the more dizzyingly

Situationist question of whether, as a result of the early involvement of Malcolm McLaren and Jamie Reid in punk, there is the 'possibility that it was in some sense already recuperated before it had even begun' (p. 144).

3. For a discussion of the formation and significance of independent record labels in the context of British punk, see Johnny Rogan's introduction to Colin Larkin, ed., *The Guinness Who's Who Of Indie And New Wave Music*, Enfield 1992, pp. 5–9. Jon Savage notes that by the autumn of 1977 the independent labels 'had combined to form an alternative, countrywide distribution system . . . [with] some degree of autonomy . . . a promise of decentralization': 'Xerox music' (Savage, *England's Dreaming: Sex Pistols and Punk Rock*, London 1991, p. 417).

4. Stewart Home, *The Assault on Culture: Utopian Currents from Lettrisme to Class War*, Stirling 1991, p. 102. In terms of record sales, Crass dominated the alternative charts with each new release for a number of years in the early eighties. Their average sales of albums up to 1995 approaches 250,000 each. Many records mysteriously disappeared or were entirely absent from the national charts – for instance, *Penis Envy* entered at number 17 in the album charts in 1981 for one week only, even though sales increased in subsequent weeks. Personal communication with Penny Rimbaud, 20 November 1995.

5. Savage, p. 584. More critical attention is starting to be paid to Crass and their culture. See my 'Postmodernism and the Battle of the Beanfield: British Anarchist Music and Text of the 1970s and 1980s', in Steven Earnshaw, ed., *Postmodern Surroundings*, Amsterdam 1994, pp. 147–66; see also Craig O'Hara, *The Philosophy of Punk: More Than Noise!!*, Edinburgh 1995. Various ex-members are themselves working on books directly or indirectly about Crass.

6. The Situationists were the largely French group of extreme left cultural/political writers and artists who influenced the events of May 1968 with their rejection of traditional left politics, replacing this with a satirical and critical construction of the spectacle, and slogans such as 'Be reasonable: demand the impossible', and 'Never work'. See Plant, *The Most Radical Gesture*, or Greil Marcus, *Lipstick Traces: A Secret History of the Twentieth Century*, London 1989.

7. Home, p. 85.

8. Crass, *Best Before 1984: Crass Singles Collection* (London 1987). This double album includes a self-written potted history of the band: 'In Which Crass Voluntarily "Blow Their Own"'.

9. I make great use in this chapter of a comprehensive 1989 unpublished interview with Crass by Jon Savage. Most of the later unannotated quotations from the band are from this interview.

10. Paul Gilroy, *'There Ain't No Black in the Union Jack': The Cultural Politics of Race and Nation*, London 1987, p. 125.

11. Dave Laing, *One Chord Wonders: Power and Meaning in Punk Rock*, Milton Keynes 1985, pp. 112–13.

12. Quoted in Home, p. 96.

13. Dick Hebdige, *Subculture: The Meaning of Style*, London 1979, pp. 104–6.

14. Unlike the Situationists and other non-Marxist subversive groups, Crass tended to avoid humour as a political strategy, especially in their later material: 'Oh yes, you can inwardly laugh at the absurdity, / Satirise the obscenity, but the hysteria soon wears thin . . . / We are ruled by dangerous mad-people / What's funny about that for fucks sake?' (*Yes Sir, I Will*, London 1983).

15. *Yes Sir, I Will*.

16. 'In Which Crass Voluntarily "Blow Their Own"'.

17. Penny Rimbaud elaborates: 'Not so much nerves as the certainty that had we released it legitimately it would immediately have been seized. By dismissing it as a bootleg smuggled in from the Continent, we were able to distribute over 20,000 copies – they were free and simply and randomly slipped into records (punk, classical, jazz, pop) by sympathetic dealers'. Personal letter, 28 May 1995.

18. Laing, p. 113.

19. Quoted in John Street, *Rebel Rock: The Politics of Popular Music*, Oxford 1986, p. 17.

20. Mark E. Smith, *The Fall Lyrics*, Berlin 1985, p. 54; 'Cash 'n' Carry' is on The Fall's album *Grotesque (After the Gramme)*, London 1980.

21. I may be getting carried away here: the Smiths (on Rough Trade), Joy Division/New Order (on Factory) are clearly other important instances of successful outfits staying with their independent labels. There's not the same political intent stated with these as with Crass, though.

22. Larkin, p. 73.

23. In *Spray It Loud* (London 1982) Jill Posener captures the variety of graffiti to be seen on British streets, explaining that 'the feminist movement, No Nukes campaigners, the anti-smoking lobby and anarchists have all become street writers' (p. 11) – suggesting street fighters, too? See in particular Chapter 2, 'Persons Unknown'.

24. This description of the film 'Autopsy' is found on the poster cover of *Stations of the Cross*, London 1979.

25. *Détournement*, Sadie Plant explains, 'is a turning round and a reclamation of lost meaning. . . . The subversions of comic strips . . . were perfect examples of such appropriation: in the pages of *Internationale Situationniste*, true love stories were confused with bubbles of political propaganda. . . . These methods were essentially reworkings of those employed by the dadaists and surrealists, extended by the situationists to every area of social and discursive life' (Plant, pp. 86–7). A clear example in punk is Jamie Reid's later-withdrawn picture sleeve for the Pistols' 'Holidays in the Sun' (London 1977), though see *The End Of Music* (p. 11) for a nice sneering critique of the Pistols' use of Situ techniques as the commodification of the spectacle.

26. Interview by Russell Southwood and Tony Nicholls, in *Leveller*, no. 25, April 1979, pp. 24–5. For a short history and survey of recent punk fanzines – DIY magazines – see Paul Rutherford's *Fanzine Culture*, Glasgow 1992; an American view of punk fanzines is found in O'Hara's *The Philosophy of Punk*, especially Chapter 4.

27. Both quotations are from *Yes Sir, I Will*.

28. Savage, p. 12.

29. A more problematic reading of this song is offered by Paul Gilroy, when he notes that '[t]he Stranglers' "I Feel Like a Wog" and the Clash's "(White Man) in Hammersmith Palais" both featured almost continually in the Rock Against Communism chart in *Bulldog*, the paper of the Young National Front. They held the number one and number two positions as late as September 1982' (Gilroy, p. 124).

30. The song is 'Punk is Dead', from *The Feeding of the Five Thousand*, London 1978.

31. Researching this a couple of years after I first analysed 'Women', I dug out letters from Crass, from a trunk in an attic, including this one, the first:

25 April 1979.

dear George,

. . . I find a lot of 'feeding of the 5000' a bit moderate now, at the time we were pleased with it, but inevitably, much of it now sounds thin. I'm sorry you find 'women' contrived, I don't think it is, it was recorded live and isn't played around with at all. You probably won't like the new recording we've done of Asylum for the same reason, we're hoping to get it pressed ourselves, we want to get it out on record because what it says matters to us. fuck comes up a lot because I suppose that's the way we speak, it wasn't fabricated, honest!! . . .

Penny Rimbaud

How ironic: as a teenage fan I apparently dislike the piece; as a thirtysomething academic, it's the first one I ever discuss.

32. Southwood and Nicholls, p. 24.

33. 'In Which Crass Voluntarily "Blow Their Own"'.

34. Peter Murray and Linda Murray, *The Penguin Dictionary of Art and Artists*, Harmondsworth 1986, pp. 206–7.

35. 'In Which Crass Voluntarily "Blow Their Own"'.

36. Quoted in Tom Vague, *The Great British Mistake: Vague 1977–92: A Fourteen and a Half Years' Struggle Against Lies, Stupidity and Cowardice: A Reckoning with the Destroyers of the Punk Rock Movement*, Edinburgh 1994, p. 31.

37. 'In Which Crass Voluntarily "Blow Their Own"'.

38. Interestingly, though, the record is dedicated 'In loving memory of Wally Hope', the instigator of the Stonehenge Free Festivals. Penny Rimbaud cites Wally Hope as a major inspiration behind the formation of Crass. He has written to me that 'More than any other single event, Wally Hope's death led to the formation of Crass. . . . Crass in part succeeded in avenging Wally's death.' Personal letter, 28 May 1995.

39. 'In Which Crass Voluntarily "Blow Their Own"'. As an antidote to the occasional factual (as opposed to rhetorical) hyperbole by Crass, it's worth noting that a reader's survey undertaken by the British anarchist fortnightly *Freedom* in 1993 found only 7 out of 100 readers who described themselves as 'anarcho-pacifists'. Other self-descriptions included anarcho-communist (21), green anarchists (14), anarcho-syndicalists (12). Quoted in Andy Chan, 'Anarchists, Violence and Social Change: Perspectives from Today's Grassroots', *Anarchist Studies*, vol. 3, no. 1, Spring 1995, pp. 45–68.

4 Evereeebodeee's freee; or, Causing a public new sense? Rave (counter)culture

1. Nigel Fountain, *Underground: The London Alternative Press, 1966–74*, London 1988, pp. 26–7.

2. I'm not terribly happy with using the term 'rave' in this chapter, since, as anyone involved in the scene knows, rave refers to a specific time and music – the late eighties after acid house parties, and an identifiable dance music that predates the splintering of the music into techno, hardcore, jungle and so on. I am using it, though, as a convenient umbrella term to discuss both the commercialization of the late eighties dance scene and the move towards free parties and festivals. There simply isn't a better term. Actually the resurgence in the currency of 'rave' can be put down to the British government, which, as we'll see in Chapter 6, uses it in the text of the Criminal Justice and Public Order Act 1994.

3. Daniel A. Foss and Ralph W. Larkin, 'From "The Gates of Hell" to "Day of the Locust": An Analysis of the Dissident Youth Movement of the 1960s and Its Heirs of the Early 1970s – The Post-movement Groups', *Theory and Society*, vol. 3, no. 1, Spring 1976, p. 47.

4. Antonio Melechi, 'The Ecstasy of Disappearance', in Steve Redhead, ed., *Rave Off: Politics and Deviance in Contemporary Youth Culture*, Aldershot 1993, p. 29.

5. Melechi, p. 33.

6. One of the slogans from May 1968 in Paris was 'Sous les pavés, la plage'.

7. Kristian Russell, 'Lysergia Suburbia', in Redhead, *Rave Off*, p. 119. Some clubbers moved on from Ibiza to the resort of Rimini in Italy. More recently still, acid beach parties attract dance tourists to sites clearly resonant of the hippy trails of the sixties: Goa in India, Ko Phangan in the Gulf of Thailand, for instance.

8. Melechi, p. 36.

9. Russell, pp. 126–7.

10. Russell, p. 97.

11. Okay, more self-importantly serious pop music fans. You know, like me. At school, I sneered at Oxford bags and Wigan Casino.

12. Steve Redhead, 'The Politics of Ecstasy', in *Rave Off*, p. 23. This is also the focus of Sarah Thornton's *Club Cultures: Music, Media and Subcultural Capital* (Cambridge 1995). Thornton interestingly looks at the rave scene in order to question the standard 'mainstream–subculture divide' (p. 95) which situates subculture as resistance. While denying that challenging this paradigm constitutes a retreat from political engagement, however, it's only in her conclusion that Thornton mentions the direct-resistant politics of rave through free parties and opposition to the Criminal Justice Act.

13. An old cinema/bingo hall was squatted for a series of free parties. Handy hint: to throw police off the scent of illegality, publicity was in the form of invitations to a 'midsummer event for social workers and their clients in the Notting Hill area, by kind permission of the authorities concerned' (Alan Beam, *Rehearsal for the Year 2000 (Drugs, Religions, Madness, Crime, Communes, Love, Visions, Festivals and Lunar Energy): The Rebirth of the Albion Free State (Known in the Dark Ages as England): Memoirs of a Male Midwife (1966–1976)*, London 1976, p. 137)! In the nineties in Brighton, anti-Criminal Justice Act group Justice! squat a derelict courthouse. A bit like an Albion Free State manifesto, a sign lists a number of facets of the current (I hesitate to say new) DIY culture, including 'Grow fins and swim' and 'Never laugh at fat bastards in clouds' (Nicholas Saunders, *Ecstasy and the Dance Culture*, London 1995, p. 174).

14. Clubber and writer Mary Anna Wright comments on this description of an underground party: 'I think this illustrates how *different* rave is from previous scenes. On E you don't spit on people – you embrace them. That vibe was the sacred part of the rave experience – it is still there in places today. A celebration of positivity.' Personal letter, 29 September 1995.

15. Theodore Roszak, *The Making of a Counter Culture: Reflections on the Technocratic Society and Its Youthful Opposition*, London 1970, p. 73.

16. Russell, p. 125.

17. Douglas Rushkoff, *Cyberia: Life in the Trenches of Hyperspace*, London 1994, p. 12.

18. Rushkoff, p. 13.

19. Rushkoff, p. 16. Some of the religious possibilities of rave are taken up through trance, shamanism, the

spirituality of the earth and so on. Others are seemingly more prosaic: rave vicars holding Christian services, exhorting youth to SWALLOW GOD.

20. Rushkoff, p. 161.

21. Mary Anna Wright, personal letter, 29 September 1995.

22. Quoted in Richard Lowe and William Shaw, *Travellers: Voices of the New Age Nomads*, London 1993, p. 168.

23. Derek Jones, ed., *Equinox: Rave New World. An Edited Transcript*, p. 15. Programme first shown on Channel 4 Television, 6 November 1994.

24. Philip Tagg, 'From Refrain to Rave: The Decline of Figure and the Rise of Ground', *Popular Music*, vol. 13, part 2, May 1994, pp. 209–10.

25. Quoted in Jones, p. 13.

26. For a more comprehensive story see Harry Shapiro, *Waiting for the Man: The Story of Drugs and Popular Music*, London 1988.

27. For extensive colour examples of flyers and some analysis of their contribution to dance culture see Mike Dorian, *High Flyers*, London 1995.

28. Tagg, p. 213.

29. Nicholas Saunders: 'Designer drugs: the term was originally used to mean compounds that were designed to have the same effect as illicit drugs without being illicit themselves. However, the term is often used to mean new drugs which have been designed to have a particular effect' (p. 16). I use it largely in the second sense.

30. Shapiro, p. 146.

31. Jones, p. 9.

32. Mary Anna Wright, personal letter, 29 September 1995.

33. Tagg, p. 210.

34. Rushkoff, p. 117.

35. Quoted in Russell, p. 152.

36. Hillegonda Rietveld, 'Living the Dream', in Redhead, *Rave Off*, pp. 43, 58.

37. Rietveld, p. 64.

38. Quoted in Russell, p. 135.

39. Rietveld, p. 62.

40. Shapiro, p. 109. Of course, there exists anyway a familiar criticism of the innate conservatism of the mod scene and its various revivals around the Union Jack and versions of Englishness: maybe mod was subculture's precursor to something like Thatcherism.

41. Quoted in Melechi, p. 37.

42. For example, how do we read the fact that, in 1994, rave firm Dance For Life sought to arrange with the Ministry of Defence to hold huge all-night raves at the now disused Greenham Common airbase? As an emblematic retreat from engagement? Or as a knowingly ironic celebration of the success of past political campaigns?

43. Redhead, p. 7. A real sense of such pleasure – and not a little aspirational smugness – can be gleaned from Jonathan Fleming's book *What Kind of House Party is This? The History of a Music Revolution*, Slough, Berkshire 1995. There's little actual comment however on the ideas mentioned in its subtitle – of music revolution – or in its cover blurb: 'from the fifties came ROCK 'N' ROLL, in the seventies it was PUNK ROCK, by the nineties it's called HOUSE MUSIC'.

44. Sarah Thornton, 'Moral Panic, the Media and British Rave Culture', in Andrew Ross and Tricia Rose, eds, *Microphone Fiends: Youth Music and Youth Culture*, London 1994, pp. 180, 179.

45. Melechi, pp. 34–5. The bhangra music and dance scene of Asian youth was itself invisible for many years – does that factor alone make it too 'move to a new order of politics and resistance'?

46. Quoted in Lowe and Shaw, p. 164. Though there is an anarchist politics of the party, as Hakim Bey explains, tongue only slightly in cheek: 'Let us admit that we have attended parties where for one brief night a republic of gratified desires was attained. Shall we not confess that the politics of that night have more reality and force for us than those of, say, the entire US Government? Some of the "parties" we've mentioned lasted for two or three *years*. Is this something worth imagining, worth fighting for?' (Bey, *TAZ*, p. 134)

47. Dave Hesmondhalgh, 'Technoprophecy: A Response to Tagg'. *Popular Music*, vol. 14, part 2, May 1995, p. 262.

48. Both quotations are from Rushkoff, p. 19.

49. Hesmondhalgh, pp. 261–3.

50. Jones, p. 17.

51. Tagg, p. 214. Though out of date for rave music, Andrew Goodwin's 'Sample and Hold: Pop Music in the Digital Age of Reproduction' does offer a good discussion of sampling and other technological interventions. It's in Simon Frith and Andrew Goodwin, eds, *On Record: Rock, Pop and the Written Word*, London 1990.

52. Russell, p. 124.

53. Quoted in Jones, p. 20.

54. Rushkoff, p. 113. Perhaps he really didn't mean 'teeming'.

55. Quoted in Rushkoff, p. 156.

56. Russell, p. 142.

57. Saunders, pp. 6–9.

58. Quoted in Rushkoff, pp. 158–9.

59. Russell, p. 143.

60. Rushkoff, p. 18.

61. The British practice is sometimes overlooked, though, in favour of earlier US events. Thus Russell (p. 137) argues: 'Like the Californian "Be Ins" and "Trips" festivals of 1996 and 1967, these outdoor events, in particular, evoked the same social sensations and sense of unity.'

62. Aitken, 'Twenty Years of Festivals', p. 20. The subsequent quotation comes from a personal letter, 18 April 1995.

63. Tagg, p. 219.

64. Writing in *Festival Eye* of Summer 1990, Alex Rosenberger observes that '[o]ver the past year, links between "house culture" and "festival" culture have been getting more and more obvious. First it was Smileys, bandanas, and an interest in psychedelic drugs; then it was large gatherings out in the open with loud music, and that brought the inevitable media hysteria . . . [and] crazy games of "cops and convoys". . . . *Ravers seem to have squeezed 20 years of "hippydom" into just two*' (p. 13; my emphasis).

65. Spider of Circus Normal, quoted in Lowe and Shaw, p. 88.

66. John, of Bristol Free Information Network, personal letter, 29 September 1995.

67. Mary Anna Wright, 'The Rave-Scene in Britain: A Metaphor for Metanoia', unpublished dissertation for MSc in Human Ecology, University of Edinburgh 1993, p. 18.

68. 'Interview with Aztek', in *Eternity*, no. 31, July 1995, p. 37.

69. Quoted in Lowe and Shaw, p. 169. Two years later, Spirals in Europe returned voluntarily to face trial; the prosecution collapsed and they were acquitted through lack of evidence. Some more traditional free-festival-goers have resented the invasion of the rave scene, calling this particular free sound system Spiral Bribe or Spiral Tripe.

70. 'Sunnyside at the Feel Good Factory', in *Eternity*, no. 31, July 1995, pp. 14–15.

71. Quotations are taken from *The Story of Exodus: A Movement of Jah People, Documented and Presented by Squall: The Magazine for Sorted Itinerants*, London 1995.

72. See *The Story of Exodus* and Tim Malyon's piece 'The Trial of Exodus' in Saunders, for further details.

73. Saunders, p. 177.

5   Direct action of the new protest: eco-rads on the road

1. John of the *Aufheben* collective, 'The Politics of Anti-Road Protest: The No M11 Link Road Campaign and Its Dilemmas', in Clare Zine, ed., *The End of the Beginning: Claremont Road, E11 Not M11*, Leeds/London 1995, pp. 72–3, 75; George Monbiot, 'Whose Land is it Anyway?', *Creative Mind*, no. 27, Summer 1995, p. 9. In relation to Monbiot's criticism of direct action's over-reliance on the negative, see however Neil Nehring, *Flowers in the Dustbin: Culture, Anarchy, and Postwar England*, Ann Arbor, Michigan 1993. Concluding maybe a little predictably with the punk of the Sex Pistols, Nehring none the less constructs what he terms 'cultural anarchism' to argue for 'the usefulness of negation as a reminder of what all dissident politics have in common – contumacy, the angered resistance of authority' (p. 16).

2. Earth First! was founded in the USA around 1980 and in Britain as recently as 1991. I think it's fair to say

that in general terms they have different perspectives, British activists offering a more wide-ranging political critique. Whereas early Earth First! activists in the USA emphasized their non-revolutionary positions, their direct action campaign focusing on simply preserving the American wilderness, in Britain Earth First! is fundamentally more radical, more located in a wider context of social criticism.

3. Iain Donald, 'Off Paper and On to the Land: The Contemporary Grassroots Environmental Movement: Where Does It Come From? Where Is It Going?' Unpublished dissertation for BSc. (Hons) Environmental Quality and Resource Management, University of the West of England, 1995, p. 57. This dissertation includes very useful transcripts of personal interviews undertaken by Donald, called 'Dialogues with the Dongas'.

4. A cartoon from *The End of the Beginning* book by Claremont Road activists showing 'M11 squatters violently evicted' contains groups of people standing around passively while the direct activists do the real work up on the roof. A representative of *Socialist Worker* says: 'Don't worry, we have a new issue'; a Freedom Network member proclaims: 'We are the young people, we are the naive people'; a Liberty representative says: 'This is an infringement'; the Road Alert! member asks: 'Has anyone seen the paperclips?' In Zine, p. 38.

5. Quoted in the *Guardian*, 6 May 1995, p. 27.

6. On the fiftieth anniversary of VE Day in May 1995, 'activists in London squatted a tube station to remind us of direct action during the blitz and post-war for decent housing'. *Counter Information*, no. 43, August/September/October 1995.

7. Most of these examples are taken from April Carter's *Direct Action and Liberal Democracy*, London 1973, pp. 15, 17.

8. However, the swift expansion of anti-roads protest recently is evident in the newness of the language and names that have gained currency: Dongas, Wanstonia, Leytonstonia, Cuerdenia, Scaffoldistas, digger-diving, cherry-pickers, lock-ons . . .

9. This and the subsequent quotation are taken from Carter, pp. 3, 24. It's worth noting that, while direct action has maintained an aura of the subversive, the fanatical, it's actually with the state rather than the individual that its excesses lie. As V.G. Kiernan succinctly puts it, 'its extremist and most acceptable form is war'. In 'Patterns of Protest in English History', in Robert Benewick and Trevor Smith, eds, *Direct Action and Democratic Politics*, London 1972, p. 25.

10. John Jordan, 'An Art of Necessity', in the visual newspaper *Claremont Road E11: A Festival of Resistance*, London 1995, no pagination.

11. Quoted in Donald, p. 37.

12. Craig O'Hara, *The Philosophy of Punk: More Than Noise!!*, Edinburgh 1995, p. 75.

13. O'Hara, pp. 105, 107.

14. Quoted in Fiona Stephens and Wenda Shehata, eds, *The Siege of Shoreham: Reflections from the Front Line*, Brighton 1995, pp. 2, 8, 42 and from the Foreword respectively.

15. Quoted in the *Observer*, 19 June 1994, p. 3.

16. Barbara Bryant, Twyford campaigner and local Conservative councillor, was one of the 'pearls-and-twinsets' brigade (as she puts it) the media were surprised to see protesting with travellers and so on. Her book, *Twyford Down: Roads, Campaigning and Environmental Law*, London 1996, tells the complex story of the lengthy pre-Dongas Tribe struggle against the road.

17. Alexandra Plows, 'The Donga Tribe: Practical Paganism Comes Full Circle', *Creative Mind*, no. 27, Summer 1995, p. 26.

18. André Gorz, *Dear Motorist . . . The Social Ideology of the Motor Car*, pamphlet extracted from *Ecology As Politics*, Oxford, no other publication details, p. 2.

19. Anthony Esler, *Bombs, Beards And Barricades: 150 Years of Youth in Revolt*, New York 1971, p. 18.

20. Linda Grant, 'Just Say No', *Guardian*, Weekend magazine, 3 June 1995, p. 18. Colour-supplement stories on the new protest spectacle and action have flourished; I think without exception, every one I've read offers some degree of sympathy with anti-roads campaigns, and is interspersed with full- or double-page ads. for new cars.

21. Jo Waterworth, personal letter, 6 July 1995.

22. *Schnews*, no. 9, 10 February 1995.

23. Plows, 'Practical Paganism', p. 25.

24. Quoted in Donald, p. 50.

25. Alexandra Plows, 'Eco-philosophy and Popular Protest: The Significance and Implications of the Ideology and Actions of the Donga Tribe', *Alternative Futures and Popular Protest*, vol. 1, Manchester 1995, no pagination.

26. A version of this is published in Earth First!'s *Do or Die*, no. 5, 1995, as 'The Rise (and Fall?) of the Ego-Warrior', pp. 88–9.

27. Plows, 'Practical Paganism', p. 26.

28. Donga Alex (Alexandra Plows), personal letter, 10 October 1995.

29. This and the following quotation are taken from Plows, 'Practical Paganism', pp. 25 and 27 respectively.

30. Quoted in Richard Lowe and William Shaw, *Travellers: Voices of the New Age Nomads*, London 1993, p. 116.

31. Their innocence can perhaps be seen in their expression of shock at discovering 'once we slipped out of the boundaries of society to create our own alternative, how we became targeted, stereotyped and persecuted by that society' (Plows, 'Practical Paganism', p. 25).

32. This and the following quotation are taken from Plows, 'Practical Paganism', pp. 28 and 29 respectively.

33. Donald, p. 67.

34. Plows, 'Practical Paganism', p. 25.

35. John Vidal, 'The Real Earth Movers', *Guardian*, section 2, 7 December 1994, p. 24.

36. Bellamy's subsequently published children's book called *The Roadside*, describing a place in which 'where the old track used to wind, a great six lane road' now runs, turned Earth First!'s reviewer apoplectic with rage. The reviewer quotes from the book: 'Hedgerows have gone . . . the road runs through a deep cutting . . . Despite the cars roaring past only a few metres away, the vixen dozes peacefully in the sun. She knows that her cubs are safe to chase butterflies.' All is well in *The Roadside* because '[t]he road builders have done a good job'. Just like at Twyford Down? *Do or Die*, no. 5, 1995, p. 64.

37. Plows, 'Practical Paganism', p. 25.

38. Jonathon Porritt, 'The Environmentalist's Conclusions', in Bryant, *Twyford Down*, p. 299.

39. I don't know if Rudyard Kipling, that great writer of the Downs and constructor of certain types of Englishness, was invoked, but he certainly should have been.

40. *Schnews*, no. 10, 16 February 1995. In custody, the protesters went on hunger strike. Presumably the magistrates had visions of a suffragette-style situation, which they certainly didn't want on their patch.

41. *Schnews*, no. 9, 10 February 1995.

42. Plows, 'Practical Paganism', pp. 25–6.

43. Plows, 'Eco-philosophy and Popular Protest'.

44. Quoted in Donald, p. 72.

45. Quoted in Donald, p. 68.

46. Only riot vans, dogs, tractors, helicopters, cameras, and Criminal Justice Act section 61 eviction notices were used.

47. Quoted in the local newspaper, *Gazette and Herald*, 10 August 1995, p. 7.

48. Iain Donald tells me that after the event they discovered that the fair Charter of 1499 had been granted by Henry VII to the abbess of an abbey in Winchester. For the Dongas this was not just a delicious coincidence, but further proof of the spiritual power and energy of their original birthplace at Twyford Down, outside Winchester.

49. Iain Donald, personal letter, 2 October 1995.

50. Donga Steff, quoted by Iain Donald in a personal letter, 20 October 1995.

51. Donga Alex, personal letter, 10 October 1995.

52. Andrew Ross, *Strange Weather: Culture, Science and Technology in the Age of Limits*, London 1991, p. 46.

53. Ross, p. 70.

54. Quoted in Donald, p. 73.

55. Quoted in Grant, p. 22.

56. After Twyford, some Dongas went west in search of a low-impact sustainable lifestyle, as travellers reclaiming ancient trackways, on the Freedom Trail; others headed east, into the city, to maintain the more confrontational direct action approach at the No M11 Link Campaign.

57. Gorz, pp. 5, 6.

58. Patrick Field, 'Roots of Resistance', in *A Festival of Resistance*.

59. Roger Geffin, Secret Squirrel and Yellow Pinky, 'News From the Autonomous Zones', *Do or Die*, no. 4, 1994, p. 21. The subsequent quotations about the Chestnut Tree and eviction orders are taken from p. 22.

60. Taken from an unpublished longer version of Phil McLeish's piece 'A View From the Tower', in *A Festival of Resistance*.

61. Zine, p. 9.

62. John of the *Aufheben* collective, 'The Politics of Anti-Road Protest', p. 75. This piece was written during the campaign, and discusses many of the practical and theoretical issues and problems, in particular of Claremont Road.

63. The spectacular nature of the art/performance aspect is well documented in the photographs of *A Festival of Resistance*.

64. This and the following quotation are taken from Zine, pp. 10, 9 respectively.

65. Polysemic dissent has its dangers, too. An eco-rads action against opencast mining in Wales in 1995 rather lost some of its thrust in reports as it sought to link environment and Criminal Justice Act. This was quite successfully picked up and used by defenders of the mine as an instance of the wacky confusion of protesters. The danger of senseless acts of beauty, I suppose, is that the subversive irony of the interrogation of 'sense', common or -less, can be overlooked or sidestepped.

66. John of the *Aufheben* collective, 'The Politics of Anti-Road Protest', pp. 82–3.

67. McLeish, 'A View From the Tower'.

68. As with Twyford Down, other organizations have sprung from the inspiration and energy of the No M11 Link direct action campaign. The nascent Brixton-based Reclaim the Streets group received a massive boost by the actions in this campaign. In a version of the street transformation of Claremont Road, in 1995 Reclaim the Streets spread sand on the tarmac outside Goodge Street underground station in London, set up deckchairs and held a beach party in the middle of a central London road. This was a terrific literalization of that Situ slogan, slightly inverted: *sur* not *sous le pavé, la plage*.

69. *Do or Die*, no. 4, June 1994, Update.

70. As in the name of Greg Piggot's exhibition of photographs of M65 actions, shown at the University of Central Lancashire in early 1995: 'Cuerdenia Rising'.

71. *Schnews*, no. 20, 28 April 1995.

72. Helen Prescott, 'Take to the Trees', *Creative Mind*, no. 26, Spring 1995, pp. 11, 13.

73. *Do or Die*, no. 5, 1995, carries detailed reports of both the M65 and M77 campaigns.

74. *Road Alert! Newsletter*, no. 4, September 1995. Activists who commented on the manuscript of this chapter when it was passed round the Road Alert! office in November 1995 were unanimously critical of my suggestion that these living spaces constituted 'a politicized retreat into the pleasure sites of childhood'. In their words, such spaces are 'innovative, low-tech, good defensive tactics, cheap and easy to build with readily available materials, low-impact, movable, and don't leave marks'.

75. Hakim Bey, 'The Temporary Autonomous Zone', in *TAZ: The Temporary Autonomous Zone, Ontological Anarchy, Poetic Terrorism*, Brooklyn, NY 1991, p. 101.

76. Don't they? Do they?

77. Alan Beam, *Rehearsal for the Year 2000 (Drugs, Religions, Madness, Crime, Communes, Love, Visions, Festivals and Lunar Energy): The Rebirth of the Albion Free State (Known in the Dark Ages as England): Memoirs of a Male Midwife (1966–76)* London 1976, pp. 159, 161.

78. Sadie Plant, *The Most Radical Gesture: The Situationist International in a Postmodern Age*, London 1992, p. 92. The Kabouters quotation below is taken from Plant, pp. 92–3.

79. Stewart Home, *The Assault on Culture: Utopian Currents from Lettrisme to Class War*, Stirling 1991, p. 66.

80. The phrase is by Claremont Road protester Phil McLeish in 'A View From the Tower'.

6   Caught in the Act

1. James Morton, *A Guide to the Criminal Justice and Public Order Act 1994*, London 1994, p. 3. This book contains the full text of the Act, as well as guiding commentary.

2. Quoted in *United You're Nicked: New Statesman and Society Criminal Justice and Public Order Bill Supplement*, London 1994, p. vi.

3. Subcultural style as export rhetoric isn't always such a positive thing: Germany could no doubt have done without the British template for its neo-Nazi skinheads, for instance.

4. On the other hand, I'm advised that, by some readings, the attempt to provide legal definitions of groups and events in the Act can be viewed as preferable to having a wider definition which judges themselves can fill in possibly to the even greater detriment of those the Act is used against. By this argument the text of the Act is the focus rather than leaving things to the vagaries of British judges. This apparently makes for clearer accountability on the part of the government.

5. Tim Malyon, in *United You're Nicked*, p. vii.

6. Quoted in *United You're Nicked*, p. vi.

7. A response to this aspect of the Act in 1995 has been that 'many Travellers have tried to provide their own sites but have run head first into an inflexible planning system. A planning consultant reported to Friends, Families and Travellers that of 37 cases he'd dealt with, only two were passed by the planning authority'. *Friends, Families and Travellers Newsletter*, November 1995.

8. Morton, p. 40.

9. Liberty, *Defending Diversity and Dissent: What's Wrong with the Criminal Justice and Public Order Bill*, London 1994, p. 10.

10. Wright, writing in Nicholas Saunders, *Ecstasy and the Dance Culture*, London 1995, p. 172.

11. On the other hand, maybe it is straightforward. The stated aims of the council- and police-led *Report of Working Party following Illegal Invasion of Castlemorton Common near Malvern, Hereford and Worcester, May 22 to 29 1992* include formulating steps 'to ensure, as far as possible, that an invasion such as that which took place at Castlemorton in May 1992 cannot occur again – anywhere' (p. 1). The working party's main recommendations were twofold: new laws to combat mass trespass and the preparation of plans to deal with any attempt at repetition (p. 2). These appear to translate directly into sections of the Criminal Justice Act. The idea of a sympathetic strategy by government – such as offering sites, as was done at Watchfield for the People's Free Festival in 1975 – would seem to be more remote than ever. Significantly, while the report offers (prejudice under the form of) recommendations on everything from restricting the payment of travellers' state welfare benefits to compensation for local landowners, under one subject area alone it offers 'No recommendations' whatsoever: this is the issue of temporary sites for travellers, places to live, places to hold festivals. The report from the working party – which included three senior police officers from West Mercia constabulary – also mentions without comment or criticism that '[i]n the recent past there have been several incidents where police have used extra-legal powers and tactics' (p. 8). *Extra*-legal – is that the same as *illegal?*

12. Josef Skvorecky, 'Red Music', in *The Bass Saxophone*, London 1980, p. 10.

13. DJ Aztek, interviewed in *Eternity*, no. 31, p. 40.

14. I've found it difficult on occasion not to hit either a paranoiac note (as here) or a potentially excessive one (as with the Nazi comparison) when writing about such a comprehensive series of laws as the Criminal Justice Act.

15. See Hillegonda Rietveld, 'Living the Dream', in Steve Redhead, ed., *Rave Off: Politics and Deviance in Contemporary Youth Culture*, Aldershot 1993, pp. 47–9.

16. Morton, p. 37.

17. The following is taken from a Spiral Tribe leaflet distributed at later free raves: '1000 people were dancing at an Easter party run by Spiral Tribe on Acton Lane, London. At approximately 2.30 a.m. police suddenly sealed off the building. . . . The police then prevented anyone entering or leaving the premises – anyone who attempted it was maliciously beaten to the ground with truncheons and kicked. By 3.30 a.m. a massive force of riot police wearing padded jackets and helmets and wielding shields and batons stormed the building. No warning was given. Sledge hammers and a JCB digger were used to collapse the walls in on the people trapped inside. When they finally got into the building they indiscriminately beat up men, women and children.'

18. Yes and no, I'd reply: yes, its recognizable characteristics are indeed written into the law; no, it's not the music that's banned but unlicensed mass events outdoors at which that and other music is played.

19. George Monbiot, 'Whose Land Is It Anyway?', *Creative Mind*, no. 27, Summer 1995, pp. 7–8.

20. Morton, p. 38.

21. Simon Fairlie, 'On the March', *Guardian*, section 2, 21 January 1994, p. 14.

22. Quoted in *United You're Nicked*, p. xiv.

23. Morton, p. 36.

24. Quoted in the *Observer*, 19 June 1994, p. 3.

25. Liberty, pp. 16–18.

26. *Aufheben*, no. 4, Summer 1995, p. i.

27. Catherine Muller, personal letter, 8 October 1995.

28. A protester, quoted in *Schnews*, no. 43, 6 October 1995: 'One of the great things about rave music is that it winds up the old Bill something chronic.' This *Schnews* includes a special anniversary report on the Battle of Hyde Park.

29. 'The Criminal Justice Bill Riot: Eyewitness Reactions', Leeds, no date, no pagination.

30. In John of the *Aufheben* collective, 'The Politics of Anti-Road Protest: The No M11 Link Road Campaign and its Dilemmas', in Clare Zine, ed., *The End of the Beginning: Claremont Road, E11 Not M11*, Leeds/London 1995, p. 77.

31. *Aufheben*, no. 4, p. 9.

32. *Counter Information*, no. 41, October/November/December 1994. The criticism of the London-based Freedom Network may be equally explicable as a Scottish reaction against the perceived dominance of the South-east of England even in the culture of resistance.

33. *Schnews*, no. 38, 1 September 1995. The first year of Justice? and *Schnews* is documented in their book *Schnews Reader*, Brighton 1995.

34. *Aufheben*, no. 4, p. 20.

35. *The Book: Directory of Active Groups in the UK*, Brighton 1995, first edition, p. 2.

36. DJ Weasel, 'The International Free Party Network: United Systems', *Eternity*, no. 31, July 1995, p. 20.

37. In Saunders, p. 173.

Conclusion; or, Work in progress; or, Et cetera

1. Dick Hebdige, 'After the Masses', in Stuart Hall and Martin Jacques, eds, *New Times: The Changing Face of Politics in the 1990s*, London 1989, pp. 87–8.

2. Steven Englander, Preface to ADILKNO, *Cracking the Movement: Squatting Beyond the Media*, translated by Laura Martz, Brooklyn, NY 1990, p. 10.

3. Jill Bruce, 'The Time, the Place and the People', in Richard Barnes, *The Sun in the East: Norfolk and Suffolk Fairs*, Kirstead, Norfolk 1983, p. 134.

4. Quoted in Nicholas Saunders, *Ecstasy and the Dance Culture*, London 1995, p. 173.

5. Quoted in *The Story of Exodus: A Movement of Jah People, Documented and Presented by Squall: The Magazine for Sorted Itinerants*, London 1995, p. 2.

6. *The Book: Directory of Active Groups in the UK*, Brighton 1995, first edition, p. 3.

7. Phil McLeish, 'A View From the Tower', in *Claremont Road E11: A Festival of Resistance*, London 1995.

INDEX